THE MURDER CLUB

"Well, I do not like accidents," replied Mrs Mush, "there's no meaning in them: but," she added confidentially, "I dearly like a murder. Of course I do not wish for murders," she continued, in a tone of resigned virtue: "but when there is one, why, I like it. It is human nature."

(Julia Kavanagh, *Sybil's Second Love*, 1867)

THE MURDER CLUB

Guide to

SOUTH-EAST ENGLAND

Devised and Edited by Brian Lane

HARRAP
London

ACKNOWLEDGEMENTS

Sincere thanks go primarily to Derek Johns, Publishing Director of Harrap, whose imaginative response to the proposal for these *Guides* provided their initial impetus, and whose continued encouragement and practical support have ensured their realization. Thanks also to our editor, Roy Minton, whose knowledge and understanding has saved us from more than a few pitfalls; and to Tim Pearce, who helped turn our ideas into books.

On the Murder Club side there are people too numerous to mention whose contributions to our Archive of illustrations and texts have made the compilation of these books possible. In particular, credit must be given to Steve Wheatley, whose work on the overall concept of the *Murder Club Guides* was of immense value, as were his written contributions to Volume One. And to John Bevis whose creative application to the layout and overall appearance has helped make the concept a tangible reality.

For the kindness and generosity we have been shown in scores of libraries and museums, large and small, all over Britain, and for all those people who knew about things and were willing to share, we hope these books may represent our thanks.

First published in Great Britain 1988
by HARRAP Ltd
19-23 Ludgate Hill, London EC4M 7PD

ISBN 0-245-54685-5

Designed by Brian Lane and John Bevis

Typeset in Times by
Facet Film Composing Limited
Leigh-on-Sea, Essex

Printed by Biddles Limited,
Guildford and King's Lynn

THE MURDER CLUB
GUIDE TO SOUTH-EAST ENGLAND

CONTENTS

General Introduction

On Apologias

Madame Life's a piece in bloom
Death goes dogging everywhere;
She's the tenant of the room,
He's the ruffian on the stair.
(W.E. Henley, 1849-1903)

A disturbing by-product of the new fashionable 'humanism' and its inseparable partner 'attitude-baring' is that the individual is under constant pressure to apologize for his passions. And nothing needs an apologia quite as much as a fascination with the darker sides of humankind.

There can be few notions more difficult to promote than that an interest in, say, the ritual of Magic does not of itself lead to nocturnal harvesting of the parish graveyard; or that a diet of gangster movies results in St Valentine's Day madness. An interest in crime is viewed as decidedly sinister; but a fascination with the crime of Murder – be it as academic or aficionado – renders a person particularly vulnerable, particularly in need of an apologia.

And so, for all those members, and prospective members, and closet members of The Murder Club; for all those readers of these, its regional *Guides*, here are some excellent precedents for our common need to justify.

One of the earliest examples can be found in the first issue of what was to become a popular illustrated weekly paper for a number of years around the turn of the century. Though its name was *Famous Crimes Past and Present*, like so many similar magazines of the period "crime" meant "murder". Editor Harold Furniss wrote, "Down the vista of crime which stretches from the first transgression of our Father Adam to the last little boy punished for stealing a pennyworth of sweets, there stand at intervals landmarks – milestones, as it were – on the road of iniquity. These are the doings of great criminals, of men whose cunning, wickedness or brutality have thrown out their lives into relief against the sordid background of everyday transgressors. It is of these that we propose to write, and we do so with a two-fold purpose; firstly that those who are interested in criminology, and desirous of furthering the science by which the moral welfare of the country is preserved may have before them a reliable record of typical criminals; and secondly, that as the natural bent of man tends towards crime, we may provide him with reading matter, interesting and dramatic, which will afford him food for thought."[1]

That there was a lighter side to the "interest in criminology" even earlier is evidenced by David Jardine's *Criminal Trials* being published, in 1835, by The Society for the Diffusion of Useful Knowledge as part of its series 'The Library of Entertaining Knowledge'. Just why such material should be considered 'Entertaining' is spelt out by another chronicler of the Courts, Horace Wyndham: "Of course, the real truth is (as De Quincey, who was something of a connoisseur on such matters, has asserted) crime in itself is intrinsically interesting. We may protest to the contrary, but there is no getting over the fact that the traffic of the dock does make an appeal. An extended one, too. Still, there is abundant reason for this. After all, 'crime books' are concerned with human happenings, with real life, with the stir and fret and thrill of everyday occurrences. Again, crime is essentially dramatic, and touches the whole emotional gamut. Thus, there is tragedy; there is comedy; there is melodrama; and there is occasionally sheer farce. Even romance, too, at times. Anyway, plot and passion and swift moving incident from the rise to the fall of the curtain. Hence, not nearly so astonishing that such volumes are popular as that they are not still more popular."[2]

Other writers have sought to give equal stress to the 'Useful' and to the 'Entertaining' sides of the crime story. Few people have done more consistently to popularize the twilight world of the criminal than the much respected writer, broadcaster, and former barrister, Edgar Lustgarten: "The main aim of one approach is to probe psychology – and thereby to illuminate and instruct. The main aim of the other is to tell a story – and thereby to divert and entertain."[3] But whichever of these two caps Mr Lustgarten chooses to wear, he is clear on the moral foundation of his apologia, "Certainly the arrangement adopted in the construction of the book does not signify any departure by the author from the received opinion that murder is the wickedest and gravest of all crimes."[4]

A different approach is taken by Colin Wilson, whose prolific path has taken him through such dangerous territory as Black Magic, Extra-Terrestrialism, ESP, Assassination, and Murder. One of his contentions is that the study of murder is a necessity – indeed, an obligation – if one is to understand the counter-balance, which is man's great creative potential. We have to be very grateful to Wilson for much of our contemporary understanding of 'criminality', though it is an approach which has has led to accusations of pomposity – not much dispelled by his published feelings about some fellow-authors: "It will be observed that my references to certain other writers on murder – particularly Edmund Pearson, William Roughead and William Bolitho – are hardly complimentary. I dislike the 'murder for pleasure' approach. I consider this book, like the *Encyclopaedia of Murder*, as a tentative contribution to a subject that does not yet exist as a definite entity, a science that has not yet taken shape."[5] Wilson's co-author on the *Encyclopaedia of Murder* was Patricia Pitman, who took a rather less pedantic view of the task in hand, concluding that the fascination with murderers is that they are so utterly different from us, and that that fascination is perfectly natural. Further, she brings a refreshing down-to-earthness to it all by adding that, aside from psychological justifications, the *Encyclopaedia* can provide "...plots for novels, questions for quizes, and innocent entertainment for eerie winter evenings."[6]

But what of the "murder for pleasure" approach so despised by Wilson?

The late Edmund Pearson, tireless recorder of the classic American murders and controversial authority on the Lizzie Borden case does, it is true, seem to take a wholesome relish in the retelling of a great murder story; England's own 'Brides in the Bath' killer, George Joseph Smith, he laments as a man "who only went to ruin because, like so many great artists, he could not resist one more farewell performance" [see *Murder Club Guide No.2*].[7] In the essay 'What Makes a Good Murder?', Pearson treats 'collectors' of murders with the respect that he feels due to a discerning cognoscente, noting that "...failure to recognise the elementary principle of an attractive murder is characteristic of many who should be better informed".[8]

Back on this side of the Atlantic, Pearson would recognize a soul-mate in Nigel Morland, who steers a course happily between detective fiction and criminology; he too is adamant about quality in a murder – "the critical eyes of aficionados recognise two distinct divisions of murder in the United States. There are the common-or-garden majority, whose ultimate destiny is the pages of popular magazines with lurid covers. The second, numerically minute, division is concerned with murders acceptable to the discerning taste, and here time has made certain classics".[9]

Edward Spencer Shew was one of the pioneers, with Wilson and Pitman, of the encyclopaedic approach to the recording of murder, and in the frank introduction to his indispensible *Second Companion to Murder*, Shew comes dangerously close to appearing to enjoy his subject: "Here the emphasis falls upon naked violence, raw and uncompromising, like the mallet strokes which destroyed Francis Mawson Rattenbury [see *Murder Club Guide No.6*], or the blows of the iron-stone brick with which Irene Munro was battered to death upon the sands of the Crumbles [see *Murder Club Guide No.2*]. Here murder wears its most savage face;[10] a face that Ivan Butler recognises: "it is in the strange vagaries of human behaviour that the persisting interest lies...the bizarre, the mysterious, the tragic, the gruesome, the just plain vicious".[11]

Two novel and distinguished vindications are advanced by Gordon Honeycombe in his introductory pages to *The Murders of the Black Museum* – "But the Black Museum made me realise what a policemen must endure in the course of of his duty; what sights he sees, what dangers he faces, what depraved and evil people he has to deal with so that others may live secure".[12] And later, "Murder is a very rare event in England. Its exceptional nature is in fact part of its fascination."

A counterpoint to this approach is provided by journalistic investigators, such as Paul Foot and Ludovic Kennedy. Their immediate motivation is the righting of a particular injustice, but they also have a wider purpose. As Kennedy writes in his introduction to 'Wicked Beyond Belief': "...once we start selecting those whom we think worthy or unworthy of Justice, we shall all in the end be diminished; for even if Justice is sometimes rough in practice, it is not for Cooper and McMahon alone that this book has been assembled; but for all those who, if Justice is allowed to go by default, may come to suffer in their time."[13] Kennedy's intention is to expose those attitudes and processes of the police, the courts, lawyers and judges which create an institutional tendency towards injustice.

A more academic, but no less absorbing, motive for the study of Murder derives from the fact that murder cases have tended to be so much better documented than the less notorious fields of human endeavour. The wealth of detailed information which can be gleaned from Court testimony and newspaper reports provides an eloquent picture of the everyday behaviour, social conditions, and moral attitudes of times past. We would, undoubtedly, be far more ignorant of conditions in London's East End in the 1880s if it were not for Jack the Ripper; the description of repressive middle-class life presented by the cases of Dr Crippen and Major Armstrong [see *Murder Club Guide No.4*] is, surely, as vivid as any novelist could invent; an examination of the predicament of Florence Maybrick [see *Murder Club Guide No.3*] or Edith Thompson provides a telling case study of the moral taboos of their time.

To be generous to the field, an example should be given of the "There but for the Grace of God..." argument. Take Tony Wilmot's introduction to *Murder and Mayhem*, "Why do we like reading crime stories, especially murder? For murder, that most heinous of crimes, both horrifies and fascinates at one and the same time...Could it be that deep down, we suspect that we are capable of committing murder, or other serious crimes, if we knew we could get away with it? That, perhaps, the only thing that holds us back is the fear of being caught and paying the price?"[14]

Probably not. But the one certainty is that there are as many reasons for a fascination with the "ruffian on the stair" as there are people to be fascinated by him.

References

1 *Famous Crimes Past and Present*, Ed. Harold Furniss. Vol.1. No.1, 1903.
2 *Famous Trials Retold*, Horace Wyndham. Hutchinson, London. 1925.
3 *Illustrated Story of Crime*, Edgar Lustgarten. Weidenfeld and Nicolson, London, 1976.
4 *Ibid.*
5 *A Casebook of Murder*, Colin Wilson. Leslie Frewin, London, 1969.
6 *Encyclopaedia of Murder*, Colin Wilson and Patricia Pitman. Arthur Barker, London, 1961.
7 *Masterpieces of Murder*, Edmund Pearson.

Hutchinson, London, 1969.
8 *Ibid.*
9 *Background to Murder*, Nigel Morland. Werner Laurie, London, 1955.
10 *Second Companion to Murder*, E. Spencer Shew. Cassell, London, 1961.
11 *Murderers' London*, Ivan Butler. Hale, London, 1973.
12 *Murders of the Black Museum 1870-1970*, Gordon Honeycombe. Hutchinson, London, 1982.
13 *The Luton Murder Case*, Ed. Ludovic Kennedy. Granada Publishing, London, 1980.
14 *Murder and Mayhem*, Ed. Tony Wilmot. Harmsworth Publications, London, 1983.

Maps

The complexity of Britain's road system – particularly around the crowded inner-city areas – makes it impractical to provide a detailed road map to the regions covered in this series of *Guides*. Instead, individual cases are accompanied by a map of the immediate area, marked where possible with the nearest British Rail station as well as locational information relevant to the text.

To give an overview of the areas covered, each county is prefaced by a map on which the murder sites are numerically plotted and listed.

KEY TO MAPS

No.27 The Ship Inn Buildings and locations relating to text are set in box rules

⊖ Underground stations   Grassland and parks

━━━■━━━ British Rail stations   Woodland

Location Locations at time of crime   ═════════ Footpaths

Location Locations in 1988   River or coastlines

Location Photographs

In keeping with the status of this series of books as Guides, maps have been supplemented, where possible and appropriate, with photographs of buildings and locations relevant to the crime under discussion; in many cases, however, the precise spot on a landscape has been buried either by time or by the ubiquitous developer. Further research may unearth more precise information, and the compilers would be most grateful to receive it.

Public houses come quite naturally to the foreground in many of these cases, and provide a genuine excuse for refreshment in the amateur 'murder hunt'; but it should be remembered that those many private houses whose history has been blackened by dark deeds are not public monuments, and their present occupants' privacy should be respected.

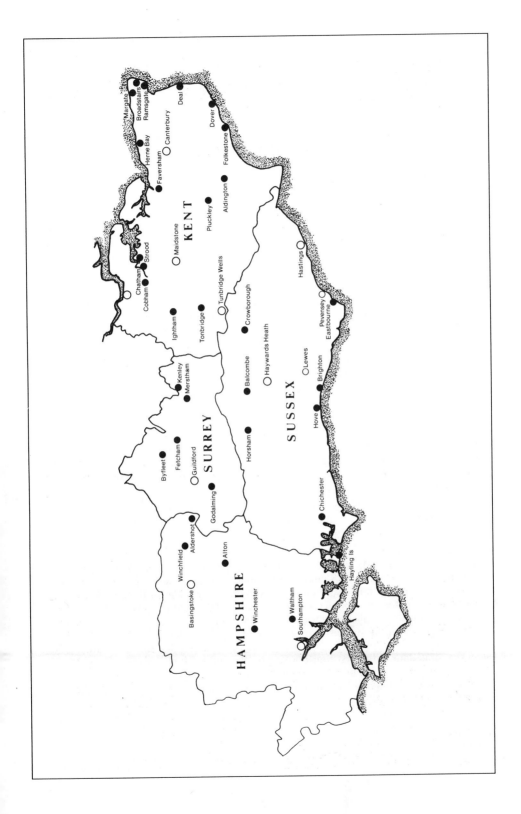

THE MURDER CLUB

Background

In the October of 1985, when Steve Wheatley and I first began to mould our mutual interest in Crime and Criminology into some more tangible form, it was as an occasional fireside activity. The first manifestation was the manuscript for a book of Execution Broadsheets. From there, as winter deepened, and the fireside became host to more frequent discussion, the ambitious concept for a new kind of periodical devoted to the Crime of Murder began to creep from our meditations. And the more of the blood-red wine that was sipped, and the more nimbly the shadows from the flickering flames darted about the room, the more of a good idea it seemed. It even stood up to the cold, thin reality of winter daylight.

It was, we decided, to be called *The Murder Club Bulletin* – though heaven knows why, the 'Club' wasn't due to emerge from the moving shadows until the next season's firelight. Indeed, at the time the first rough plans were put on to paper the 'Club' fitted round the editorial desk with more than enough room to spare.

It must have been around the mid-winter of 1986 that somebody said something like: "We've got the *Murder Bulletin,* what about the *Club?*"

I should say, though, that in the intervening months we had gradually begun to put together what will become a complete regional documentation of British Murders since the beginning of the seventeenth century; it's a big job. People in various parts of the country heard about it, and started to send us things – notes about famous local murders, regional press cuttings, pictures. We discovered people like Mr Mackintosh who had traced the last resting place of Bella Wright, the victim of the Green Bicycle Mystery in 1919, and had set up a fund to give Bella a modest memorial. We were becoming a Club!

Discussion began to revolve more and more around what we, as committed enthusiasts, would want out of a Murder Club if we were 'them'. The list on page 191 reveal some of those decisions which have already been adopted; other paths await discovery.

So, in the middle months of 1987 we had a prototype *Bulletin,* we had the partially clad skeleton of *The Murder Club,* and we had something else – we had a series of books demanding to be written; a series of Guides to the darker sides of Britain's landscape. Then came our first meeting with Harrap – long-established publishers of true-crime works – and their Publishing Director, Derek Johns. Derek it was who responded enthusiastically to the proposal for a series of eight *Murder Club Regional Guides;* Derek it was who enthusiastically adopted the suggestion to launch *The Murder Club* on the same date as the first four books – on the 30th of June, this year. And by the next season of flickering fires, Criminology will no longer be the exclusive preserve of the scientists, the lawyers, and the journalists. Our Members will already have become arm-chair detectives.

Brian Lane

London
April 1988

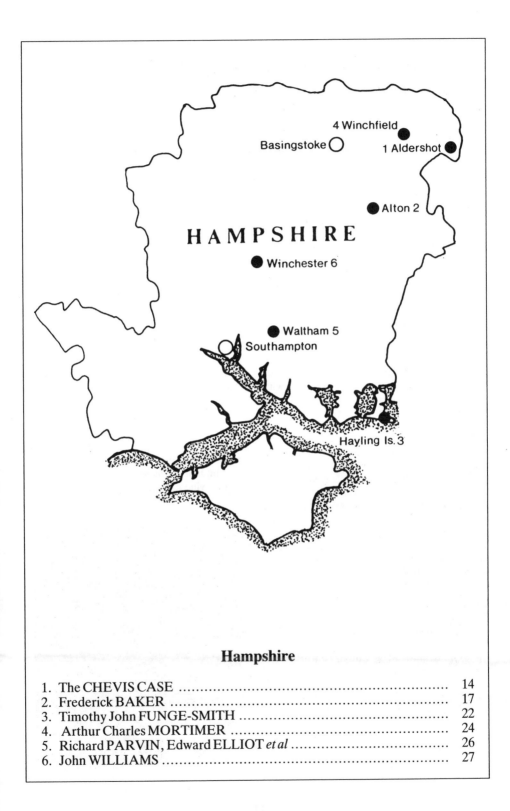

Hampshire

"A large cold bottle, and a small hot bird"*

The Murder of Lieutenant HUBERT GEORGE CHEVIS
by an Unknown Assassin

on the 21st of June 1931
at his home in Blackdown Camp, Aldershot

Any man who has risen to the rank of lieutenant in the professional Army, and is part of a long family military tradition, has to have some awareness of his own mortality; the reluctant acceptance that the nature of his calling may demand of him the ultimate sacrifice on "some foreign field". But to be struck down by a silent and unknown assassin in the middle of a family dinner within the security of an Army camp at Aldershot is the least of his expectances. But in one of the most baffling mysteries of the century, that is exactly what did happen.

In June 1931 Lieutenant Hubert George Chevis, a young Artillery officer, was occupying a bungalow on the Blackdown Camp, near Aldershot. He also kept a family house in London in which his wife and two children resided during the week while he was on duty, and the family was reunited at the bungalow for weekends. On the 21st of the month the Chevis cook, a Mrs Yeomans, took delivery of the brace of partridges which Mrs Chevis had ordered from a local poulterer as the basis for a modest celebration dinner. It was the weekend of the annual Aldershot Tattoo – always a special date for military personnel in the area – and the Chevises had planned to take the children with them to see the spectacle.

The cook hung the birds in the ventilated meat safe outside the house, and there they remained until mid-afternoon, when they were transferred to the oven to roast while Lieutenant and Mrs Chevis entertained friends to late-afternoon cocktails. When their guests had gone the couple sat down in anticipation of their evening treat, served, in accordance with quaint military protocol, by

the Lieutenant's batman, Private Nicholas Bulger. Mrs Chevis took command of the carving, and with their accompanying vegetables the partridges looked a meal fit for a king – or a general, at least.

Hubert Chevis lifted a forkful of bird to his lips expectantly; chewed; swallowed; and grimaced: "It tastes horrible!" Mrs Chevis was less adventurous, and merely touched a piece of partridge flesh with her tongue: "Fusty!" was her verdict, and with evident annoyance and disappointment Chevis ordered his batman to dispose of the rest of the dinner in a place where the dogs couldn't get it.

Within minutes Hubert was feeling more unwell than angry; within fifteen minutes he had lost the use of his legs and was in the grip of strong convulsions; within the hour he was in a military hospital fighting for his life. The battle was lost in the early hours of the following morning. Mrs Chevis, who had

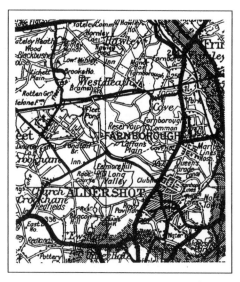

---

*"When I demanded of my friend what viands he preferred, He quoth: 'A large cold bottle, and a small hot bird'." (Eugene Field, 1850-1895, *The Bottle and the Bird*)

also had contact with the evidently contaminated poultry, suffered milder symptoms and eventually responded to treatment.

According to procedure in cases of violent or inexplicable death, the police were informed, a post-mortem examination arranged, and a coroner's inquest convened. The inquest was formally opened on July 23rd, but immediately adjourned pending the analyst's report.

On the following day Sir William Chevis – Hubert's father – was preparing for his son's funeral when a telegram boy delivered a message. It read, simply, "Hooray Hooray Hooray", and was signed on the back "J. Hartigan, Hibernia [a Dublin hotel]". The police, to whom Sir William immediately communicated the telegram, took a very grave view indeed; for sick though the message was at the time and under the circumstances of Sir William's recent bereavement, it was highly suspicious in view of the fact that no mention of the tragedy had yet been made public, and assuming, as was natural, that the words "Hooray" celebrated Lieutenant Chevis's death, the sender could only be acting on first-hand knowledge.

Developments in Eire came swiftly; the Guarda had interviewed the staff and guests of the Dublin hotel named on the cable, and eliminated any connection between it and anybody named Hartigan. They had seen the Post Office clerk who took the telegram, and he was able to give a useful description, which happened also – and here the investigation seemed to be making progress – to fit a man who had purchased a quantity of strychnine from a local chemist. However, this was where the trail went cold, and when the inquest on young Chevis was resumed in the West Surrey Coroner's Court on August the 11th, there was little more to add.

The coroner opened by recapping on the known facts of the case: that the partridges had been the vehicle for a poison – strychnine – which had been responsible for the death of Hubert Chevis and had been near fatal for his wife; that the grieving parent had received an unfortunately worded telegram, which was subsequently investigated by the Irish police.

The coroner next took time to admonish the *Daily Sketch* for having published – without consultation or permission – a facsimile of the "Hooray" telegram. This publicity made

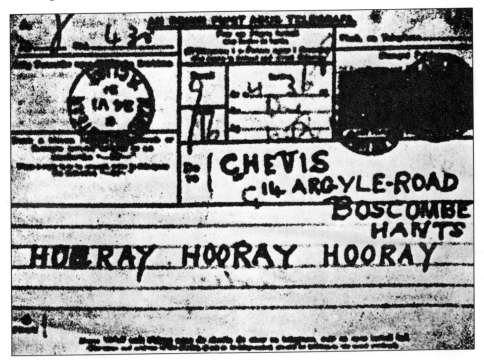

it impossible for the police to determine whether a series of subsequent messages – all purporting to come from J. Hartigan – were genuine or hoaxes. One of these was a postcard, mailed in London, to the editor of the *Sketch*; it read "Dear Sir, Why do you publish a picture of the Hooray telegram? J. Hartigan." This was followed by a further telegram to Sir Wiliam Chevis, this time postmarked Belfast and bearing the portentous message: "It is a mystery they will never solve. J. Hartigan. Hooray."

Witnesses were then called to elaborate, for the benefit of the jury, their part in the story of the Lieutenant's mysterious death:

Hubert's brother, Captain Chevis, testified that he had seen the telegram on the day of the funeral, and that he did not know anybody of the name or description of the sender.

Mrs Chevis confirmed that her husband had no Irish connections, or any friends or relatives named Hartigan. The rest of her evidence was a simple relating of the sequence of events which led to the tragedy of her husband's death.

Of more significance was the testimony of Dr J.H. Ryffel, Home Office analyst in charge of the Chevis case. Tests on the stomach contents of the deceased, and on the vomit and fæces of Mrs Chevis, revealed abnormal quantities of strychnine hydrochloride; in Hubert's case easily sufficient to cause his death, though not enough to cause the rapid death associated with this kind of alkaloid poisoning. He accounted for Mrs Chevis's survival by one of two possibilities – either her contact with the meat had been mercifully brief, or only one of the brace of birds had been poisoned – Mrs Chevis's portion suffering only from secondary contamination during the cooking. This latter theory could not be verified due to the efficient carrying out of the Lieutenant's order to destroy the meal. There had been traces of poison in the dripping and gravy left in the pan, indicating that the partridges had been interfered with before cooking – most likely when they were in the cold safe outside the house. Furthermore, by the nature of the poison, it would have to have been injected into the bird(s) for the flesh to be so heavily impregnated as to cause death from such limited contact with the meat. Dr Ryffel concluded by saying that three birds from the same batch had been randomly selected from the poulterer's stock, tested and found to be 'clean'.

Neither Bulger the batman nor Mrs Yeomans could add significantly to the story, both stating in answer to the now familiar question that they knew nobody who went under the name of Hartigan. There was, though, a small ripple of interest when Nicholas Bulger admitted he was born in Ireland. But everything that could have been said had quite obviously been said, and it remained only for the coroner to sum up the evidence for the benefit of the jury.

He emphasized that the only conclusion it was possible for him to reach, was that Lieutenant Hubert Chevis had died from asphyxia following strychnine poisoning. The poison had been administered in the flesh of a partridge which had been eaten by the deceased, but no evidence was yet available to indicate how or by whom the birds were poisoned. He could therefore form no opinion as to whether death had been accidental or murder.

This might seem an over-cautious conclusion to present to the jury, but it was quite in keeping with the responsibility of the coroner's inquest to consider only the indisputable evidence presented to it. To the layman, of course, it is quite obvious that Hubert Chevis *was* murdered – the telegram from 'Hartigan' indicates that. But, as Hartigan had pointed out earlier, "it is a mystery they will never solve".

The jury took just five minutes to return an open verdict. Which is where the case still stands: an unsolved and apparently motiveless killing.

[*See Appendix One for a note on strychnine as a poison.*]

The Partridge

The Killing of Sweet Fanny Adams
The Murder of FANNY ADAMS
by FREDERICK BAKER
on Saturday the 24th of August 1867
in Flood Meadow, Alton

THE ALTON MURDER!

THE POLICE NEWS EDITION
OF THE LIFE AND EXAMINATION OF

FREDERICK BAKER.

Price One Penny.

PUBLISHED AT THE ILLUSTRATED POLICE NEWS OFFICE.
275, STRAND.

DETAILED ACCOUNT OF THE MURDER

Few cases of modern times have created a greater amount of interest than the barbarous murder of a child at Alton. Each separate circumstance in connection with the crime seems only to serve as a link in one long chain of guilt and horror. It seems hardly possible that a man of mild demeanour, such as the accused is said to possess, should have suddenly been prompted by some demoniacal spirit to slay an innocent and inoffensive girl, and to after-wards mutilate the remains of the fair little creature he had sacrificed at the altar of his own wicked and brutal passions. The quiet town of Alton has not been for the last half-century desecrated with the crime of muder – not until Fredrick Baker chose to give its peaceful lanes, its green meadows, and fertile hop gardens an unenviable and painful notoriety. By this time the sad story of a child being spirited away by a fiend in the shape of a man, for the purpose of being cruelly butchered, is known throughout the length and breadth of the land. The hideous mutilation of the body after the murder – the villainous circumstances preceding it – the consternation which seized the town of Alton when the alarm of "murder" was raised on Saturday, created a most marvellous effect. Horror appeared depicted vividly upon the faces of the population during

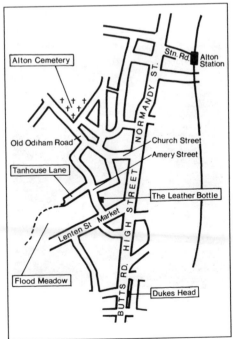

Sunday, Monday, and Tuesday, and was scarcely less manifest on Thursday at the final examination of the prisoner.

The facts which have already transpired show that, about half-past one o'clock on the afternoon mentioned, a little girl named Fanny Adams, eight years of age, left her home [in Tanhouse Lane] near the church, in company with a younger sister and a playmate named Minnie Warner, for the purpose of playing in the meadow [Flood Meadow] adjoining Amery Farm, which is situated a few yards distant from the home of the deceased. The meadow is crowned by a hop garden of considerable extent, approached by a grassy and sequestered lane, from the entrance of which, a charming view of the old town is obtained. It was in the hop ground referred to that the crime, of which full details have now come to hand, was committed. It appears that at two o'clock the children, having partaken of dinner, were engaged in play near the entrance to the secluded lane, when a man, described as wearing a black coat, with light vest and trousers, and who was sitting on the

The Murderer carrying his victim into the hop plantation

gate, beckoned Fanny Adams, the unfortunate deceased, towards him. All the children approached, and singling out the deceased, he offered her a halfpenny to accompany him for a walk in the adjacent hop-garden. Seeing that the other children were disposed to follow he distributed amongst them three halfpennies, telling them to run away and buy some sweets. They accordingly did so, and as they were leaving, saw that the man had taken hold of the girl's hand and was leading her up the lane. They also saw the poor child begin to cry, and heard the man say these words: "Don't cry, my dear; keep quiet, and if you will come up into the hop-garden I will give you some more money." From this time until seven o'clock in the evening nothing more was heard of the deceased. The child not coming home for tea, her mother became alarmed at her absence, and made inquiries, but nothing was elicited beyond the statement of her companions, that she had been seen going up the lane with a strange man. Between seven and eight the same evening a labourer named Thomas Gates, returning from work, had occasioned to cross the hop-ground, when he was horrified at beholding the dissevered head of a child resting upon two hop-poles placed at the foot of the hedge, and lying horizontally on the ground. The man took up the head and ran with it to the row of cottages at the foot of the meadow, in one of which the parents of the unfortunate child reside. The neighbours, who were standing in groups talking about the missing child, on seeing the head immediately declared it that of Fanny Adams.

With a coolness which would seem almost incredible, the man Gates took the head to the father's cottage. All doubts were then set at rest, the poor mother identifying the head as that of her daughter, and immediately falling into hysterics.

The police were at once communicated with, and search was made for the remaining portions of the body. The larger part of the population of the town having speedily become acquainted with the barbarous fate of the child, scoured the hop-ground and adjoining fields to discover, if possible, the body of the deceased. Within about twenty yards east of the hedge, and between the growing hops, were found a leg and a thigh, with a stocking and boot on, and near the

the intestines entirely removed, leaving the mere frame of the body only. The right ear was picked up in a corner of the hop-field by itself. No traces of the eyes were at this time discovered, and the right breast was also missing. In consequence of the disjointed and mutilated condition of the whole body, it is impossible for the medical gentlemen who have examined the remains to determine whether the poor child had been violated. An ineffectual attempt appears to have been made to cut off the left arm from the shoulder. The deceased child was the fourth of a family of six children, and was a tall, comely, and intelligent child. She bore the appearance of being several years in advance of her age and was of a lively and cheerful disposition. The clothes worn by the unfortunate child were found scattered about the plantation. They were much torn. The dissevered remains were placed in a trunk and conveyed to the police station. In the meantime, Superintendent Cheyney obtained a description of the man in whose company the ill-fated girl was last seen, and, aided by his local knowledge, he concluded that the person described exactly answered to a young man named Frederick Baker, whom he knew as in the employ of Messrs Clements, solicitors, of the town. He thereupon proceeded to the office of Messrs. Clements about 9 o'clock in the evening, and saw the accused sitting apparently engaged in his ordinary avocation. Superintendent Cheyney then inquired if he had heard of the murder, to which the accused replied, "Yes; and they say it is me, don't they?"

Leaving Baker in charge of a police-constable, for the purpose of making further inquiries, the Superintendent shortly afterwards ascertained that the prisoner was the man who had given some coppers to the children, as previously alluded to, and on returning to the office, accompanied by one of the children, he asked him if the statement were true. He admitted the fact, but said he was innocent of the crime of murder. He was identified by the child, and the Superintendent removed him to the police-station on suspicion of being the murderer.

same spot the right arm and hand severed from the elbow, were discovered. A little further to the right, the left hand, severed from the wrist, was found, and some distance below were the mutilated remains of the trunk. The other foot, which was the left, was picked up by a young man named Henry Allen in a field adjoining the hop plantation, where it had evidently been thrown with sufficient force to carry it over two high hedges and an intervening lane. The left arm was also picked up in this field. Horrible to relate, the eyes had been gouged out with almost scientific skill. At this time the intestines and heart were missing, but on the following (Sunday) morning further search was made when both these portions were discovered, the former not far from the spot where the trunk had been found, and the heart in an adjoining field where it had been thrown. The body displayed several fearful stabs and gashes, the ribs being severely punctured, the calves of the legs and thighs had been completely ripped up, and

The melancholy news having rapidly spread, and an immense concourse assembled in the High-street outside the office, whose menacing behaviour and threatening language necessitated recourse to stratagem on the

19

part of the Superintendent to effect the prisoner's removal. He was accordingly taken through the back premises, and safely lodged in a cell at the station. Here he was closely searched, and in order that no link in the chain of evidence might be missing, Mr Cheyney caused him to be stripped. This was done, and all his garments taken from him. The light tweed trousers were marked with blood. On both legs there were signs of very recent washing, and they were still quite damp. The socks worn by the prisoner were wet, the result evidently of a recent washing. The front of the waistcoat was splashed with blood, and the wristbands of the shirt were saturated with blood. The prisoner's boots were sodden with wet, leading to the supposition that he had washed them in the rivulet near the scene of the murder. In his pockets were found the sum of £1 6s. 1d. in money and two pen-knives, one of which contained three blades and the other two. Neither of these appeared to be of sufficient strength for the committal of the atrocious crime, and no sign of blood could be discovered upon them. The prisoner was asked if he could account for the state of his clothing, and he answered that he could not; but as to his trousers legs he had, when out, the habit of stepping into the water. It appears that on the day of the murder the prisoner left his lodgings to proceed to business, at ten o'clock in the morning, and his landlady said that he did not return during any portion of the day. He seems to have left the office of Messrs Clements at one o'clock, to have returned again at four, and it is stated that between that hour and the time of his apprehension he was in and out of the office several times.

The prisoner, since his confinement at the station, has not in any way referred to the dreadful deed with which he is accused, but has maintained the closest reticence. On Sunday, the greatest excitement prevailed in the town, and thousands of persons visited the site of the harrowing tragedy, where pools of the life-blood of the innocent child were painfully visible. The morbid feeling animating the public was conspicuously developed by the denudation of the hops and the cutting off of pieces of the plants and hedges growing in the immediate vicinity.

The prisoner was taken on Monday before E. Knight, Esq., one of the magistrates, and at the request of Superintendent Cheyney was remanded until after the coroner's investigation. In searching the prisoner's desk at the office on Monday, a well-kept diary, in the prisoner's handwriting, was discovered. Under the date "Saturday, August 24." the following entry was written in a bold and unfaltering hand, "Killed a young girl; it was fine and hot."

[The prisoner] bears but an indifferent character in the town, and it is related that a fortnight ago he accosted a lady in a secluded pathway in Alton, and made improper overtures to her. These she resisted, and ran away. The prisoner, not succeeding in overtaking her, pelted her with stones. He has always been looked upon as a man of great animal passions.

THE INQUEST

On Tuesday, Mr Robert Harfield, the deputy-coroner for Hampshire, held an inquiry at the *Duke's Head Inn*, Alton, respecting the death of Fanny Adams, aged seven years and four months, who was alleged to have been murdered and mutilated by a solicitor's clerk named Frederick Baker.

The jury having been sworn, proceeded to view the remains of the child, and on their return to the inquest-room, the accused man, Frederick Baker, was brought into the court handcuffed. He looked pale, but self-possessed, and is by no means of a forbidding cast of countenance . . .

. . . Mr Louis Leslie, MD, police surgeon, said that he had examined the parts of the body of the child. There was the trunk, head, arm, and legs – one foot was separated from the leg at the ankle-joint. The outer tissues were entirely gone; the right ear was severed from the head, and a very deep cut divided the vessels from the muscles, extending from above the ear to the end of the lower jaw, entering the cheek and dividing the muscles of the face as far as the angle of the nose. There were three incisions on the left side of the trunk between the ribs, the largest incision being three inches in length, the other two were one inch long. There was a deep cut in the left arm, dividing the muscles, but not parting the arm from the trunk. The left arm was cut off at the elbow joint. The left leg was nearly cut off, but it just hung onto the trunk. In front of the left

Murder and mutilation of the body

of "Wilful murder against Frederick Baker, for killing and slaying Fanny Adams." The warrant was then made out for the committal of the prisoner to Winchester Gaol, to await his trial on the charge of murder.

On Thursday the prisoner, Frederick Baker, was before the Court at Alton, charged on suspicion of being the murderer of Fanny Adams. The proceedings were a mere recapitulation of the evidence taken before the coroner.

The chairman inquired whether the prisoner wished to make any statement.

Prisoner: "I am not careful to answer the charge at present: I am as innocent as the day I was born."

A large crowd awaited the removal of the prisoner outside the Town Hall, and it was with some difficulty that the police were enabled to protect him from the violence of the mob, who hooted and conducted themselves in a most threatening manner. The prisoner was evidently alarmed, and entered the fly engaged for his conveyance with all possible speed. He was accompanied by Superintendent Cheyney, and has since been removed to Winchester Gaol.

thigh there was a deep incision, dividing the muscles. The foot was cut off. On the right side there was a deep incision between the fourth and fifth ribs. The leg was torn from the trunk, and there was a deep incision in it. The chest was completely empty. There were five incisions in the liver, three in the lungs, and the heart was entirely separated from the larger vessels. The spine was dislocated. In fact, the body was hacked to pieces. The dismemberment of the body took place after death. A post-mortem examination of the head showed a contused wound completely dividing the scalp. Witness believed that the blow must have been very severe, and he thought it had been inflicted by a stone. Such a blow would cause immediate insensibility, and death might follow. It was quite impossible to say whether any acts of criminal violence had taken place, the body was so cut up . . .

. . . the coroner then asked the accused, Baker, whether he desired to make any statement, and the accused replied, "No, sir, only that I am innocent." The coroner then summed up, and the jury returned a verdict

The remains of the unfortunate child, Fanny Adams, were interred at the Alton cemetery, on Wednesday afternoon. The burial service was impressively read by the Rev. W. Wilkins, curate of Thedden, and a large number of persons assembled to witness the funeral. Wreaths of flowers were placed upon the coffin, and subsequently upon the grave. The parents of the unhappy victim followed, and their grief appeared to be almost unbearable.

At the subsequent trial, Mr Justice Mellor summed up with strict impartiality, and expressed no opinion on the controversial subject of Baker's insanity or otherwise; but he admonished the jury that there must be no compassion in their verdict. Three courses lay before them – eiher to find the prisoner guilty, not guilty, or not guilty on grounds of insanity. He reviewed the evidence at some length, and then dismissed the jury, who were only absent fifteen minutes. They returned with a verdict of Guilty, and the prisoner was sentenced to death, the judge expressing his concurrence in the verdict.

The prisoner became very depressed while awaiting the execution of the sentence, and at length he unburdened his conscience and related the main details of his revolting crime.

Asked what possible motive there could be for such brutality, he declared that an irresistible desire to slay came over him when the child cried at being taken away from her companions, and that he killed her with a large stone. The mutilation was an afterthought. He felt that he must become saturated with blood, and that he experienced no natural horror or repulsion while engaged in this revolting work of decapitation and disembowelling. He stated that he had walked about some time with the heart, smoking hot from the child's body, in his hand, but that he had thrown it into a field (where it was found) when he heard someone approaching . . .

Baker expressed great sorrow and sympathy for the parents of the child and begged for their forgiveness. Little or no effort was made to obtain a revision of the sentence, and this fiend underwent the penalty of his crime shortly after the trial at Winchester, many thousands being present at his execution. He showed much fortitude at the last, and said that he deserved his fate.

[*This text has been adapted from newspaper and other contemporary reports of the crime*]

To the Memory of Fanny Adams
Fanny's grave in Alton churchyard, one hundred and twenty years after her death

The Gardener's Tale
The Murder of MICHAEL ROBERTSON
by TIMOTHY JOHN FUNGE-SMITH
on Friday the 7th of October 1984
at Hayling Island

On the night of Friday, October 7th, 1984, Mrs Yianoulla Robertson reported finding the battered body of her husband Michael in the grounds of their home at Salterns Lane, Hayling Island.

Forty-one-year-old Robertson, an executive with the IBM company, was rushed to Southampton General Hospital suffering from severe head injuries from which he died on the 9th of October, without regaining consciousness.

The police investigation, led by Detective Chief Superintendent John Wright, the head of Hampshire CID, first concentrated on piecing together Mr Robertson's movements during the evening hours leading up to his death. According to Greek-born Mrs Robertson, her husband went out earlier in the evening to collect a take-away meal, and police believed that the victim may have visited several public houses in the seafront area of Hayling Island; subsequently, an appeal was made for witnesses who saw Robertson on that evening.

Events began to move quickly then, and by the morning of the 11th October, a man was in custody and officers were about to arrest the victim's wife. At a brief sitting of the Havant magistrates court, 37-year-old Yianoulla Robertson was charged that "on a date unknown, between January 1st and October 10th, 1984, [she] solicited Timothy John Funge-Smith to murder her husband". Mrs Robertson was remanded in custody to appear again before the court in eight days.

Funge-Smith, 41, with an address at The Seafront, Hayling Island, appeared in court the following day, Wednesday, and was remanded in custody on the charge of murdering Michael Robertson, for whom he had worked as a general gardener.

When Timothy Funge-Smith came to trial at the beginning of March 1985 it was before Mr Justice Tudor Evans at the Winchester Crown Court. The jury heard how when the prisoner had first been interviewed by the police he invented the alibi that he had been drinking in a local public house at the time of the attack on his former employer Michael Robertson. But, revealed Mr Roger Titheridge QC prosecuting, when he learned that the investigating officers had found the murder weapon – a three foot galvanised pipe – and furthermore that it bore his palm print, Funge-Smith had telephoned the murder incident room and confessed to the crime. Also appearing in the dock was 37-year-old David Stacey, who admitted attempting to pervert the course of justice by giving the prisoner an alibi.

Sentencing Funge-Smith on the 5th of March, Mr Justice Tudor Evans told him: "Whatever your motives, this was a brutal murder for which the sentence is prescribed by law"; that sentence was imprisonment for life. In an unusual move from the Bench, the judge imposed an order under the Contempt of Court Act prohibiting publication either of the prisoner's motive, or of a conversation he is said to have had with the dead man's widow, who had also been charged.

A month later, on the 25th March, Mr Christopher Leigh, representing the Director of Public Prosecutions, applied for this order to be rescinded; its original purpose – to ensure an unbiased trial for Mrs Robertson – being redundant as there was insufficient reliable evidence on which to pursue the case against her.

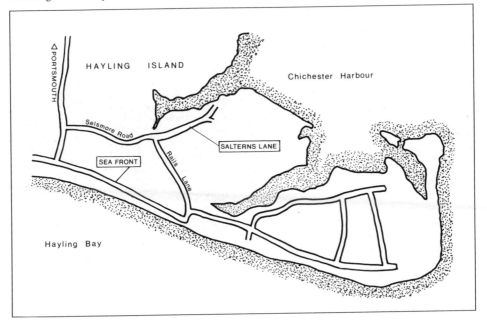

A Very Strange Pastime

The Murder of Miss PHYLLIS OAKES
by ARTHUR CHARLES MORTIMER
on Thursday the 8th of August 1935
on the Railway Bridge outside Winchfield

There can be few more extraordinary stories than that of the killing of poor Phyllis Oakes; and few more extraordinary killers than Arthur Charles Mortimer.

Arthur, you see, had a very strange and anti-social pastime – his greatest pleasure derived from driving his motor-car at women cyclists, knocking them of their mounts, and subjecting them to such further indignities as circumstances permitted, or fancy led.

It was on the morning of August 7th 1935 that Mrs Alice Series, a lady in service, had her unfortunate meeting with Arthur Mortimer, a 27-year-old lance-corporal stationed with the 1st Welch Regiment at Aldershot. It took place at Stratfield Saye, in the Hampshire countryside between Basingstoke and Reading. Having forced Mrs Series into the side of the road with such suddenness as to hurl the luckless woman into the ditch, Arthur reversed, wound down his window, smiled, and apologized: "So sorry, trouble with the steering. Look!" He points to the steering wheel; as Alice Series staggers up and nears the open car window, Arthur Mortimer lands her such a punch on the head as to loosen several of her teeth; after thumping her several times more as she lay stunned on the ground, Mortimer made off in a puff of exhaust. Under the circumstances it seems purely incidental to say that the car was a stolen one.

Before abandoning the vehicle to its rightful owner, however, Arthur Mortimer indulged his hobby once more. The victim this time was Nellie Boyes – another domestic servant as it later transpired; the location was Hartley Wintney; the *modus operandi* was the same. The plucky Nellie, though, was a more equal match and, after giving her assailant the rough edge of her tongue, frightened him off with threats of the police.

On the following morning Arthur Mortimer was out and about early, in Farnborough. He was stealing another car.

Driving through Winchfield, the prospect of sport manifested in the persons of 20-year-old Phyllis Oakes and her sister Betty, who were cycling in single file along the road where it bridges the railway line; riding ahead of her sister, Betty Oakes was horrified to hear a crash from behind, and turned in time to see Phyllis bouncing off the bonnet of Arthur Mortimer's car.

That afternoon brought fresh prospects of pleasure in the neighbouring county of Surrey. Where Mrs Lilian Rose Harwood (unbelievably, another servant) was cycling at Crastock, near Knaphill. Mortimer left her unconscious where she had fallen into the ditch; minus her handbag and the thirty shillings that it contained.

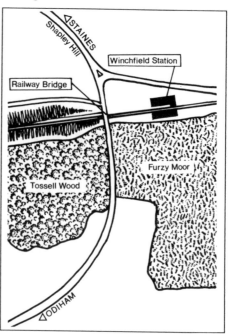

Such very odd behaviour could not long escape the notice of the police, not least since Phyllis Oakes was in a serious condition in hospital and her sister was crying vengeance. The law caught up with Arthur Mortimer just outside Guildford, and despite a chase full of heroic endeavour, he eventually crashed into a police road-block set up specifically for that purpose. He emerged shaken and bruised, but in a great deal better bodily condition than most of his victims. On the passenger seat of his car was Lilian Harwood's handbag; in his pocket was Lilian Harwood's thirty shillings.

A charge of grievous bodily harm against Miss Oakes was quickly changed when that unfortunate young woman succumbed to her injuries, and Mortimer faced trial for murder before Mr Justice Finlay at the Winchester Assizes in November.

The defence was the obvious one – that Phyllis Oakes's death was an accident; the kind of accident that was becoming all too common with the emergence of the motorcar as a form of popular transport. But it was a defence that may in retrospect have been unwise.

It is a characteristic of British justice that in the main everything is done to ensure that the accused gets a fair and unbiased trial. fo. example, only one charge is presented against a prisoner at a time – which means that other crimes, other convictions, are kept from the jury, lest they be unreasonably prejudiced against him. However, with a defence of "accidental death" it is possible for the prosecution to call "Evidence of System"; that is to say that evidence of similar crimes committed by the prisoner may be introduced to show whether the death was accidental or designed. And in Arthur Mortimer's case it was very damaging evidence indeed. In mitigation of his behaviour, it was pointed out that Arthur had suffered epileptic fits since an accident at the age of twelve, and that at seventeen he was suffering badly enough to be admitted to a mental institution for six months.

But after a three-day trial, Arthur Mortimer was found guilty of murder and sentenced to be hanged by the neck . . .

There was little punishment that would have made much difference to Mortimer – clearly mad as a hatter, he was reprieved on the evidence of the statutory medical enquiry that followed all captial sentences since the Criminal Lunatics Act of 1884. He spent the rest of his days in prison under medical supervision, well out of harm's way.

The Waltham Blacks

The Murder of the Bishop of Winchester's Gamekeeper
by RICHARD PARVIN, EDWARD ELLIOT,
ROBERT KINGSHELL et al
in the year 1723
on Waltham Chase, near Winchester

It is not often that an individual criminal case will make any lasting mark on legal history; on the one hand, the Law tends to be a ponderous process, notably resistant to change; on the other, criminals tend to be, as a category, an unimaginative section of humankind, rarely necessitating law to be rewritten for their benefit.

However, like all generalizations, the exceptions can be dramatic – indeed, often out of any proportion to the apparent mediocrity of the crime. Such a case was Dr William Palmer, notable British multiple poisoner, against whom there was such ill-feeling in his native Staffordshire that it was impossible to guarantee an impartial trial. It was necessary for Parliament to pass the Palmer Act before he could be tried in London's Old Bailey – in May 1856 [see *Murder Club Guide No.4*].

In 1817 Abraham Thornton, who had inex- plicably been acquitted of the atrocious rape and murder of Mary Ashford [see *Murder Club Guide No.4*] was rearrested on a Writ of Appeal by Mary's elder brother, against whom Thornton invoked the obsolete right of Trial by Combat (or Trial by Battle). This could clearly not be countenanced in the comparative enlightenment of the nineteenth century, and Thornton again escaped the consequences of his crime. Parliament shortly afterwards passed an Act by which Trial by Combat was abolished.

Previous to both these examples, the misdeeds of a gang of ruffians operating in the county of Hampshire prompted, in 1723, the passing of the notorious Waltham Black Act, whose effect was to increase the number of capital offences on the statute from around 36 to over 150. The following is a brief contemporary account of the Act and the crimes that led to its being passed.

Richard Parvin, Edward Elliot, Robert Kingshell, Henry Marshall, Edward Pink, John Pink, and James Ansell

The WALTHAM BLACKS, who were executed at Tyburn, 4th of December, 1723, for Murder and Deer-Stealing

These men belonged to a gang of daring plunderers, who carried on their depredations with such effrontery that it was found necessary to enact the law hereafter recited in order to bring them to condign punishment; and it was not long after it was in force before it took due effect upon them.

Having blackened their faces they went in the daytime to the parks of the nobility and gentry, whence they repeatedly stole deer, and at length murdered the Bishop of Winchester's keeper on Waltham Chase; and from the name of the place, and their blacking of their faces, they obtained the name of the "Waltham Blacks."

The following is the substance of the Act of Parliament on which they were convicted: "After the first day of June, 1723, any person appearing in the forest, chase, park, etc., or in any high road, open heath, common or down, with offensive weapon, and having his face blackened, or otherwise disguised, or unlawfully and wilfully hunting, wounding, killing or stealing any red or fallow deer, or unlawfully robbing any warren, etc., or stealing any fish out of any river or pond, or (whether armed or disguised or not) breaking down the head or mound of any fishpond, whereby the fish may be lost or destroyed; or unlawfully and maliciously killing, maiming, or wounding any cattle, or cutting down or otherwise destroying any trees planted in any avenue, or growing in any garden, orchard or plantation, for ornament, shelter, or profit; or setting fire to any house, barn or outhouse, hovel, cock-mow or stack of corn, straw, hay, or wood; or maliciously shooting at any person in any dwelling-house or other place; or knowingly sending any letter without any name, or signed with a fictitious name, demanding money, venison or other valuable thing, or forcibly rescuing any person being in custody for any of the offences before mentioned, or procuring any person by gift, or promise of money, or other reward, to join in any such unlawful act, or concealing or succouring such offenders when, by Order of the Council, etc., required to surrender – shall suffer Death."

By a vigilant exertion of the civil power all the above-mentioned offenders were taken into custody, and it being thought prudent to bring them to trial in London, they were removed thither under a strong guard and lodged in Newgate. On the 13th of November, 1723, they were brought to their trial in the Court of the King's Bench, and being convicted on the clearest evidence were found guilty and sentenced to die; and it was immediately ordered that they should suffer on the 4th of the next month. One circumstance was very remarkable on this occasion: the judge had no sooner pronounced the

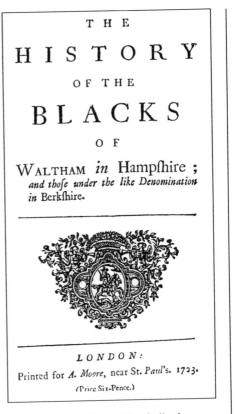

THE

HISTORY

OF THE

BLACKS

OF

WALTHAM *in* Hampſhire ;
and thoſe under the like Denomination in Berkſhire.

LONDON:
Printed for *A. Moore*, near St. *Paul's*. 1723.
(Price Six-Pence.)

sentence than Henry Marshall, the man who had shot the keeper, was immediately deprived of the use of his tongue; nor did he recover his speech till the day before his death.

The Winchester Tragedy
The Murder of MARY THOMAS
by JOHN WILLIAMS
on Sunday November the 4th [1810]
in a field outside Winchester

A COPY OF VERSES
addressed to
The Fair Sex

Young women all, of each degree,
  Of every rank and station,
Draw near and listen unto me,
  I give a true relation.

Of a young woman lost thro' love,
  Mary Thomas was her name,
She yielded to a false young man,
  And lost both life and fame.

Near Winchester the maiden dwelt,
  There led a happy life,
Until shy Cupid's dart she felt,
  Which sorrow brought, and strife.

Williams was a handsome youth,
  To court her he did come,
And by his false deceitful arts,
  Has sealed her fatal doom.

For she did yield her honour up,
  And by him was beguiled,
She drank of sorrow's bitter cup,
  By proving next with child.

He did desert and hate her then,
  And for to end the strife,
The shocking resolution form'd,
  To take away her life.

He artfully a letter penn'd,
  'Twas filled with love's deceit,
And unto her the same did send,
  Requesting she would meet

Him, at a certain time and place
  Accordingly she came,
Together lovingly they talk'd
  Through many a field and lane.

At length being in a private place,
  Together they sat down,
He cut her throat! O shocking case,
  His wickedness to crown.

He hid her body, but twas found,
  To gaol he was convey'd,
And at the assizes will be try'd,
  On the charge against him laid.

The
Winchester Tragedy
A true and particular account of a cruel and

INHUMAN MURDER

Committed on the Body of

MARY THOMAS

Near Winchester in the County of Hants, by

JOHN WILLIAMS

A Young Farmer, in the same Neighbourhood, on Sunday last, NOVEMBER 4th

Mary Thomas, the ill-fated young woman who is the subject of this history, was born near Winchester, in the County of Hants, where her parents, who are labouring people, now reside. She learned to read and write at a charity school, and was bred up as a labourer; when old enough she went into service, and lived at several places of reputation. Being a comely young woman she had several sweethearts; and had not attained her 18th year when she became acquainted with John Williams, a young farmer, who lived near Winchester.

Being a likely young man, and having much to say for himself, he soon gained her love; she believed him sincere, not reflecting:

*That man was made for to deceive.
And foolish women to believe.*

As they lived near each other their meetings were frequent, and his promises of marriage so repeatedly made, that she vainly flattered herself the time was not far distant when she should be united to a person she sincerely loved, and be happy. But John was all deceit, and aimed at her ruin; which under promise of marriage, and various other artifices, he totally effected. Repeated meetings of criminality produced the usual consequences and the deluded girl found herself pregnant; with the addition to her misery, that where she expected the most comfort she found the least, for John Williams not only evaded his promise, but entirely forsook her. She seldom saw him; and when she did, met with cold indifference and ill-treatment. Where he once loved, he now hated; and was continually ruminating how to get rid of her and the infant in her womb. This cruel treatment of an unfortunate girl whom he had seduced,

28

was increased by his fixing his eyes on a farmer's daughter, whose uncle had left her £200, and he was determined, if possible, to obtain her hand. The only obstacle to this was the pregnancy of Mary Thomas, for he had conversed with the other woman and everything seemed to favour his wishes. He formed various schemes to get rid of the poor girl, till at length the devil put it into his head to murder her. This dreadful resolution being formed, the next consideration was how to effect it: he resolved to decoy her out the following Sunday, to a private place, and there perpetrate the bloody deed. In pursuance of this plan, he sent the following letter by a young man who assisted him at the same farm:

Dear Mary,
    I hope these few lines will find you in good health, as I am at present; and to let you know, I shall be glad if you can contrive to meet me about four o'clock tomorrow afternoon, and I will wait for you in the lane below farmer Gough's field. I beg you will not fail coming, as I have something very particular to propose to you, which may be of the greatest benefit to us. So no more at present from,
                Your Loving Friend,
                    John Williams

On receiving this letter she was somewhat comforted, and having obtained leave to go out on Sunday, she sent the following answer:

Dear John,
    Your letter revived my drooping spirits; and, God knows, I have need of some comfort under my afflictions, which I have by my own indiscretion, brought upon myself. I will not fail of meeting you at the place appointed; and still I remain,
                Yours, the afflicted
                    Mary Thomas

Punctual to the time, she met him at the appointed place, when after walking together till they came to an unfrequented path, they sat down on a bank. Here putting his arms round her neck as if going to kiss her, he, with a knife which he had concealed in his hand, cut her

throat in a dreadful manner and dragged her body to a ditch, threw it in, and covered it with brambles. Thus, having perpetrated the cruel act, he stay'd out till dark, and then returned home, and shifted his clothes, which had a great deal of blood on them. The poor girl's mistress was very uneasy at her staying out all night, and made every enquiry the next day, without hearing any tidings of her, and Williams being questioned, denied having been in her company on Sunday. As she had been observed to be in a melancholy way, a suspicion arose that she had destroyed herself; her father and others, searched the ponds and fields round about. At last they found some blood, and by tracing it to the ditch they discovered the body. Williams was apprehended, and on searching his apartments, his bloody clothes were found, and in one of the pockets the letter he received from the deceased. Notwithstanding these evidences of his guilt, he persisted in denying the crime. Now the Coroner's jury being met, he was brought to the room, and was desired to touch the body, which he did, when it bled at the nose* – By this circumstance, he was so shocked, that he was fully committed to take his trial at Hants Assizes.

[*From a contemporary broadsheet*]

*See *Murder Club Guide No.1* for a note on Touching the Corpse.

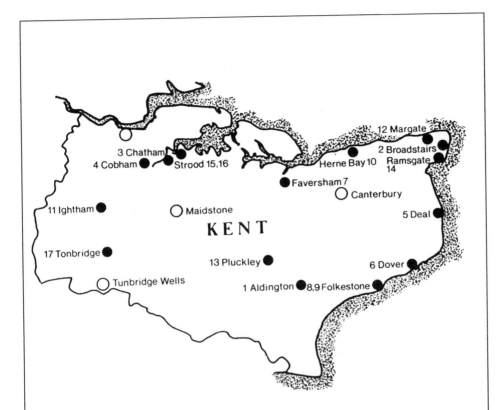

Kent

Another Notch for Four-Day Johnny

The Murder of HUBERT RODERICK TWELLS BUXTON
and his Wife ALICE
by HENDRYK NIEMASZ
on Friday the 12th of May 1961
at Pantile Bungalow, Frith Road, Aldington

Among all the sights that the milkman is traditionally supposed to enjoy on his early rounds, corpses do not often feature. Which is probably why David Pilcher will never forget that spring morning of May 13th, 1961. It was eight o'clock as he whistled his way up the back path through the trim garden of the Pantile Bungalow carrying the daily two pints. It had been a morning much like any other. But that was about to change; change very much for the worse.

As he approached, David Pilcher saw lying across the porchway where he was accustomed to leave the milk the almost naked body of a woman. He needed no close examination to tell him that she was dead: the still, staring eyes, the savagely battered body, and the blood, everywhere. If he had been able, Pilcher would have fled back to his milk float, but it was all he could do to force his numb legs to turn around, his appalled brain to direct him back down the path into Frith Road.

Summoned by the terrified roundsman, Police Constable Allen arrived on the scene with all the haste demanded by such a dramatic and ghastly event. Though no less shocked than David Pilcher, Allen was nevertheless able to bring his police training to bear on the situation; his more developed sense of observation taking in details that had been lost to the milkman. Beneath the drying blood, PC Allen recognized the features of Mrs Buxton; Alice Buxton. She was lying twisted on to her back, dressed as if she had got out of bed in a hurry, naked but for a pink slip and a hastily pulled on cardigan. Beside the body the policeman's eye took in the bloodstained double barrel section of a broken shotgun, and recognized it as a possible murder weapon.

The constable's horrified concentration was at once broken by the noise of a dog whimpering somewhere inside the house, and in following the sound he discovered the second corpse. Lying on the scullery floor was the man he knew as Mr Hubert Buxton. He too was partly dressed, and by the condition of the man's head Allen knew that he had been shot to death.

In no time the Pantiles Bungalow was playing host to some of the great luminaries of forensic investigation – Detective Chief Superintendent James Jenner, head of Kent CID, Detective Chief Superintendent John Du Rose, whose legendary speed in solving crimes resulted in the nickname 'four-day Johnny', and Detective-Sergeant Roy Habershon, both of Scotland Yard's Murder Squad, and Professor Francis Camps, pathologist to the Home Office.

While Camps took charge of the post-

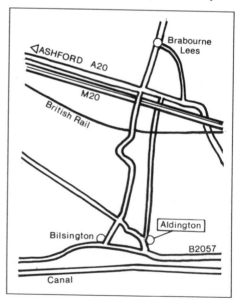

mortem arrangements, Habershon and Du Rose set about piecing together a background to the double murder and its unlucky victims.

It is often only when confronted with such a tragedy that we realize how little we really know about the people who go quietly about their business on the periphery of our lives. So it was with the Buxtons; what could their neighbours tell police about the couple who had occupied the Pantile Bungalow for the past two years?

He was Hubert Roderick Twells Buxton, a 35-year-old gardener employed in the extensive grounds of the de Pomeroy estate – Pantile House – here in the village of Aldington, between Ashford and Hythe. He seemed an agreeable fellow, but beyond that nobody could add anything. His wife (or more correctly, his common-law wife) was called Alice. She had been born in Belgium and was thought to be a couple of years older than Hubert. The couple had always seemed happy and devoted to each other; and that was the sum total of personal facts on the late Mr and Mrs Buxton.

It was Du Rose's painstaking search of the bungalow that provided the first and most significant clue to the killer's identity, and to a possible motive. On the floor of the bedroom he found the scraps of what looked like a torn-up letter, most of them under the bed. Realizing the potential importance of such evidence, Du Rose and Habershon pieced the scraps together, to find the letter had been written to Alice Buxton at an address in Belgium. Despsite the hesitant use of the English language, it was clear that this was a love letter of some passion; it was signed "bye bye, Hendryk, kiss you. XXX". The date suggested that the letter had been posted on May 8th, five days before.

Du Rose now set about the task of supplementing the sketchy portraits he had of Hubert and Alice Buxton, in the hope that it might shed light on the effect of Hendryk's letter. From Buxton's employer, Miss Gladys Etta de Pomeroy, he learned that the man had taken up the post of gardener – and the bungalow, which came with the job – in April 1959. He was by her account an excellent gardener, a man of quiet temperament and sober habits. Miss de Pomeroy had also

Hendryk Niemasz in his familiar motor-cycle gear

employed Alice Buxton for a short period, but that arrangement came to an end in November 1959. Since then Mrs Buxton had held a number of modest positions – in a local factory as an assembler, as a chambermaid in the Sutherland House Hotel in Hythe, and at the *Kings Head* nearby as a waitress.

In piecing together details of the twenty-four hours leading up to the discovery of the bodies, the detectives learned that Hubert Buxton had signed for the registered letter forwarded from Belgium and addressed to his wife from 'Hendryk' on the morning of the 12th. That evening, Alice was positively identified by the driver as having alighted from his bus at 4.50pm from Hythe. Three hours later Hubert had been seen by his employer still at work on the flower beds of Pantile House. At 9.15pm a local farmer noticed a light-coloured car parked on the verge in Frith Road, just down from the bungalow.

At the same time information was coming in from Belgium about Alice Buxton's earlier life. She had been born Alice Gyesel in February 1923 and had been an apprentice dressmaker. During the liberation of Belgium in 1944 she had met a driver in the

Royal Engineers named Richard Bateman whom she later married. After demobilization they moved to Evesham, where Bateman set up as a market gardener. Hubert Buxton became not only the Batemans' lodger, he became Alice's lover and, some said with no complaint from Bateman, ran away with her, eventually settling in Aldington. This much she had confessed to her mother on a trip home.

It was about a year after their arrival in Aldington that the lives of the Buxtons and the Niemasz family became entwined. Alice had met Mrs Grypa Niemasz on a bus on her way to work, and had invited her and her husband round to the bungalow for supper; his name was Hendryk Niemasz, and the two couples began going out together.

DCS Du Rose was beginning to feel himself making progress. He had almost certainly identified the Hendryk of the letter, and he had the bare bones of a motive. He now began to find people who could confirm his theory; people who now remembered seeing Alice Buxton in the company of a man who answered Niemasz's description. They had been seen drinking in pubs together. And Hendryk drove a cream Hillman Husky – was this the car seen parked in Frith Road on the night of May 12th?

On the following day, when the detectives ran Niemasz to ground at his home, the Polish refugee protested that he had been at home on the night of May 12th. Mrs Buxton, he said, was just a family friend: "I have wife! I want no Alice or other woman!" And the letter to Belgium? Well, he had just written to ask her on what date she returned to Dover so that they could all go down and meet her; so his English was not so good! And the kisses at the end of the letter? "Everyone put kisses!"

Hendryk Niemasz remained dubiously in the clear for a further couple of days until, acting on instinct, Du Rose, Habershon, and some local detectives returned to the Niemasz house, more particularly to the smallholding at the rear, and more specifically still, the shed which contained the hay that was the pigs' bedding. When they found the broken stock of a shotgun buried in the hay alongside some live cartridges it was the one piece of tangible evidence the Yard men needed for an arrest: the arrest of Hendryk

Niemasz. John Du Rose had lived up to his nickname once again!

By the time it reached Lewes Assizes the case against Niemasz was watertight. Not only did the concealed shotgun stock match exactly with the broken part found next to Mrs Buxton's body, but it also bore her killer's fingerprints. Mrs Niemasz broke down after the arrest and confessed that her husband's alibi was false, that he had been out of the house late on the night of the murder. A pair of bloodstained trousers was found – in the pocket was Alice Buxton's address in Belgium, and the receipt for the registered letter that Niemasz sent to that address.

In the face of overwhelming evidence, Hendryk Niemasz's defence seemed a paltry and unnecessary gesture. He had nothing to do with the murder, he pleaded; he had paid a man he knew simply as 'George' to commit the crime, a man he had met in a pub in Gillingham and had bought for £60. A hunt was mounted for the shadowy 'George', but it was to nobody's surprise that he was never found. Throughout the four-day trial the prisoner listened and spoke through Mrs Jadwiga Sutton, the Polish interpreter appointed by the court for his benefit; but when the black silk square was placed on Mr Justice Pilcher's wig Hendryk Niemasz needed no translation.

The jury had taken only an hour and quarter to decide that it was Hendryk Niemasz and not the illusory George who had been responsible for the double killing – a verdict manifestly unpopular with the prisoner who asked through his interpreter why the court wished to kill him.

Quite why Niemasz felt that it was necessary to slaughter the Buxtons is uncertain. In a statement made by Grypa Niemasz, her husband had told her that Alice was demanding that he run away with her, and threatened to tell the police that he had promised to kill Hubert if he didn't. Hendryk himself told the police another version – that Alice Buxton had given him a pistol and insisted that he shoot not only her husband but Grypa as well. The exact truth of what went on in Hendryk's mind we will never know; he was hanged at Wandsworth Prison on Friday the 8th of September, 1961.

A Very Happy, United Family

The Murder of her Sister-in-Law LILIAN
by EDITH DAISY CHUBB
on Thursday the 6th of February 1958
at 105 Hugin Avenue, Broadstairs

All happy families resemble each other, each unhappy family is unhappy in its own way.
(Leo Tolstoy, *Anna Karenina*)

It is an apparently curious fact that the great majority of murders are committed within the close confines of the family; and far from infrequently in the communal home. But a closer look is rewarded by at least one useful observation – that members of a family, unlike friends, can rarely choose each other, and a family created cannot, like a failed friendship, be easily undone, which may help us understand why, though blood may be thicker than water, quite a lot if it seems to get spilled.

Edith Daisy Chubb was a drudge. She had not been born so, but at the age of forty-six she found herself with sole responsibility for a thoughtless, ill-tempered husband, an elderly mother, five children, and a domineering sister-in-law. In addition to her seemingly endless domestic commitments, Edith Chubb kept the family just this side of poverty by working a gruelling 12-hour three-day-a-week shift as a cleaner in the Haine Hospital near her home in Broadstairs; ironically she was a trained nurse. Edith was constantly tired, constantly in debt and, like too many women forced into this position, an eternal silent martyr. That was probably the cause of the trouble that was building up for the Chubbs; had she allowed herself now and again to express her rightful indignation at her lot, the pressure might have eased. As it was, something obviously had to break under the strain. It happened to be Edith Chubb's reason, and the violent outrush of all her frustrations, all her disappointments, had to go somewhere; it happened to be in the direction of Miss Lilian Chubb.

Sister-in-law Lily was a maiden lady of a type popularly characterised on the English comedy stage – that is to say, she was middle-aged, prim, opinionated and over-bearing. Miss Chubb was employed as a sales assistant in the ladies wear department of a big store in Cliftonville, and in perfect keeping with the rest of her character, she left home on the dot of 8.40 every morning, and left work on the dot of 6 every evening.

The morning of the 6th of February 1958 was the one day that she varied the habit – and then it could hardly be said to be the result of a temporarily wayward spirit. Because this was the day that Edith's mind chose to seize up. Her husband had left for work, the children for school; the two women were alone in the house. "I felt irritated by the way she put her tea-cup down," recalled Mrs Chubb; "I followed her down the stairs, and pulled hard on her scarf . . . I didn't mean to hurt her . . . just to shake her up. She fell backwards onto the floor, striking her head on the bannister." Outside the front door, the milkman could be heard making his daily delivery; inside, Lilian made a low, groaning

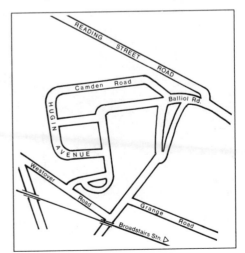

sound, and Edith put her hand over her mouth to stop it . . .

That evening there was great surprise in the Chubb household – Lilian was late home! Consternation when she did not come home at all; and it was Edith Chubb who next morning went to the Broadstairs police station to report her missing. That was at around 10am. One hour later the police returned her visit; Lilian Chubb had been found, in a hedge in Reading Street Road. She was dead; the doctor said it was strangulation. Edith could hardly believe her ears: "I just can't imagine anything like this happening; we are a very happy, united family."

It was only after Miss Lily had been given the questionable privilege of a post-mortem by one of the country's leading forensic pathologists, that Edith Chubb's story was seriously doubted. Professor Francis Camps confirmed that Lily Chubb had died from strangulation, and he also identified the probable cause of the strangely situated patches of lividity on the body. The state of lividity, or hypostasis, is simply the result of the blood in the body – no longer circulating after death – finding its own level and coagulating in the vessels; thus, those parts of the corpse that are in contact with a hard sur-

face, such as the floor, or constricting pressure, such as collars and waistbands, will not show the characteristic livid patches where the blood lies. Based on this principle, it was Camps's contention that the body of Lilian Chubb had been sat upon a chair shortly after death and left on it for some time before disposal. Incidentally, Camps confided, the pressure on the throat could easily have been exerted by a woman.

The victim's movements on the day of the crime were the next to come under police scrutiny; or rather, it was the lack of movements that started Chief Inspector Everitt and his team looking for a killer literally closer to home. It had already been established that Lilian Chubb had not reported for work on the morning of the 6th; what is more, none of the neighbours, who were familiar with her punctual nature, had seen Miss Chubb leave at her customary time that morning. So, reasoned the officers, she must have died in the house.

Edith Chubb made her confession to Chief Inspector Everitt without too much prompting: "I knew," she said, "that I should have to tell you before long."

Edith Daisy Chubb

The forlorn, long-suffering Mrs Chubb stepped into the witness box at her trial, and with the help of her defence counsel began the long recitation of depressing events in a deeply depressing life: "Lily was so smug; nobody knows what she was like . . ." Poor Lilian, she became the focus, rightly or wrongly, for all Edith's discontent. Then finally: "Something came over me. I pulled the scarf tightly round Lily's neck. She didn't struggle . . . When I realized she was dead I was horror-struck." Edith Chubb put her victim in the old invalid chair that was in the garden shed, and pushed it back into the shed. Next morning early she covered the corpse with a rug and wheeled it down the Reading Street Road where she dumped it: "It didn't take me long."

And it didn't take the jury long either, to reach their verdict. They had heard medical evidence from Edith's doctor, Gordon Marshall, who testified that she was a woman close to breaking-point. Mrs Evelyn Cook, the matron of Haine Hospital, where the prisoner had worked, agreed that Mrs

Chubb was a sick woman. Mr Justice Jones, however, was careful to redress this balance of sympathy when he spoke about the incident of the milkman on the doorstep: "This woman is a trained nurse, and you may think that the simplest thing in the world would have been for her to deal with the situation and the deceased would have recovered quite quickly . . . You must ask yourselves whether the most natural behaviour on the part of a nurse would have been to render some first-aid." He added that, at the very least, the jury must return a verdict of manslaughter. And that is what they did.

The next four years, during which Edith Chubb was a guest of Her Majesty, were probably the most relaxed of her life.

The Man who Wanted to Die
The Murder of THOMAS FREDERICK HOUGHTON
by ROBERT ALEXANDER BURTON
on Tuesday the 22nd of July 1862
on the Chatham Great Lines

There are cravings of the human mind for which no philosophy can account. To some men death seems sweeter than life, and they long to die, though they may shrink from cutting with their own hands the tie that binds them to existence. But never, so far as I am aware, has the craving for death taken a more morbid, a more ghastly, and a more unaccountable shape than in the case of Robert Alexander Burton, who had such a yearning to die on the gallows that he perpetrated a cold-blooded murder with no other object than to experience the sensation of being hanged. Here was a youth who actually courted death by the hangman's rope, who was fascinated by the idea of thus making his exit from the world – had dreamed of it and brooded over it until he could no longer resist the temptation to do that which should satisfy his unholy craving, and realise his unnatural desire. A madman, surely, you will say.
(*Famous Crimes Past and Present*, 1904)

At a late hour on the night of Wednesday, July 23rd 1862, Police Constable 469 Hibbert was amazed to be accosted by a young man who calmly stated that his name was Robert Alexander Burton, and that he wished to confess to the brutal murder of a nine-year-old child.

Recovering his composure, PC Hibbert encountered no resistance in escorting the youth Burton back to the police station at [Rochester]. Here he was able to confirm that just such a crime as his charge described had been discovered on the previous afternoon. The victim, a Thomas Frederick Houghton, was found where he had been slain, at the entrance to one of the airshafts ventilating the tunnel through which the London, Chatham and Dover Railway passed under the open area of land known as Chatham Great Lines.

Taken before Superintendent Everitt, Robert Alexander Burton gave the following extraordinary testimony, faithfully recorded by Constable Hibbert:

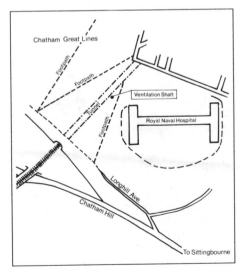

The bleak Chatham Great Lines in 1987

"I was feeling weary of life and, therefore, determined to kill someone. I did not care one jot who it might be – one person would answer the purpose as well as another in my anxiety to be hanged. Walking through the street I came upon the deceased boy with his mother, and at once resolved in my mind that this poor child should be my victim. After following them for some distance, I saw the mother go into her house after giving the child permission to play on the Lines. This was at about two o'clock on Tuesday afternoon. I then followed the boy to the place where the body was discovered and, thinking it was a favourable place for carrying my intention into effect, went up to the unfortunate child, and after accosting him, knocked him down, and dragged him a short distance. The boy struggled very much, and made every effort to free himself. But I succeeded in getting a knife from my pocket and with it cut the boy's throat, severing the windpipe." [The accused – if so one can call a self-confessor – in answer to the Superintendent's remark that there were several bruises about the face of the deceased, said he only gave one cut on the throat, and denied anything else.] "The boy, after receiving the wound in his throat, struggled very much and seized my hands. But I shook him off and, as he did not die quickly enough, I knelt on the child and pressed both hands tightly round his throat until the blood ran from his eyes and nose, and he was dead. After, I proceeded across the Lines, and met a gentleman dressed in black coming towards me; fearing that he might see my hands, which were covered with blood, I hastily thrust then in the pockets of my trousers. I then went to the military bathing pond and washed the blood off my hands, face, and clothes; and also cleansed the blood from the knife. Afterwards, I went into town, and the same night hid the knife in a water-closet of a house at the rear of the *Dark Sun* public house, in the High Street at Chatham."

When Burton was taken before the magistrates it was through streets thronged with angry crowds, mostly of women, who shook their fists at him and screamed, "Oh! the bloody murderin' villain! – to kill a poor innocent child! Let's get at him and tear the eyes out of him!" and other oaths and expletives less delicate. Seemingly offended by these undignified outcries, Burton was constrained to remark to his warder to the effect that, "I'd as soon treat some of those women as I treated the boy. It would be a good riddance to clear some of them off with a knife."

But the youth's murdering days were to be severely curtailed, and though a history of insanity running through the family seemed to have been demonstrated, this defence found no favour with the jury. It was their verdict that obliged the judge to intone the fearful words of the sentence of death and when this dread speech had been delivered to a hushed court, a single joyful voice broke from the dock – "Thank you, my Lord!"

Robert Alexander Burton's dream came true on Wednesday the 11th April 1863; his irrepressible craving for death was finally gratified outside Maidstone Gaol, where he looked up at the scaffold with a smile, the sight of the dangling rope seeming to give him genuine pleasure.

The Fairy Feller's Master Stroke
The Murder of ROBERT DADD
by his Son RICHARD
on Monday the 28th of August 1843
at Cobham Park, Cobham

Born the fourth of seven brothers and sisters, Richard Dadd first saw the light of day on August the 1st, 1817. The boy's father, Robert, was a native of Chatham, and in the business of apothecary and chemist in the High Street of that town; his mother was the former Mary Ann Martin, of whom we know little beyond the fact that she did not live to see Richard's seventh birthday.

The Dadds were a cultured, moderately prosperous, middle-class Victorian family, and their fourth son received his education at Rochester Cathedral Grammar School, supplementing his classes with drawing lessons from William Dadson, whose Academy was situated not far from Robert's shop in the High Street.

In 1834, in furtherance of Robert Dadd's new career as carver and gilder, the family removed to London, where they took up residence at number 15 in respectable Suffolk Street, Pall Mall East. In January 1837 Richard entered into full-time study at the Royal Academy School of Art; here he embraced the painterly principles of the exclusive 'Clique', and became a member in such company as Augustus Egg, William Powell Frith, John Phillip, and H.N. O'Neill. His artistic promise was recognized by the award of three silver medals, and his subsequent exhibitions with the Society of British Artists, and the Royal Academy, established for him a small reputation and several commissions. He also began to receive the private patronage of Sir Thomas Phillips, a solicitor of Newport, and a former mayor of the town.

It was as companion and draughtsman to Sir Thomas that Richard Dadd departed England on July the 16th, 1842, following that requisite of Victorian middle-class pursuits –

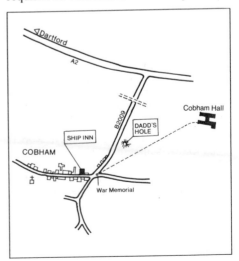

The Grand Tour. During the remainder of 1842 and the early part of 1843, the couple travelled through France, Greece, Italy, and the Middle East. Despite the onset of mental disturbance (aggravated, some say, by sunstroke from the fierce Egyptian sun*), Richard managed to complete many estimable watercolours and drawings throughout the trip. Unfortunately, by the time our travellers began the return, by way of Malta, Naples, and Rome, Richard had become convinced that he was pursued by devils; the more disturbing since one of the chief of these emissaries from Hell he imagined to be his companion Thomas Phillips. It may or not have been some comfort to Phillips to know that a fellow-demon took the shape of the Pope, whose assassination Dadd seriously considered until he saw the pontiff so heavily guarded.

It says a great deal for family loyalty that though Richard arrived home in May clearly very seriously disturbed, nobody felt that the situation demanded any urgent remedial action. The after-effects of the sunstroke, avowed his father, would pass with rest and quiet. Any invocation of that nineteenth-century bugaboo "insanity in the family" was strenuously resisted. Indeed, the painter had resumed his work; locking himself in his studio with the vast quantity of eggs and ale which lately formed his diet, Richard began to make a number of portraits of his friends, likenesses to which had been added a deep red gash across the throat.

By the month of August Richard's behaviour could be ignored no longer, for his manic flights from imagined persecution had become a public as well as a family embarrassment. On Saturday, August 26th, he was examined by Dr Alexander Sutherland, physician at St Luke's Asylum; the doctor advised that Richard was no longer responsible for his actions, and that he should be confined.

Still unconvinced of the urgency, Robert Dadd allowed himself to be persuaded to take a trip with his son on the following day; a trip during which Richard promised to "unburden his mind". Cobham had always

*Geraldine Norman in her *Dictionary of Nineteenth Century Painters and Paintings* perpetuates Dadd's occasional notion that he became subject to the arbitrary will of the god Osiris.

The Ship Inn, *Cobham*

been a favourite haunt of the Dadds, and father and son arrived in the village at about six o'clock in the evening, alighting at the *Ship Inn*, where they supped and arranged for lodging for the night. In the following hours Richard was frequently overheard pestering his reluctant father to take a stroll, to which the latter finally acceded, the pair walking off through the darkening acres of Cobham Park. Close by a large chalkpit (called Paddock Hole then, but subsequently changed to Dadd's Hole), the young man made a frenzied and murderous attack on his father and after a desperate struggle left the latter dead.

The remains of Robert Dadd were found the next morning by a butcher passing on his way to Wrotham Market; examination revealed the corpse to be a bloody mass of stab wounds and razor cuts, and the hunt began for his killer . . . his son.

But dishevelled and bloody though he was, Richard Dadd was on his way to France, fleeing via Rochester, through Dover and in a hired boat over the Channel to Calais, and down towards Paris. Meanwhile in London a

Part of the depression known as Dadd's Hole

paper had been found written in Richard's hand. The document comprised a list of names of several eminent people – headed by Robert Dadd, and including the Emperor Franz Ferdinand I of Austria. It proved to be Richard's assassination list.

Though hardly a tragedy of national importance, the case did receive some attention from the press, and beneath the heading "Murder at Cobham Park", the *Illustrated London News* reported:

> A rumour was prevalent during the week that the wretched parricide Dadd (the particulars of whose atrocity appeared in our late editions last week) had been arrested at Calais by one of the old Bow-street officers, on Monday last; but we regret to state that this is not the fact, and that the savage maniac is still prowling about in quest, perhaps, of other victims.
>
> (9th September, 1843)

The fugitive might have remained undetected for some time longer, had he not made an incomprehensible – and fortunately incompetent – attempt to cut the throat of a fellow passenger on the stage-coach they shared at Fontainebleau*. As a result Richard was arrested by the French police, and in accordance with their customary treatment of the criminally insane, committed to an asylum without benefit of trial. It would probably have been better for all concerned if the unhappy fellow had been allowed to remain confined in Clermont – certainly his family approved, and had even made arrangements for special food to be provided for Richard's comfort. But for complicated, and rather vague, 'political' reasons the Home Office was unwilling to let things remain as they stood, and Richard Dadd was extradited to England to be taken before the Rochester Magistrates, and remanded by them to the Assize at Maidstone, where:

> No doubt can remain in the mind of anyone who was present at the examination that the unfortunate young man is altogether irresponsible for his own acts. While in the presence of the bench his

---

*In mitigation, Martin Hardie (*Water Colour Painting in Britain*) suggested that the forest surroundings at Fontainebleau reminded Dadd of Cobham Park and so revived his condition.

demeanor underwent various and instantaneous changes. The opinion of the bench was unanimous and decided as to the state of his mind, and there is little doubt that the last public scene in this melancholy tragedy has closed, and that this once promising artist will be removed to a place of permanent safe-keeping without coming to trial.

(*Illustrated London News,* August 1844)

He was indeed found unfit to plead his case in a court of law and – in the manner of his

Richard Dadd at work on Contradiction: Oberon and Titania *at Bethlem Hospital, ca. 1856*

times and class – quietly relegated to the roll of inmates of the Bethlehem (or Bethlem; or Bedlam) Hospital at Southwark.

More fortunate than many in his position, Richard came to the enlightened notice of Dr Edward Monro, who encouraged him to take up painting again, and in collaboration with Dr W. C. Hood, Resident Physician at Bethlem from 1853 and a great admirer of Dadd's work, was responsible for promoting the most brilliantly productive four decades of the painter's life. Here in the Hospital,

The Fairy Feller's Master Stroke, *Tate Gallery, London*

and later in the newly instituted Broadmoor Asylum for the Criminally Insane, the academic achievement of Dadd's youth was transformed into intense and obsessive alegories crowded with the unreal denizens of his fantasies – the fairies, goblins, and spirits that characterize his most popular works.

At the end of 1885, Richard Dadd became fatally ill with consumption; on January 8th of the following year he died, and was buried in the small cemetery at Broadmoor.

The Half-Hanging of Ambrose Gwinett

The Fictitious Murder of Mr ROBERT COLLINS
by AMBROSE GWINETT
on Wednesday, the 17th of September 1709
in an Unnamed Inn at Deal

THE LIFE
AND UNPARALLELED
VOYAGES AND ADVENTURES
OF
AMBROSE GWINETT

Written by Himself*

I was born of reputable parents in the city of Canterbury, where my father dealt in slops [sailors' clothing and bedding]. He had but two children, a daughter and myself; and having given me a good school education, at the age of sixteen he bound me apprentice to Mr George Roberts, an attorney of the same town, with whom I stayed four years and three quarters, to his great content, and my own satisfaction.

My sister being come to woman's estate, had now been married something more than a twelvemonth to one Sawyer, a seafaring man, who having got consider-able prizes (my father also gave him £200 with my sister) quitted his profession, and set up a public house within three miles of the place of his nativity, which was Deal, in the county of Kent.

I had frequent invitations to pass a short time with them; and in the Autumn of the year 1709, having obtained my master's consent for the purpose, I left the city of Canterbury on foot on a Wednesday morning, being the 17th day of September; but through some unavoidable de-lays on the road, the evening was con-siderably advanced before I had reached Deal; and so tired was I, being unused to that way of travelling, that, had my life depended on it, I could not have got as

* In fact it was written by Isaac Bickerstaffe.

far as my sister's that night. At this time there were many of her Majesty Queen Ann's ships lying in the harbour, the English being then at war with the French and Spaniards; besides which, I found this was the day for holding the yearly fair; so that the town was filled to that degree that a bed was not to be gotten for love or money. I went seeking a lodging from house to house to no purpose, till, being quite spent, I returned to the public house where I had first made inquiry, desiring leave to sit by their kitchen fire to rest myself till morning.

The publican and his wife where I put up happened, unfortunately for me, to be acquainted with my brother[-in-law] and sister, and finding by the discourse that I was a relation of theirs, and going to visit them, the landlady presently said she would endeavour to get me a bed, and going out of the kitchen, she quickly after called me into a parlour that led from it. Here I saw sitting by the fire side a middle-aged man in a night gown and cap, who was reckoning money at a table. "Uncle", said the woman as soon as I had entered, "this is a brother of our friend Mrs Sawyer: he cannot get a bed any-where, and is tired after his journey. You are the only one that lies in this house alone, will you give him part of yours?" To this the man answered that she knew he had been out of order, that he was blooded [bled] that day, and consequent-ly a bedfellow could not be very agree-able. "However", said he, "rather than the young man shall sit up, he is welcome to sleep with me." After this we set a while together, when, having put his money in a canvas bag into the pocket of his nightgown, he took the candle, and I followed him up to bed.

How long I slept I cannot exactly determine, but I conjectured it was about three o'clock in the morning when I awakened with a cholic, attended with the most violent gripes; I attributed this to some cabbage and bacon I had eaten that day for dinner, after which I drank a large draught of milk. I found my chum awake as well as myself. He asked me what was the matter. I informed him, and at the same time begged him direct me to the necessary. He told me when I was down stairs I must turn on my right hand, and go straight into the garden, at the end of which it was, just over the sea. "But (adds he) you may find some difficulty opening the door, the string being broken which pulls up the latch. I will give you a pen knife, which you may open it with through a chink in the boards." So saying, he put his hand into his waistcoat pocket, which lay over him on the bed, and gave me a middle-sized pen knife. I hurried on a few of my clothes and went downstairs; but I must observe that in unclasping the pen knife to open the door of the necessary, according to his directions, a piece of money which was stuck between the blade and the groove in the handle, fell into my hand. I did not examine what it was, nor indeed could I well see, there being then but a very faint moon light; so I put them together carelessly into my pocket. I apprehended I staid in the garden pretty near half an hour, for I was extremely ill, and, by over-heating myself with walking the preceding day, had brought on the piles; a disorder I was subject to since my youth. These seem trifling circumstances, but afterwards turned out of infinite consequence to me. When I returned to the chamber, I was surprised to find my bedfellow gone; I called several times, but receiving no answer, took it for granted he had withdrawn into some adjoining closet for his private occasions. I therefore went to bed and again fell to sleep.

About six o'clock I arose, nobody yet being up in the house. The gentleman was not yet returned to bed, or if he was, had again left it. I dressed myself with what haste I could, being impatient to see my sister; and the reckoning being paid overnight I departed.

I will not trouble you with a relation of the kindness with which my sister and her husband received me. We breakfasted together, and I believe it might have been about eleven o'clock in the fore-noon when standing at the door, my brother-in-law by my side, we saw three horsemen galloping towards us. As soon as they came up they stopt, and one of them lighting suddenly seized me by the collar, crying, "You are the Queen's prisoner." I desired to know my crime. He said I should know that as soon as we came back to Deal, where I must immediately go with them. One of them told my brother that the night before I had committed murder and robbery.

Resistance would have proved as vain as my tears and protestations of my innocence. In a word a warrant was produced and I was carried back to Deal attended by the three men; my brother and another friend accompanying us, who knew not what to say, or how to comfort me.

Being arrived in town, I was immediately hurried to the house where I had slept the previous night, the master of which was one of the three men that came to apprehend me, though in my first hurry I did not recollect him. We were met at the door by a crowd of people, every one crying "Which is he? which is he?" As soon as I entered, I was accosted by the publican's wife, in tears. "Oh! cursed wretch, what hast thou done? Thou hast murdered and robbed my poor dear uncle, and all through me, who put thee to lie with him! But where hast thou hid his money? And what hast thou done with his body? Thou shalt be hanged upon a gallows as high as the May pole." My brother begged her to be pacified, and I was taken into a private room. They began to question me as the woman had done, about where I had put the money, and how I had disposed of the body. I asked them what money, and whose body they meant? They then said I had killed the person I had lain with the preceding night for the sake of a large sum I had seen him with. I fell down upon my knees, calling God to witness I knew nothing of what they accused me. Then somebody cried out, "Carry him up the stairs;" and I was brought to the chamber where I had slept. Here the man of the house went to the bed, and turned down the sheets, pillows and bolster dyed with blood. He asked me did I know anything of that? I declared to God that I did not. Says a person who was in that room, "Young man, something very odd must have passed here last night, for lying in the next chamber I heard groanings, and going up and down stairs more than once or twice." I told them the circumstances of my illness and that I had been up and down myself, with all that passed between my bedfellow and me. Somebody proposed to search me; several began to turn my pockets inside out, and from my waistcoat tumbled the pen knife and the piece of money I have already mentioned. Upon seeing these, the woman immediately screamed out, "O God! There is my uncle's pen knife!" Then taking up the money and calling the people about her, "here is what puts the villain's guilt beyond a doubt; I can swear to this William and Mary guinea; my uncle has long had it by way of a pocket-piece and engraved the first letters of his name upon it." She began to cry again, while I could do nothing but continue to call Heaven to witness that I was as innocent as the child unborn.

After this they carried me down to the necessary, and here fresh proofs appeared against me. The constable, who had never left me, perceived blood on the edges of the seat, (which might have been the hemorrhage of the night before). "Here," said he, "after having cut the throat, he let the body down into the sea." This everybody immediately assented to. "Then," said the master of the house, "it is vain to look for the body any further, for there was a spring tide last night, which has carried it off."

The consequence of these proceedings was an immediate examination before the justice of the peace; after which I suffered long and rigorous imprisonment in the county town of Maidstone. For some time my father, my master, and my relations were inclined to think me innocent; and in compliance with my earnest request, an advertisement was published in the *London Gazette*, representing my deplorable circumstances and offering a reward to any person who could give tidings of Mr Richard Collins (the name of the man I was supposed to have murdered), either alive or dead. No information, however, of any kind came to hand. At the Assizes therefore, I was brought to trial; and circumstances appearing strong against me, I received sentence to be carried in a cart the Wednesday fortnight, to the town of Deal, and there to be hanged before the inn-keeper's door where I had committed the supposed murder; after which I was to be hung in chains within a little way of my brother's house.

Nothing could have supported me under this dreadful condemnation, but a consciousness of my not being guilty of the crime for which I was to suffer. My friends now began to consider my declarations of innocence as persisting in falsehood to the perdition of my soul; many of them discontinued their inquiries after me, and those few who still came to visit me, only came to urge me to confession. But I was resolved I would never die with a lie like that in my mouth.

The Monday was now arrived before the fatal day, when an end was to be put to my miseries. I was called down into the court of the prison; but I own I was not a little shocked when I found it was to be taken measure for the irons in which I was to be hung after execution. A fellow prisoner appeared before me in the same woeful plight (he had robbed the mail) and the smith was measuring him when I came down; while the gaoler, with as much calmness as if he had been ordering a pair of stays for his daughter, was giving directions in what manner the irons should be made so as to support the man, who was remarkably heavy and corpulent.

Between this and the day of my execution, I spent my time alone in prayer and meditation. At length Wednesday morning came, and about six o'clock I was put into the cart; but sure such a day of wind, rain, and thunder, never blew out of the Heavens. It pursued us all the way; and when we arrived at Deal, it became so violent that the sheriff and his officers, who had not a dry thread upon them, could scarce sit their horses. For my own part, my mind (God help me) was with long agitation become so unfeeling, that I was in a manner insensible to every object about me; I therefore heard the sheriff whisper to the executioner to make what despatch he could without the least emotion, and suffered him to tuck me up like a log of wood, unconscious of what he was doing.

I can give no account of what I felt while I was hanging, only that I remember, after being turned off, something for a little appeared about me like a blaze of fire; nor do I know for how long I hung, no doubt the violence of the weather favoured me greatly in that circumstance. What I am now going to tell you I learned from my brother, which was that after having hung about half an hour, the sheriff's officers went off and I was cut down by the executioner; but when he came to put the irons upon me, it was found a mistake had been made, and that the iron of the other man had been sent instead of mine. This they remedied as well as they could, by stuffing rags between my body and the hoops that surrounded it. After a while I was taken according to my sentence, to the place appointed, and hung upon a gibbet which was ready prepared.

The cloth over my face being but lightly tied, and suffering no pressure from the iron, which stood a great way from it, was, I suppose, soon detached by the wind, which was still rather violent, and probably its blowing on my face expedited my recovery; certain it is, that in this tremendous situation I came to myself.

It was, no doubt, a very great blessing that I did not immediately return so perfectly to my senses as to have a feeling of things about me; yet I had a sort of recollection of what had happened, and in some measure was sensible where I was.

The gibbet was placed in one corner of a small common-field, where my sister's cows usually ran, and it pleased God that about that time a lad who took care of them came to drive them for evening milking. The creatures which were feeding almost under me, brought him near

the gibbet; when, stopping to look at the melancholy spectacle, he perceived that the cloth was from off my face and, in the very moment he looked up, saw me opening my eyes and moving my under jaw. He immediately ran home to inform the people at his master's. At first they made some difficulty to believe his story; at length, however, my brother came out, and by the time he got to the field I was so much alive that my groans were very audible.

It was now dusk. The first thing they ran for was a ladder. One of my brother's

men mounted, and, putting his hand on my stomach, felt my heart beating very strongly. But it was found impossible to detach me from the gibbet without cutting it down. A saw, therefore, was got for that purpose and, without giving you a detail of trifling circumstances, in less than half an hour, having freed me from my irons, they got me blooded, and put me into a warm bed in my brother's house.

It is an amazing thing, that, though upwards of eight persons were entrusted with this transaction, and I remained three days in the place after it happened, not a creature betrayed the secret. Early next morning it was known that the gibbet was cut down, and immediately it occurred to every body that it was done by my relations in order to put a slight veil over their own shame by burying the body; but when my brother was summoned to the mayor's house in order to be questioned, and he denied knowing anything of the matter, little more stir was made about it; partly because he was so greatly respected by all the neighbouring gentlemen, and in some measure, perhaps, because it was known that I continued to persist strongly in my being innocent of the fact for which I suffered.

Thus, then, was I most miraculously delivered from an ignominious death, if I may call my coming to life a delivery after all I had endured. But how was I to dispose of my life now I had regained it? To stay in England was impossible without exposing myself again to the terrors of the law. In this dilemma a fortunate circumstance occurred. There had lain for some time at my brother's house, one or two of the principal officers of a privateer that was preparing for a cruise, just then ready to sail. The captain kindly offered to take me aboard with him. You may guess little difficulty was made on our side to accept of such a proposal; and proper necessaries being quickly provided for me, my sister recommended me to the protection of God and the worthy commander, who most humanely received me as a sort of under-assistant to his steward . . .

[*There follows an account of the "Voyages and Adventures . . . to the West Indies, and being taken by the Spaniards, amongst whom he met with the supposed Murdered Mr Collins, and proposed to return to England together. The Accident that threw Ambrose into the hands of Pirates; his Extraordinary adventures with them; and being again taken by the Spaniards, and there condemn'd to the Galleys. His being taken by the Algerines, and carried into Slavery, and, after many Hardships, returned to England"*]

Behind Closed Doors
The Murder of Mr EDWARD ADOLPHUS WALSHE
by THOMAS WELLS
on Friday the 1st of May 1868
at the Dover Priory Railway Station

It had taken penal reformers many years to achieve the modest aim of getting the squalid ritual of judicial hanging carried out in private. On the 26th of May, 1868, Michael Barrett, the Fenian, was the last person to suffer public execution [see *Murder Club Guide No.1*]; on May 29th the Capital Punishment Within Prisons Bill was given Royal Assent, within three months, nineteen-year-old Thomas Wells became the first person to be executed in private. The following description of this significant development in the treatment of offenders, derives from the *Dover Chronicle* of August 15th, 1868, and is based on eye-witness accounts of the lacklustre crime of a rather pathetic youth:

EXECUTION OF THE MURDERER WELLS

Thomas Wells, the murderer of Mr Walshe, the stationmaster of the Dover Priory Station of the London, Chatham and Dover Railway, expiated his great crime at the county gaol in Maidstone on Thursday morning last [August 13th, 1868]. Without at any time formally confessing that he had committed the murder, Wells never either denied his guilt or attempted to palliate his conduct, and there is every reason to believe that he died deeply penitent. From the moment the Judge assumed the black cap, at the trial three weeks ago, and slowly, solemnly, but still sternly, even though his voice was here and there rendered indistinct by emotion, passed the Sentence of Death, no hope was held out to the prisoner [though] he may have thought that mercy would have been extended to him at the last moment, perhaps on the ground of his extreme youth alone. But the crime could not be condoned.

He must have remembered the faults he committed that led to poor Mr Walshe's complaint of his conduct. The correction that followed galled his stubborn spirit, and aroused in him feelings that had hitherto, however bad they were, lain dormant. He uttered, in his deep and bitter passion, his intense hatred of his master, the threats which were so fully consummated only a short time subsequently. The readers know the rest of the story only too well. How, on the morning of a bright May day, the first of the most charming of the Spring months, he hid a loaded gun in some part of the station, in order to use it with deadly result when the opportunity occurred. How he was called into the station-master's office, was rebuked in his presence by Mr Cox, the superintendent, who told him he would be reported to a yet higher authority; and how, three or four minutes afterwards, Mr Walshe, a kind, genial, good-hearted gentleman, who would not have intentionally harmed a fellow-creature at any price, lay weltering in his blood on the floor of his own private office, shot through the brain as he stood whilst Mr Cox indicated the letter complaining of Wells to his superior officer. And how the murderer, rushing from the scene of the awful catastrophe, with the mark of Cain on his brow, was discovered by the police in an empty carriage with a recently discharged weapon in his hands, and the conclusive chain of evidence, irrefutable, though purely circumstantial, by which the crime was brought home to him – all these dreadful details are already deeply engrafted on the minds of most people, and repetition would be as tedious as it would be unnecessary and painful. Sufficient it is to say that Wells was put on his trial for wilful murder, and the clever defence of the learned counsel who appeared for him, and who contended that the lad must have been insane, had no weight with the jury, who returned the verdict of guilty which led to the prisoner being sentenced to be hanged by the neck until he was dead.

During the space of time which elapsed between his conviction and Thursday morning, he was, on several occasions visited by his relatives . . . He implored the forgiveness of Mrs Walshe, the widow of the murdered man, and of Mr Cox, and in both cases it was readily extended towards him, Mr Cox and Mrs Walshe both expressing the hope that he would do all that lay in his power to leave this world deeply penitent for his crime.

The day fixed for the execution came at last, and, owing to the fact that this was the first hanging under the provisions of the new Bill to provide for private executions, the public have looked forward to the event with a kind of morbid interest which is always displayed in anything unusual, but more particularly when it is in the slightest degree connected with the horrible. One means of gratifying this peculiar taste has, by the new Act, been done away with, for the spectacle of a man being hanged in accordance with the claims of the law will no longer be one that will fall to the lot of the public at large in Great Britain . . . That the abolition of public executions is a wise piece of legislation there can be no doubt, especially taking into consideration the way in which the provisions of the scheme were carried out on Thursday in the case of Wells. Perhaps one of its greatest effects is that which it has upon the prisoner condemned to death. It is well known that, in the majority of cases where a man was sentenced to be publicly hanged, he steeled himself up to a kind of bravado, in order, poor deluded mortal, to show the two or three thousand people who,

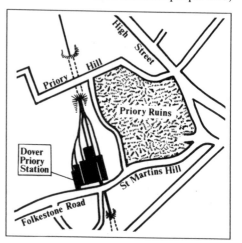

with eager faces staring towards the drop, had come miles to witness the death of a fellow creature, that he had died "game". What a mockery! But now there will be no more of this. The hoots, and the yells, and the cheers, that have greeted various male-factors at the moment of their execution, will not again be heard. The prisoner knows that he is to meet his death within the precincts of the gaol, surrounded by high and dreary walls that shut out the world and hope at the same time, or, in the presence of warders and other gaol officials, in whose breasts no sympathy dwells, and of gentle-men representing the Press who look at the tragedy as a piece of routine duty, a duty of a solemn nature, but still one that does not permit the display of anything like senti-ment. Thirteen of those gentlemen, amongst them being George Augustus Sala and Edmund Yates, representing respectively the *Daily Telegraph* and the *Morning Star*, met at the gaol at Maidstone at ten o'clock on Thursday morning, and waited in one of the offices of the South Division, until notice was given that their presence was necessary at the place of execution. The minutes pas-sed by with a painful slowness. Warders were running here and there, engaged in mysterious duties connected with the approaching catastrophe, and the bell of the prison was tolling a death knell. The morn-ing was a very dull one; the sun not shining, the atmosphere was close and oppres-sive, and a drizzling rain was falling. The condemned man, we were told, was at that moment with the chaplain, who had left him late on the preceding night, and joined him again early that morning, when Wells par-took of the Holy Communion. At about ten o'clock on Wednesday evening he was ex-cited and hysterical; he had that afternoon seen his father for the last time, and the interview, together with the awfulness of his doom, completely unnerved him, whilst his father was carried away in a fit.

However, Wells afterwards grew more com-posed, and no longer babbled of home, and of friends, but fell asleep at about eleven o'clock. His rest was comparatively undis-turbed during the night, and he rose early on Thursday morning, partook of a slight meal, and then devoted himself to his spiritual duties for a time, but the hysterical fits again returned, and at half-past nine o'clock it was

feared he would not be able to sustain himself to the last. Mr Robert Furley, the Under-Sheriff of the County, made the usual formal demand to the Governor at about ten o'clock to deliver up the body for execution according to law; and at five and twenty minutes past ten o'clock Calcraft, the hang-man [see *Murder Club Guide No.3*], was introduced to the cell where the prisoner had partaken of the Communion shortly before. It was not the condemned cell, for there is no such place in the gaol, but was a small room adjoining the debtors' quarters, and looking out into a small passage leading directly to the yard where the execution was to take place. Calcraft has been described on many occasions. He is a man of middle stature, about sixty-five years of age, with grey hair and on Thursday, was attired in a rusty suit of black. He was assisted by Smith, of Dudley, a man who carries on the busi-ness of a cattle dealer in that place, and who is the hangman for the Midland Counties. It was he who hung Palmer at Stafford [see *Murder Club Guide No.4*]; and on the last two occasions we saw him officiating at that place he appeared on the scaffold wearing a large white smock, one side of which he coolly lifted in order to draw the usual white cap from his trousers pocket. Now he was dressed in a velvet coat and waistcoat, with drab trousers, and shoes with light coloured uppers. The Press did not witness the pinioning, which was the work of but a few minutes, but in a short time they were called out of the room where they had been staying, and, having been conducted through two large cells, emerged into the passage before referred to, leading to the yard. Wells was at this moment being con-ducted on to the drop; in fact, he had already reached it, and was being guided by Smith into the proper place on the trap door. This drop was under a small shed at the end of the courtyard, and the spectators, who now comprised the chaplain, the governor of the gaol, the Under-Sheriff, the surgeon, the representatives of the Press, two inhabitants of Maidstone, and the carpenter who had built the drop (who was in attendance for fear of any accident) stood behind a wood barrier, stretched across the court, about four yards from the drop. The beam from which the rope dangled, the ominous slip-knot at the end, supported the low roof of the shed, and underneath the drop, which

was painted a light drab colour – "black would look so gloomy", we heard one of the officials say – was a small pit, lined with white-washed bricks. The culprit had, therefore, neither to descend nor ascend any steps, and was not called upon to drag one heavy foot after another up the stairs of a scaffold.

Now, as he stood there, helpless in the hands of his executioners, one could not help pitying him. He appeared to be almost unconscious, and before he left his cell, brandy and sal volatile had to be administered to him. His elbows were strapped close to his sides, and his wrists were also bound up in strong leather thongs. His shoulders, either from the strapping, or else from the fright of the victim, were elevated to his ears, and his face, which on the day of the trial was so composed, was now distorted by fear; his lips were parched, and terribly swollen, his eyes were fixed upon vacancy, and over his countenance was suffused a most ghastly livid colour. The chaplain stood in front of him, grasping the lad's clasped hands, and praying with a fervency that affected all present.

Wells seemed to hear the prayers, for his lips every now and then moved, and a low mumbling sound was heard. While all this was going on, the two hangmen were silently making every arrangement. Calcraft, so soon as Wells, supported on either side by a warder, was in the centre of the drop, fixed the noose round his neck, quickly, but taking care that the knot should press under the ear; and Smith, kneeling down, passed a strap round the legs of the condemned man, and tightly buckled them together. Directly Wells felt the rope round his neck, he moistened his lips, and with difficulty commenced singing. The chaplain stopped praying, and, amid a silence broken only by the shuffling of the hangmen, Wells sang:

> Happy soul, thy days are ended,
>   All thy mourning days below,
> Go, by angel friends attended,
>   To the throne of Jesus go.

The hymn was one he came across in one of the prison books, and he sang it several times during the two or three days that immediately preceded the execution. The words of the first two lines were distinctly heard by the group of spectators, but when he had got so far the white cap was drawn over the quivering face, and the voice was so muffled that the remaining words were inaudible. But the verse was finished. The lips could be seen moving under the cap, and a low sound reached the bystanders. Then some one made a sign to Calcraft, who pressed Wells' clasped hands in his own, stepped to the back of the drop, and motioned to Smith, who stood on the steps leading underneath, his right hand grasping a lever. What followed is soon told. There was a rusty grating noise, that jarred terribly on the ears of those present, a dull thud from the heavy trap door falling against the sack of straw that had been placed there to prevent its rebounding, and the soul of Thomas Wells was swung into Eternity.

Calcraft immediately went down the steps, and steadied the body, but did not press on it as he sometimes does, to hasten death. He stayed there for about two minutes, and then slunk away with a shuffle that is peculiar to him, without having spoken a word to anyone. Smith stayed for a few moments longer, contemplating, with the rest of the spectators, who had now been admitted through the barrier, the repulsive spectacle of the body of a fellow-creature dangling between heaven and earth. Wells did not seem to die very hard. When the drop fell there was that mighty heaving of the frame which always follows asphyxia, a low gurgling noise, and a few convulsive struggles.

The cap, which beforehand hung loosely over the face, is now distended from the protuberation of the features consequent on strangulation. The neck turned a deep scarlet, and then a livid blue colour; the hands, tightly clenched together as when the drop fell, became of a dark hue. Some one at last draws a deep breath, and says in a low voice, "He's dead!" No. There is another convulsive heave of the body, then a tremble, and now all is over. Justice is satiated; the law which demands a life for a life is satisfied. A corpse is suspended at the end of a rope, dressed in the dark corduroy uniform of a porter of the London, Chatham and Dover Railway – the same clothes in which Wells was arrested, tried, and convicted. In the button hole of his waistcoat there was a faded geranium. It had been given him by one of the friends who visited him.

The bystanders now leave the gaol, for the inquest is not to take place until half-past two o'clock, and it is yet only ten minutes to eleven. From a temporary flag-staff erected over the entrance to the gaol hangs listlessly a black flag, which was raised at the moment the drop fell as a signal to the outer world that the sentence of the law had been carried into effect. The symbol of death was observed by comparatively few people, for, although it was market day in Maidstone, there was not the slightest excitement manifested. A group of idlers, numbering about fifty persons, most of them tramps and beggars, had gathered in front of the gaol, and were gazing at the ominous flag with much intentness. Several of them asked those who had witnessed the execution whether Wells had died easy, and this was the only public curiosity displayed during the whole day. At half-past eleven the flag fell, the staff was taken down, the only indication at the gaol that a man had been executed was the notice, signed by the Governor and the Under-Sherriff, to certify that sentence of death had been duly carried out.

The inquest was held in the afternoon, before Mr Dudlow, the coroner for that division of the county, and twelve inhabitants of the town, who had been summoned as a jury. The proceedings were exceedingly formal. The Coroner explained to the jury that they were empanelled under the provisions of a recent Act of Parliament, which provided for the private hanging of culprits sentenced to death. They were afterwards to meet, view the body, and hear evidence to show that the law had been duly carried into effect. The jury then went and viewed the body, which had been cut down after hanging an hour, stripped of the greater part of its clothing, and laid in a plain elm coffin, over the bottom of which were spread a few shavings. To look at the dead face, no one would have thought that it was of a man who had been hanged. There was very little distortion, although the lips were much swelled and the eyes bulged out a great deal under their lids. The jury next inspected the gallows, and then returned to the cell in which the inquest was held. The Governor of the gaol (Major Bannister) proved that the dead body just seen was that of Thomas Wells, condemned to death for murder; and the surgeon proved that death had resulted from hanging according to the law. The jury then returned a verdict that the deceased had been hung as the law directed, and the proceedings terminated.

The first private execution in this country was thus finished, and that it is in every way preferable to the old disgraceful plan, everyone who reads the details of the proceedings will admit. There was no crowd of thousands of people, no unruly mob to make the violent death still more hideous than it is in any shape; the depraved taste of the masses will no longer be gratified by a public strangulation of a fellow creature, and the supreme penalty of the law is rendered all the more awful in its influence for the good, and greatly strengthened, we fervently trust, in its moral effects.

[See also Appendix Three to this volume.]

The Lamentable and True Tragedie of Master Arden of Feversham

The Murder of THOMAS ARDEN
by his Wife ALICE and her three Accomplices MOSBIE, SHAGBAG and BLACK WILL

on the 15th of February 1550
at his home in Abbey Street, Faversham

The conversion of real-life drama into a literary or a theatrical drama can ensure its elevation to immortality. Would the story of William Corder and Maria Martin have survived without the rash of melodramatic theatricals celebrating The Murder in the Red Barn; whence Eugene Aram without his illustrious biographers Thomas Hood and Bulwer-Lytton. And will John Reginald Christie's body be forever surmounted by Richard Attenborough's head?

One of the earliest English dramatizations of true-crime was the Elizabethan play *The Lamentable and True Tragedie of Master Arden of Feversham*. The fact that the drama has endured is in a great part due to the way in which the unknown author* departed from the prevailing tendency of Elizabethan theatre to take as its subject matter the royal court and "diplomatic service" to deal with more fundamental social and domestic preoccupations, painting as it does a realistic (if sordid) picture of low-life and base passions; passions and intrigues that result in the foul murder, in 1550, of Thomas Arden (or Ardern, or Arderne) in his own front parlour.

Arden was a Kentish gentleman and former mayor of the town of Faversham. He had made a good and profitable marriage to Alice Misfin (or Morfyn), step-daughter of Sir Edward North, and his civic responsibli-

ties included the Commissionership of the Customs of the Port of Faversham. He was later granted some of the Abbey lands by Sir Thomas Cheney, in the processs of which he is said to have defrauded a man named Greene – an accusation voiced especially loudly by the victim, and one which was to play a seminal role in Arden's death.

Alice's dowry having been secured, and her family connections established, Thomas transferred his attention to the relentless pursuit of money. Alice meanwhile transferred *her* attention to the relentless pursuit of a man named Thomas Morsby (or Mosby, or Mosbie), formerly a tailor, now engaged as her step-father's steward.

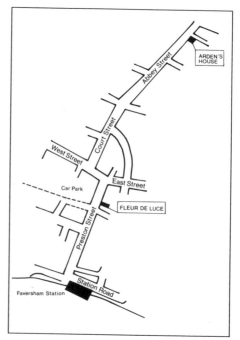

*It has been not too seriously advanced that William Shakespeare had a finger in the development of the text as the result of his visit to Faversham as a member of Lord Leicester's Players in 1590. The Bard is said to have played the part of Shakebag (or Shagbag), and in consequence "adapted" the play to give his character more prominence.

One of the earliest factual accounts of the case – Raphael Holinshed's *Chronicles* (1577) – informs us that Arden was "contented to winke at her filthie disorder, and both permitted and also invited Mosbye verie often to lodge in his house". Inevitably, the master became an unnecessary burden to the adulterous pair, and Alice and Mosbie plotted to murder him. It is quite clear who was the stronger personality and evident that Mosbie finds himself less and less enthusiastic about the scheme. Indeed, after the extraordinary device of the poisoned crucifix fails . . .

["A crucifix impoysoned
That who so looke upon it should wax blinde
And with the sent be stifeled that ere long
He should dye poysoned that did view it wel."]

. . . he resorts to employing two characters with the unlikely names of Black Will and Shagbag (or Shakebag) whose incompetence borders on the burlesque, and the man Greene, who is still smarting from the former real or imagined injustice. The conspirators rendezvous frequently over ale at the *Fleur de Luce* to formulate their plans.

Arden's House, scene of the tragedy

The Fleur de Luce, *formerly an inn, now preserved as the Faversham Heritage Centre*

There follow some of the most ludicrous assassination attempts in the history of crime, and it is a wonder that the *Lamentable and True Tragedie . . .* does not veer into concentrated farce. In one plan Will and Shagbag lay in wait for Arden in the shadows of a shop; as Arden approaches the shopkeeper happens to swing open his shutters, which catch Black Will such a crack on the head that he falls unconscious to the ground and has to be helped back to the *Fleur de Luce* by his accomplice.

Finally it is decided that Arden shall be "sent to everlasting night" in his own home, and to this end Black Will and Shakebag are secreted in the parlour, while Alice encourages her husband to play a game of tables (a sort of backgammon) with Mosbie:

Arden: Come Alice, is our supper ready yet?
Alice: Ay! when you have a game at tables played.
Arden: Come, Master Mosbie, what shall we play for?
Mosbie: Three games for a French crown, sir, and please you.
Arden: Content.

[*They go to a small table on the left of the stage and play tables on a draught-board with counters and dice. Mosbie is in the arm-chair and Arden sits on a stool. Will and Shakebag appear at the back. Will has a towel in his hand*]

Will: Can he not take him yet? what a spite is that?
Alice: Not yet, Will; take heed he see thee not.
Will: I fear he will spy me as I am coming.

complaint and lamentation of Mistresse *Arden* of
..rsham in *Kent*, who for the loue of one *Mosbie*, hired certaine Ruffians
..d Villaines most cruelly to murder her Husband ; with the farall end of her and her
Associats.   To the tune of, *Fortune my Foe*.

A Pure, vile wretch, that euer I was borne,
  Making my selfe vnto the world a scorne:
And to my friends and kinred all a shame,
Blotting their blood by my vnhappy name.

Vnto a Gentleman of wealth and fame,
  (One Master Arden, he was call'd by name)
I wedded was with ioy and great content,
Liuing at Feuersham in famous Kent.

In loue we liu'd, and great tranquility,
Vntill I came in Mosbee company,
Whose sugred tongue, good shape, and louely looke,
Soone won my heart, and Ardens loue forsooke.

And liuing thus in foule adultery,
Euen in my husband cause of iealousie,
And lest the world our actions should betray,
We did consent to take his life away.

To London faire my Husband was to ride,
But ere he went I poyson did prouide,
Got of a painter which I promised
That Mosbies sister Susan he should wed.

Into his Broth then did put the same,
He lik't it not when to the board it came;
Saying, There's something in it is not so so,
At which inrag'd, I flung it on the ground.

Yet ere he went, his man I did coniure,
Ere they came home, to make his Master sure,
And murder him, and for his faith and paine,
Susan, and store of gold that he should gaine.

Yet I misdoubting Michaels constancy,
Knowing a Neighbour that was dwelling by,
Which, to my husband bore no great good will,
Sought to incense him his deare blood to spill.

His name was Greene; O Master Green (quoth I)
My husband to you hath done iniury,
For which I sorry am with all my heart,
And how he wrongeth me I will impart.

He keepes abroad most wicked company,
With whores and queanes, and bad society;
When he comes home, he beats me sides and head,
That I doe wish that one of vs were dead.

And now to London he is rid to roare,
I would that I might neuer see him more:
Greene then incenst, did vow to be my friend,
And of his life he soone would make an end.

O Master Greene, said I, the dangers great,
You must be circumspect to doe this feat;
To act the ded your selfe there is no nede,
But hire some villaines, they will doe the ded.

Ten pounds Ile giue them to attempt this thing,
And twenty more when certaine newes they bring,
That he is dead, besides Ile be your friend,
In honest courtesie till life doth end.

Greene vow'd to doe it; then away he went,
And met two Villaines, that did dwel in Kent
To rob and murder vpon Shooters hill,
The one call'd Shakebag, t'other nam'd Black Will.

Two such like Villaines Hell did neuer hatch,
For twenty Angels they made vp the match,
And for the more when they had done the ded,
Which made them sweare, they'd doe it with al spede

Their vp to London presently they hye,
Where Master Arden in Pauls Church they spy,
And waiting for his comming forth that night,
By a strange chance of him they then lost sight.

For where these Villaines stood & made their stop
A Prentice he was shutting vp his shop,
The window falling, light on Blacke-Wilshead,
And broke it soundly, that apace it bled.

Where straight he made a brabble and a coyle,
And my sweet Arden he past by the while;
They missing him, another plot did lay,
And meeting Michael, thus to him they say:

Thou knowst that we must packe thy Master hence
Therefore consent and further our pretence,
At night when as your Master goes to bed,
Leaue ope the doores, he shall be murthered.

And so he did, yet Arden could not sleepe,
Strange dreames and visions in his senses creepe,
He dreamt the doores were ope, & Villaines came,
To murder him, and 'twas the very same.

Shakebag: To prevent that, creep betwixt my legs.

Mosbie: One ace, or else I lose the game.

Arden: Marry, sir, there's two for failing.

Mosbie: Ah, Master Arden, 'now I can take you'. [*Will, by means of the towel held in both hands, like a noose, pulls Arden off the stool*]

Arden: Mosbie! Michael! Alice! what will you do?

Will: Nothing but take you up, sir, nothing else.

Mosbie: There's for the pressing iron you told me of. [*stabs him*]

Shakebag: And there's for the ten pound in my sleeve. [*stabs him*]

Alice: What! groans thou? nay, then give me the weapon! Take this for hindering Mosbie's love and mine. [*stabs him*]

Michael: O, mistress!

Will: Ah, that villain will betray us all.

Mosbie: Tush, fear him not; he will be secret.

Michael: Why, dost thou think I will betray myself?

Will: Shift for yourselves; we two will leave you now.

Alice: First convey the body to the fields, and throw the knife and towel down the well.

Shakebag: We have our gold; Mistress Alice, adieu; Mosbie, farewell, and Michael, farewell too.

[*The body is carried out down the passage by Will, Shakebag, and Michael; Alice and Susan tidy the room. Knocking is heard at the porch door . . .*]

But true to their natures, the buffoons Will and Shakebag in carrying the body to the meadow not only lift up a handful of rushes from the floor which leaves a trail of debris to the corpse, but seem oblivious to the fact that they are implanting a trail of perfect footprints in the newly fallen snow.

Vengeance was both swift and violent. The punishment for husband killing (a category of "petit treason") was to be burnt alive at the stake, a fate Alice Arden shared with her maidservant Susan. The executions took place at Canterbury on March the 14th.

Mosbie was hanged in London, at Smithfield; Michael, the treacherous servant, was hung in chains at Faversham; and Black Will was burnt on the scaffold at Flushing. Greene and Shagbag escaped, though the latter is said subsequently to have been murdered in London.

The Blissful Decease of God's Angels

The Murder of CAROLINE and MARIA ANN BACK
by DEDEA REDANIES

in the early morning of Sunday the 3rd of August 1856
at Steddy Hole, between Folkestone and Dover

Few crueller and more unprovoked deeds of assassination than this have been recorded in the history of crime. The victims were two innocent and unoffending girls, who never injured the monster who took their lives by thought, word, or deed. In all trust and confidence they accompanied him, whom they believed to be a friend, on a night walk across the cliffs, and there they were done to death with every circumstance of atrocity. Small wonder, then, that the crime of Dedea Redanies created unexampled excitement at the time.

The motive – if ever there was one – was jealousy, but it was a jealousy for which there was not the smallest justification, seeing that no engagement had taken place between the murderer and either of the girls, that he was not the accepted lover of either, and that neither had ever professed any love for him. His jealousy – if one can dignify his passion by that name – arose from a malignant and morbid mind, and from an overweening self-esteem, and the murder was the result of the brutal savagery imbued in the man's inmost soul.

The perpetrator of these dreadful deeds, Dedea Redanies, was a native of Serbia, aged about twenty-five years. He had been quartered with the Swiss brigade at Shorncliffe for some time, and had formed the acquaintance of a man residing in Dover named John Back, a labourer, with two adult daughters, Caroline and Maria, both rather good-looking and superior girls for their position. Redanies had perhaps shown some slight preference for Caroline, but he had paid her no especially marked attentions, and there is no proof that any particular understanding existed between them.

On the evening of Saturday, previous to the murders, Redanies arrived at Back's house at about eight o'clock, and he remained for about an hour and a half. Then he went out to meet some of his companions in the town, and turned up again at Mr Back's at about quarter to three in the morning, when it was seen that he had had a drop to drink but was not actually drunk. The two girls had mentioned that they were going to Folkestone by the train that left Dover at 6.15am, and the young soldier proposed that as it was a fine night, they should walk over the cliffs with him as far as Shorncliffe Camp. This was agreed to, and Back asked Redanies to partake of some breakfast with them before they started their walk.

What happened on this fatal walk must now be disclosed. Having induced the girls to accompany him over the downs, Redanies, from an indiscernible emotion of jealousy, murdered them both. He appears to have done the deed with such skill and effect, that his victims offered no resistance, but fell with all the passiveness of sheep in the slaughter-house.

On the Sunday morning about eight o'clock, Thomas Gurling, a carpenter of Folkestone, left that town with a friend, and proceeded nearly as far as Dover. He returned as far as a place known as Stiddy [or Steddy] Hole, where he sat down upon a cliff reading Saturday's paper for half an hour. After he had rested, he got up and set out to try to find a way down to the beach, but he had not proceeded far, when he was horrified to see the bodies of two girls. He hurried to the spot, and the first he came to was the body of Maria, the younger of the sisters. He looked at her face and dress, and found that both were saturated with blood, while it did not

escape his observation that her clothes were much disordered. He called assistance and then went to the other girl, who was also quite dead. Her clothes were smothered with blood, and he noticed that her fingers were badly cut, while each girl had been terribly wounded in the region of the chest. The bodies were lying about 15 yards apart when he first saw them, and apart from the blood there were no signs of a struggle having taken place in that vicinity.

Gurling left his friend with the dead bodies and set out to procure further assistance and alarm the neighbourhood. The police speedily arrived, and with them Mr William Bateman, a surgeon of Folkestone, who at once commenced an examination of the bodies of the murdered girls. He inspected that of Maria Back before her sister, and found her dress but little disordered. She had on her gloves and bonnet, and the front of her dress was buttoned up close to her throat, but all that portion of her dress was saturated with blood. He found holes in the dress and, on removing her garments, saw four incised wounds in the chest, each about half an inch in length and penetrating deeply into the bosom. There were two wounds on each side of the chest, between the second and fourth ribs, and from the direction of the wounds he was clearly of the opinion that the arch of the aorta was wounded and that death was instantaneous.

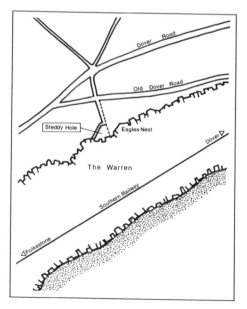

He then examined the body of Caroline Back. He found three wounds of the same sort in the chest; one of them had passed through the cartilage, another through the sternum, or chest bone, and the third was on the left breast, which, however, had not actually entered the chest. They were all stabs, and there was also a stab in the left hand. The chests of both girls were filled with blood, and the bodies were quite warm when he first saw them. On turning them over the blood gushed out of their wounds.

Early on the morning of the Monday, Redanies called at the shop of Mrs Elizabeth Attwood, at Lower Hardress, and asked if she sold paper and envelopes, and on her replying in the affirmative, he purchased two sheets of bill paper, two envelopes, a bottle of ink and a pen. He asked permission to write a letter, to which the shopkeeper agreed, and he sat down and wrote, afterwards going in the direction of the post-office.

He was next seen on the Ashford turnpike road by George Frier, the constable who was searching for him, and who at once identified him and ran to apprehend him. Redanies observed the officer coming for him and immediately put his hand to his breast, produced a knife, and threw it away. Frier was joined by another man, and together they effected the arrest of the suspected man, who was then seen to be suffering from three more or less serious wounds in the left breast, which were self-inflicted.

He was at once removed to Dover, and there it was found that the wounds he had inflicted upon himself were much more serious than was at first imagined; but strenuous efforts were made by the medical men attendant upon him in order that he might not cheat the gallows, and when December came around the prisoner was well enough to be arraigned at Maidstone.

The most interesting part of the evidence here produced consisted of the letter written by the prisoner, and addressed to Mrs Back at 3 Albion Place, Dover. The reading of the letter, which was in the German tongue, created a great sensation in the crowded court. Here is the literal translation:

August 3rd, 1856
Dear Mother Back – On the first lines I pray to forgive me the awful accident to the unlucky Dedea Redanies, which I committed upon my very dear Caroline and Maria Back yesterday morning at five o'clock. Scarcely am I able to write by heartbreak for my ever memorable Caroline and Maria Ann. The cause of my deed is (1) as I hear that Caroline is not in the family way, as I first believed. (2) Because Caroline intends to go to Woolwich. (3) Because I cannot stay with my very dear Caroline. It made my mind so scattered that I put into my mind at last rather that Caroline should die by my hands than to allow Caroline's love being bestowed upon others. However, I did not also intend to murder Mary Ann, her sister, but, not having other opportunity, and as she was in my way, I could not do otherwise – I must stab her too. Dear Mother Back, Saturday evening when I came, I had not the slightest intention to commit the fearful act, but as I learned that my dear Caroline gave me back my likeness, and as she told me she would leave, I did not know any other way in my heartbreak than that leading to the cutler's where I bought a poignard, which divided the hearty lovers. Arm-by-arm I brought both my dearest souls in the world to the unlucky place near the road before Folkestone, and requested them to sit down, but, the grass being wet, they refused to do so. I directed them, Caroline to go forward, and I went behind Mary Ann, into whose heart I run the dagger. With a dull cry, she dropped down. With a most broken heart I rushed towards Caroline, lifting my poignard in my hand towards her. "Dear Dedea," she cried, with half-dead voice, and fell down with weeping eyes. Then I rushed over and gave her the last kisses as an ever-lasting remembrance. I could not live a more dreadful hour in my life than that was, and my broken heart could not tell where my senses are gone, and I took both the black shawls of Mary Ann and my dear Caroline as a mourning suit for me, leaving the awful spot with weeping eyes and a broken heart. Never shall I forget my dear Caroline and Mary Ann, and the poignard will be covered with the blood of Mary Ann and Caroline with me, until it be put into my own breast, and I shall see again my dearest Mary

Ann and Caroline in the eternal life. Farewell, and be careless about the blissfully-deceased angels of God, and forgive the unhappy, ever-weeping

Dedea Redanies.

The extraordinary nature of this remarkable criminal is indeed exemplified in this astonishing document. The air of romantic sentiment with which he endeavours to clothe his sordid and brutal crime speaks volumes as to his enormous conceit and self-esteem. He feels himself a victim, and is overwhelmed with pity for himself. Intending to murder one sister, he kills the other because she was in the way, but he feels that he is really the one to be pitied, and is quite unable to realize the brutal nature of his cowardly crime. He can murder two girls in cold blood, and can write to their mother that they are "blissfully-deceased"!

It would be humorous if it were not so terrible.

Witnesses were called, who spoke of oddities in the manner and behaviour of the young soldier, and on these the defence relied for the acquittal of the prisoner, or, at least, for the verdict of "guilty, but insane at the time of the act". Counsel for the prisoner asked if any man who, having committed a barbarous double murder, could sit down and pen such a missive as he had sent the mother of his victims, should be considered to be in his right mind? Evidence went to prove Redanies had always been eccentric and a prey to sudden emotion. Counsel asked the jury to find that this man did these deeds, but that at the time of their commission he was not responsible for his acts.

The jury retired to consider their verdict, and were speedily in court again. They found the prisoner guilty, and the foreman added the belief that he was responsible for his actions. The learned judge then passed sentence of death in the usual form, commenting on the wickedness of the prisoner's crime, hurling, as he did, the souls of these young girls before their Maker before they had had a moment for repentance and preparation for death. He held out to the pale and shrinking man in the dock, no hope of mercy in this world, and in solemn tones besought him to make his peace with God.

The condemned man was led away, pale and violently trembling, and he passed that night in tears and tribulation.

Redanies was a member of the Greek Church, and it may be added at this point that some attempt – though rather feebly made – was put forward on the part of the Serbian government to procure, though unavailingly, a revision of the sentence. The British Government replied that under the circumstances it did not feel justified in interfering with the sentence which the nature of the crime so well deserved, and the Serbian ambassador made no further effort to save his countryman.

Dedea Redanies was hanged at Maidstone Gaol on January 1st 1857 – not an auspicious start to the New Year. Large crowds assembled in the pleasant old town to witness the execution, and half Shorncliffe Camp came over to see the last of the Serbian murderer. He seemed perfectly resigned to his fate at the last, and, though much agitated, was able to appear under the fatal beam with some show of fortitude. He died instantaneously, without a struggle, and it is said that the faces of few murderers have borne so peaceful an expression after suffering death by hanging.

It's the way you say it...

The Murder of CAROLINE ELLEN TRAYLER by Gunner DENNIS EDMUND LECKEY

on Whit Sunday the 13th of June 1943 in an empty shop, 94 Foord Road, Folkestone

Pretty Caroline Trayler was a member of that generation whose young lives were fated to be lived in the disruption and uncertainty of 1940s wartime Britain. The majority survived the bombs, and the blackouts, and the irritating personal privations; but for Caroline there was to be one blackout too many.

In 1943 she was eighteen years old, already a bride of six months, with a husband on active service with the British Forces in North Africa. And like many lively youngsters in her peer-group, Caroline was bored; the war had been going on just too long. She had a part-time job as a cinema usherette which gave her a small financial independence, but there was little enough in those days of austerity on which to spend her well-earned wages.

It might have been just another familiar Sunday evening spent with her parents behind the black curtains which kept their modest private lives from the searching eyes of the Luftwaffe's bombers. But this was Whit-Sunday, and Caroline Trayler was determined to find some pleasure in the weekend holiday. Which is probably why she ended up at the *Mechanic's Arms*; and it would be generous to her memory to suggest that it was a combination of drink and boredom that resulted in her leaving the pub at closing time on the arm of an off-duty soldier. The darkness swallowed them up; Caroline never returned from it.

When her anxious mother reported Caroline's disappearance, the police moved into a now-familiar wartime routine – first search the empty buildings and bombed sites. It took them four days, but it had been the right move – Caroline Trayler's body was found in an unoccupied shop, and a cursory glance at the body indicated strangulation compounded with violent sexual assault.

The unenviable job of forensic pathologist was to be undertaken here, as in so many cases, by the late Professor Keith Simpson, who arrived at the scene of the crime with other Scotland Yard specialists within hours. Simpson's reconstruction suggested that the 'rape' almost certainly began with Caroline's consent – the dirtied state of her calves was consistent with her lying with her legs wide apart and flat on the floor. Whether she changed her mind or found herself the unwitting consort of a sexual sadist we will never know. The bruising around Caroline's throat indicated that her killer had tried unsuccessfully to strangle her from the front, then turned her over and completed the job from behind. The pathologist then set about the gruesome task of scavenging such clues as the body could offer to the identity of its attacker. Simpson found a half dozen dark body hairs stuck to Caroline Trayler's thighs which contrasted sharply with her own auburn colouring and almost certainly came from her killer. The girl's fingernails had also become torn and broken in her last brave struggle, and scrapings from the nails contained rusty-brown fibres, in all likelihood from the assailant's clothing. All that was needed was a suspect with which to match the clues.

If Dennis Leckey, a serving Artillery gunner, had not gone absent on the day that Caroline's body was found, it is possible that the trail would never have led to him. As it was, his evident panic caused the Folkestone police to issue a nationwide description and a request for his apprehension. Gunner Leckey was picked up by an observant London Bobby named Briggs ten days later. Formally arrested, the prisoner was obliged to surrender samples of his body hairs which Professor Simpson was pleased to confirm matched those left behind in the assault on his victim. Furthermore, the couple had

Caroline Ellen Trayler

'exchanged' hairs, one of hers being found on Leckey's uniform trousers. The fibre taken from beneath Caroline's fingernail matched those of his uniform shirt. Not conclusive proof, it is true, but it was strong enough evidence to take Dennis Leckey to trial on. And it was enough to convince the jury of his guilt; to convince the presiding judge, Mr Justice Singleton, who without the least hesitation pronounced the sentence of death upon Leckey.

Now, we must remember that English law has built into it – rightly – certain safeguards for the protection of persons accused of committing a crime. One of these basic rights is that to remain silent – not to be obliged to say anything that may incriminate him until he has the benefit of legal advice – and quite properly so. An extension of this is the right of an accused not to give evidence at his own trial. And it must not be inferred from a prisoner's silence in either of these circumstances that he is making an admission of guilt.

At the conclusion of the Leckey trial, in a legal error that was as damaging to the prosecution case as it was inexplicable from so experienced a judge, Sir John Singleton not once but three times in his summing-up gave utterance to the sentiment that the prisoner's reluctance to make a statement to the police at the time of his arrest could be seen as an indication of guilt – "Of course, he is not bound to say anything, but what would you conclude?" he asked the jury. Anyway, it was enough to force the Court of Appeal to overturn the conviction, and allow Dennis Leckey – without dispute the brutal killer of poor Caroline Trayler – to walk free; society had, on this thankfully rare occasion, become victim to its own impeccably fair legal system.

The scene of the crime

The Case of the Brides in the Bath

The Murder of BEATRICE ('BESSIE') MUNDY
by GEORGE JOSEPH SMITH (alias WILLIAMS)
on Saturday the 13th of July 1912
at 80 High Street, Herne Bay

Mrs Margaret Lloyd looked up from the letter she was struggling to write and gazed adoringly at her brand-new husband. How exciting, she thought, to be married and living in London after all the dull old years at home in Bristol. And it had all happened so romantically, so quickly, she could hardly believe it was real. She studied her husband's profile carefully as he sat reading his newspaper. True, she thought, he wasn't exactly handsome, but there was certainly something about him – something so magnetic, so stylish; and with a little thrill of possessiveness she remembered the way other women blushed or lowered their eyelids when John Lloyd spoke to them. He might not be what Mother called a 'proper' gentleman, but he could quote line upon line of divine poetry, and he played the piano, and drew the sweetest, most flattering portraits of her; and his manners were beautiful. So what were a few rough edges and dropped aitches she reflected petulently, compared to the riches of such a character. Margaret Lloyd – or Margaret Lofty as she had been until only the day before – was completely happy and in love.

She took a deep breath, "I must not get over-excited", she reminded herself, "or I might find myself in the middle of another strange attack like yesterday." She had known nothing about it until she came round with dear John patting her hand and asking, "Margaret, are you all right, my dear? You blacked out for a moment." He had insisted on taking her to the local doctor, who luckily could find nothing wrong with her. She sighed: it would be too awful if anything should happen now to spoil the joy of their first few days together.

Reluctantly she refocused her thoughts on the half-filled sheet of paper in front of her. It was not an easy letter to write, telling Mother, and her sister, that she had eloped with a man whose very existence they had never even suspected. She would have to confess how she had written to him in secret, and arranged to marry behind their backs. She had been so afraid they would disapprove and spoil everything. Well, it was too late now: they would just have to get used to it.

George Joseph Smith

During the evening, after she had walked down to the postbox, John Lloyd suggested that a "nice warm bath" might relax his wife; he still thought she looked a little pale from the previous day's upset. He summoned Miss Blatch, the landlady, who was soon bustling around with hot water, soap and towels. The tub in the bathroom was tiny, and Margaret was rather tall, but still she climbed gratefully into the steaming water

61

and tried to relax, soothed by the sound of her husband playing the harmonium in the downstairs room.

She was still sitting in the bath when she became aware that the music had stopped; that the bathroom door was slowly opening. Margaret blushed as her husband crossed the room and gently put his hand on the top of her head, but as she tried to turn and smile his grip tightened; the next instant his arm was under her knees and before she had even a split second to wonder he was pushing her down, down into the bath; the water was filling her eyes, her nose, her mouth . . . then there was nothing but total swirling blackness.

Fifteen minutes later Miss Blatch was startled when a knock at the front door revealed John Lloyd holding a brown paper bag. "Oh, Mr Lloyd", she greeted him, "you did give me a start. I didn't even know you'd gone out." "Just popped along the road to get some tomatoes for Mrs L's supper," he told her with his engaging smile. "Is she out of her bath yet?" "Haven't heard a squeak from upstairs for ever so long," the landlady confided. Lloyd called up the stairs, and getting no reply, turned a face dark with concern towards Miss Blatch, "Oh dear, I do hope nothing's amiss", he said, "she has these fainting fits; she's not terribly strong, you know. I wonder, would you be so very kind and come upstairs with me . . . just in case . . ." Miss Blatch would be delighted, and they mounted the stairs together.

The sight that greeted them in the bathroom was one of horror. Margaret Lloyd's face was completely submerged beneath the water in the three-parts-full tub; her knees were raised, and she was terribly still. Between them they lifted her from the bath and summoned help from the police and from Dr Bates – the physician who had so recently attended Mrs Lloyd's fainting fit.

Miss Blatch was still telling and retelling the story to her fascinated neighbours three months later – "There was nothing they could do for the poor soul – stone dead she was; the inquest said it was a fainting fit due to the 'flu and the hot water sort of overcoming her. Poor man, he was beside himself when he saw she was dead. Mind you," she added with smugly relished disapproval,

"she hadn't played straight with him, you know; told him she was all alone in the world, she did. And then that solicitor turning up and saying her mother and sister had asked him to investigate. Mr L told him straight – 'My wife told me she had no surviving relatives', he said. 'I know nothing of any letter she might have written, or of any family to whom it might be written'. That put the legal nosey-parker in his place all right. . ."

After the funeral, Mr Lloyd (alias Smith, alias Love, Rose, Williams, James, and more) collected the £700 life assurance he had taken out on this, his sixth bigamously married wife, emptied her savings-bank account of its remaining £19, and quietly disappeared.

So ended the last in a series of fraudulent, bigamous and – in three cases – murderous episodes in the life of George Joseph Smith – the man who used the power of his charm for women to such cynical and profitable effect. And, but for a long chance, Smith might well have continued to prosper in his horrible career, claimed even more victims to his insatiable greed.

Smith's history started in Bethnal Green in

1872, born the son of an insurance company agent. A troublesome child, at nine years old he was sent to one of the harsh and brutalizing reformatories that marked that era; at eighteen he was serving six months for stealing, and in 1896, after two years' service with the Northamptonshire Regiment, he was sentenced, in the name of George Baker, to twelve months' hard labour for larceny, followed by another two years in 1901. By this time Smith, under the alias Oliver Love, was already married to his first wife, Caroline Beatrice Thornhill, a domestic servant. 'Love' shortly persuaded her to act as his accomplice in a series of break-ins in London and along the prosperous south coast, though it is unlikely that she needed much persuading; at any rate, all good things coming, as they do, to an end, Caroline was caught in 1899 and sentenced to three months in prison; he managed to escape. On her release Mrs Love evidently decided that she had had enough not only of the life of crime into which she had been introduced, but of Oliver Love as well and she made a strategic escape to Canada.

Smith flirted with several occupations before finding his true vocation – he was a baker and a gym instructor among other things, and in his spare time he was an enthusiastic writer of letters on such subjects as Manners, Objectionable Literature, and other social dilemmas, a number of which were published in the *Bath and Wilts Chronicle*.

In July 1908, disregarding his previous marriage, Smith 'married' Edith Pegler in Bristol under his own name, and of all his subsequent 'marriages' and affairs, Edith alone seems to have been the woman for whom he had any real or lasting affection. Time after crime he would return to her welcoming arms, and it was to her that he sent his last farewell as he faced death.

Although Smith had proved that he could earn his living, he found work of the sort for which he was qualified uncongenial, and he hungered for more lavish rewards. He could not help but be aware that women of nearly all stations and ages found him inexplicably attractive, and the bright idea occurred to him to maximize this gift into a positive asset. So, with what were to be horrendous consequences, Smith set about perfecting the art of living off his charms. . .

In 1909, as George Rose, he married a Miss Faulkner at Southampton, and on her he developed a technique that was to become something of a trademark. He persuaded the poor woman to make over to him any money that she had, and then one day, during a pleasant walk in the park or, in Mrs Rose's case, a visit to the National Gallery, he excused himself on some pretext and while the unfortunate woman was waiting, hastened to her home, stole everything of value – in one case going so far as to take the furniture and a piano – and disappeared for ever, leaving the lady without even a change of clothing to her name.

However, horrible as the crime against Mrs Rose had been, the fate of Smith's next wife was incalculably worse – for she was to be robbed of her very life. Bessie Mundy married 'Henry Williams' in Weymouth in August 1910, and although he robbed and deserted her soon after the ceremony they ran into each other again in 1912, and Bessie, silly girl, forgave him. They set up home once again, this time at No.80 High Street, Herne Bay. Her forgiveness was rewarded when Smith accorded her the distinction of

Popular contemporary accounts of the Herne Bay Tragedy were imaginative if inaccurate. In this version, poor Bessie chooses her own bath!

Left to right: Alice Burnham, Bessie Mundy, and Margaret Lofty

becoming the first of the 'Brides in the Bath', the one on whom he perfected his silent and ingenious slaying technique. The format never varied – from the preliminary visit to the doctor (in Bessie's case for an 'epileptic fit') through to his appearance at the street door with "something for my wife's supper" after he had committed his victim to a watery grave.

After his success with Miss Mundy, Smith was ready to murder again. He met Alice Burnham at a Congregational Chapel and, greatly against her father's wishes, married her – as George J. Smith – in Portsmouth on November 4th 1913. A month-and-a-half later, in Blackpool, he was collecting £500 life assurance on her, after a verdict of 'accidental drowning' had been pronounced by the Coroner's inquest.

Then came Alice Reavil – who became Mrs 'Oliver James' in Woolwich in September 1914. She escaped with her life, but not much else; using the classic desertion technique – this time in South-East London's Brockwell Park, Smith got away with what was left after he had already relieved Alice of her life's savings.

In between the 'marriages', George Smith was also finding the time to practise his love-'em-and-leave-'em-penniless tricks on several other ladies to whom he clearly felt no constraint to offer his hand in marriage; and he was also returning each time to the unsuspecting Edith Pegler, explaining his extended absences as 'business trips', an excuse made thinly credible by their joint ownership of an antique shop in Bristol.

The beginning of the end came for the vile Smith when Charles Burnham – father of wife number five, Alice – saw an account of the inquest on Margaret Lloyd in the *News of the World*. The circumstances of the death were identical to those in which his own daughter had so tragically and unexpectedly lost her life, and Burnham's deep dislike and mistrust of his daughter's husband immediately galvanized him into action. He was convinced that this John Lloyd was one and the same person as the George Smith who had coolly collected the life assurance on his late daughter.

He instructed his solicitor to contact Scotland Yard, and so a long and painstaking investigation was launched into the activities of George Joseph Smith. Chapter by chapter, the story was fitted together; the first link was an examination of the circumstances in which Mrs Williams (poor Bessie Mundy) had also died in her bath at Herne Bay in 1912. It was then that police came to the awful realization that Lloyd, Smith, and Williams were the same gruesome killer. And so the manhunt for Smith began, and just as police were beginning to think that their quarry might have escaped abroad he was run to ground and arrested in a solicitor's office in Shepherd's Bush. As a holding measure, Smith was initially charged with the bigamy at Bath (Edith Pegler). The next step was to exhume, one by one, the bodies of the three dead 'brides'; and this time the medical experts were of the unanimous opinion that accidental death in baths of the size of the three murder tubs was virtually impossible. With no reason to suppose that all

The History and Fate of the Seven Brides of George Joseph Smith

Name	Bride	Place of Marriage	Date	Fate of Bride	Possessions gained by Smith	Inquest	Exhumation
Oliver Love	Caroline Thornhill	Leicester	January 17th, 1898	Emigrated to Canada 1900	—	—	—
George J. Smith	Edith Pegler	Bristol	July 30th, 1908	Survived	—	—	—
George Rose	S. A. Faulkner	Southampton	October 1909	Deserted at National Gallery	£300	—	—
Henry Williams	Bessie Mundy	Weymouth	August 26th, 1910	Separated 1910–1912 Drowned in bath at Herne Bay, July 13th 1912	£2,500	July 15th, 1912 Drowning in epileptic fit	February 18th, 1915 Herne Bay
George J. Smith	Alice Burnham	Portsmouth	November 4th, 1913	Drowned in bath at Blackpool, December 12th, 1913	£140 plus Life Assurance for £500	December 13th, 1913. Accidental drowning	February 9th, 1915 Blackpool
Oliver James	Alice Reavil	Woolwich	September 17th, 1914	Deserted September 23rd, 1914, at Brockwell Park	£78, piano and furniture and clothes	—	—
John Lloyd	Margaret Lofty	Bath	December 17th, 1914	Drowned in bath at Highgate, December 18th, 1914	£19 plus Life Assurance for £700	December 22nd, 1914 and January 1st, 1915 at Islington. Accidental drowning	February 4th, 1915 Finchley

three women suffered from suicidal tendencies, they concluded that the deaths were therefore homicidal. Forensic experts later unravelled the silent murder technique used by the ingenious Smith, and demonstrated it in court.

At an identity parade, a large number of witnesses successfully picked out Smith as the man they knew under one or another of his soubriquets. Among them, triumphant in avenging his late daughter, was Mr Charles Burnham.

Smith's hearing at Bow Street Magistrates Court, where he was charged with the murder of his three 'wives' took six weeks and, six weeks after that, on June 22nd, 1915, he came to trial at the Old Bailey charged with the murder of Mrs Williams (née Mundy) at Herne Bay – incidentally, the most lucrative of his 'transactions'. 112 witnesses filed before the court during the eight-day trial, and the proceedings were nearly brought to a nasty, if wryly appropriate, conclusion when an over-zealous young detective nearly drowned a swim-suited nurse who had volunteered to help in the reconstruction of

the murder method; it proved necessary to give her artificial respiration on the courtroom floor!

The story broke in the middle of the Dardanelles campaign of the Great War, and the grey pages of the national Press, devoted almost entirely to military news, gratefully accepted the spicing of the terrible tale of 'The Brides in the Bath'. Smith became the monster anti-hero almost overnight, and women fought for places in the public gallery to catch a shuddering glimpse of the creature whose reputed magnetism had lured so many susceptible members of their own sex to ruin and even to violent death.

On July the 1st, after a retirement of only twenty-two minutes, the jury brought in their verdict, and Mr Justice Scrutton passed sentence in accordance with that verdict.

Friday August the thirteenth was an unlucky day for George Joseph Smith; they hanged him at Maidstone Prison.

[*Adapted from 'The Case of the Brides in the Bath' by Susan Dunkley*]

DROWNED IN A BATH

LADY'S SAD DEATH AT HERNE BAY

HUSBAND'S TRAGIC DISCOVERY

THE RESULT OF AN EPILEPTIC FIT

Very sad was the death of Mrs Bessie Constance Annie Williams, and very tragic the discovery of her husband Mr Henry Williams, an art dealer, living at 80, High Street, Herne Bay.

On Saturday morning, it appears, Mr Williams left the house for a stroll before breakfast, and also for the purpose of purchasing some fish. He returned; but on calling to his wife there was no response.

Having searched the house he went into the bathroom, and there found his wife lying unconscious in the bath, and with her face beneath the water, a piece of soap clenched in her right hand. He lifted her head over the side of the bath, and hurried off for Dr French, who came immediately. The lady was lifted from the bath, and artificial respiration was tried; but without avail. Mrs Williams was dead.

It seems that she had been treated for epilepsy, and apparently while having a bath

she had a seizure; she sank into the water and was drowned.

THE INQUEST

VERDICT OF
"DEATH BY MISADVENTURE"

Mr Rutley Mowll, the Coroner for East Kent, held an inquest in the Council Chamber, Town Hall, on Monday afternoon into the circumstances of the sad occurrence. Mr J.S. White was chosen foreman of the jury, who proceeded to the house to view the body.

Henry Williams, the husband, said he lived at 80 High Street, and was an art dealer. The deceased was his wife, and was 35 years of age. They had been married two years. There were no children. Deceased was very poorly during the previous week, her symptoms being nervousness and headache. She had three fits, the first on Tuesday night, another on Thursday night, and the third on Saturday in her bath. He had never known her to have fits before. Witness went with his wife to see Dr French on the Wednesday morning. The doctor sent some medicine which she took. On Friday at 1am., she had another fit when in bed and he went for Dr French who returned with witness and sounded the deceased, and asked her several questions. She had several questions. She had recovered from the fit then; but she was left in a state of nervousness, and her hands were clammy. Witness went to the surgery with the doctor and fetched more medicine which deceased took. On Friday afternoon the doctor came again, and on Friday night the deceased appeared to be all right. Witness and deceased got up at 7.30am. on Saturday, and witness, after asking if the deceased was all right, went out for a stroll and to fetch some fish. No one was left in the house when he went out, as only deceased and himself lived there. Witness returned about eight o'clock and unlocked the door. It had always been their province to lock the door, each having a key, as the slam top latch was out of order. Witness went into the dining room and called, but got no answer. He went into the bedroom; but could not find the deceased there, and so he went into the bathroom, as he remembered that the deceased had told him the night before she intended to have a bath in the morning. He there found the deceased with a piece of soap in her hand, but her head under the water. He raised her head, and called to her; but could get no reply, and he then ran for the doctor. When he left the house he had put her head on the side of the bath; but it must have slipped down again in his absence. The doctor came immediately, reaching the house as soon as the witness got to the top of the stairs. Deceased's head had sunk into the water again, the mouth being level with the top of the water. The doctor felt the deceased's pulse, and said "I am afraid she is dead." They lifted the deceased from the bath, and witness held the deceased's tongue while the doctor trid artificial respiration, but without avail, and then Dr French said, "It is hopeless."

The Coroner: Do you think she had a fit while she was in the bath?

Witness: I don't know what happened. The doctor said she might have had a fit, and fallen down and been drowned. I did not know what happened.

She did not have a bath regularly, I understand? – No.

It seems rather unfortunate she had a bath in the house by herself just after having these fits? – I did not know she would have one quite so early.

How much water was in the bath? – I should think it was about three parts full.

That means three-quarters only? – Yes, sir.

Was it hot or cold water? – It just had the chill off.

Who got the water there? – I suppose she did.

You did not get the water? – No sir, she generally does that the night before.

Did she do so then? – I don't know.

You did not go in there then? – No, sir, we generally sleep downstairs.

You had not been upstairs that morning? – No, sir.

Previous to finding her in the bath? – No, sir.

Have you been on good terms with her? – (With emotion) Yes, sir, and we have always been out together. I had only just bought a lot of new things for her, clothes and furniture, and one thing and another.

Was her life insured? – No, sir.

Had she any private means of her own? – Yes, she had private means.

Has there been any unpleasantness with members of the family? – They did not care for the marriage; but I have never seen any of them.

Did you communicate the fact of the death to them? – Yes, sir.

Whom did you inform? – I sent a wire to her uncle and her brother.

On the same day, the Saturday? – Yes, I sent after the doctor went.

Have you heard from either of them? – I had a telegram from the uncle, who said he was sorry, and he said he would like to hear from me. Her relatives I have never seen. They did not agree with the marriage at all.

Have you anything else you would like to tell us about, or you would like to say, Mr Williams? – No, sir; but I am ready to answer anything you like to ask. We were married two years ago, and the relatives did not approve of it at all.

Coroner: That has nothing to do with us at all.

The Foreman: Do I understand the water would have to be carried to the bathroom?

Witness: Yes, we had no pipes or taps.

As far as you know, the deceased would have had to carry it up? – Yes, sir.

Probably when you were out? – She might have done it the night before; but I don't know when she did do it.

A Juror asked witness if he thought his wife was alive shortly after eight o'clock, when he got home, or had she passed away then?

Witness: I can't say. I don't know whether she was in a fit, or dead, or not.

You left her in the bath during the time you went to fetch Dr French? – I got her head and bust out of the bath, got her in a sitting position.

You found no life in her then? – No, I could not make anything of her.

Another juror: How many pails would be required to fill the bath three parts full?

Witness: I can't tell you, I am sure. I never measured it.

Coroner: Was it the practice to take pails, cans, or what?

Witness: A little can or bath, and so on.

Didn't you see the cans? – There are always pails and buckets about the kitchen; but what the water is taken up in I cannot tell you.

Didn't you find any buckets or cans in the

bathroom? – There is a bucket in the bathroom now.

A bucket; it is a big pail, is it not? – Yes, it is a
pail, and there is another small bath there.

How long had you been living there Mr Williams? – Just three months.

Where did you come from? – Ashford.

Were you an art dealer there? – I have always
been dabbling in antiques, and so on.

Did you have the bath put in there? – Well,
there was nowhere else to put it.

There was no bath till you put it there? – No,
we were going to have the bath fixed up. She
bought the bath herself.

What does it empty into, a drain? – No, I
empty it into a bucket myself. That is how we
had to manage till the bath was fixed.

Foreman: Did you attempt to lift the deceased
out of the water before you went for the
doctor? – I tried to, but she was too much for
me.

Dr Frank Austin French, MRCS, LRCP,
practising at Herne Bay, said on Wednesday
morning Mr Williams and his wife came to the
consulting room. Mr Williams said his wife had
had a fit on the previous day. He asked him to
describe the fit, and Mr Williams did so,
stating there had been opening and shutting of
the mouth, and spasmodic contractions of the
extremities, arms and legs. He asked if she had
had fits before; and she replied that she had
never had any before.

He examined her tongue, as epileptics com-
monly bit their tongue; but he could not find
any evidence of this. He came to the conclusion she had had an epileptic fit, and he
prescribed a course of medicine accordingly.
The husband told him he wanted her to have
proper attention. Witness sent medicine, and
the next he heard was a call on Friday about
1am. The husband rang the bell, and said his
wife had just had another fit. He went to the
house, which was about three minutes' walk,
and found the deceased in bed. She was not in
a fit then; but further from the hands being hot
and moist – as everyone's were that night as it
was a very warm night – he found no evidence
of a fit. The deceased told him she had a
headache, and this would be quite compatible
with the after-effects of an epileptic fit. She
told him she had taken the last dose of medicine that evening, and witness suggested that
the husband should go with him and fetch
more medicine. At 3 o'clock the same afternoon he called at the house; but no one was at
home. As he was leaving the gate, the husband
and wife came up after a walk. Deceased still
complained of lassitude and headache.

On Saturday morning, about eight o'clock,
witness received a note signed by Mr Williams
to the effect: "Do come at once; I am afraid my
wife is dead." Whether he mentioned the bath
or not witness did not know. The note was
written in pencil. He did not know where it
was, he may have thrown it in the waste-paper
basket. The man who had answered the door
brought the note up to him. Witness finished
dressing and went at once to 80 High Street,
finding the deceased in the bath with her head
submerged. Witness raised her head, but made
no comment to the husband about the head
being under water, as he attended to the
woman at once. He felt the deceased's pulse,
but she was pulseless. Witness helped the
husband lift her out of the water, which he felt.
It was not hot, and he should not be surprised
if it was cold. Artificial respiration was kept up
for over half an hour, and he then came to the
conclusion she was dead.

Coroner: What was the cause of death?

Witness: In my opinion her death was due to
asphyxia, brought about by drowning.

You think so; how do you know that? – On
applying artificial respiration I found a lot of
froth come from her mouth, blowing across
the floor. She certainly had water in the stomach, because in pressing her stomach, some
water ran from her mouth, showing me she
had swallowed water.

Do you think she had an epileptic fit? – Yes;
but of course, I cannot say definitely.

Was there any sign of a fit at all? – Yes, her
face was rather blue, which looked as if she
might have met with her death in an early
condition of epilepsy.

Was she naked? – Yes.

Did you see any signs of a struggle? – None. I
saw a large piece of soap clasped in her right
hand.

If a person has an epileptic fit from which they
never come out, is there any medical sign by
which you can trace the presence of a fit? – Not
from external signs, except biting the tongue
for instance.

Was her tongue bitten? – No.

Did you look at it? – Yes, she had an upper
and lower set of teeth, and these were not
disarranged in any way; but were in position in
her mouth. I moved them before trying artificial respiration.

Is there not a clenching in epilepsy? – There
are spasmodic contractions in different stages.
There is clenching in the first stage.

You think death was due to drowning, really?
– Yes.

You think she had an epileptic seizure? I
think so, yes. Although I had never seen
her in an epileptic fit, and I had small
grounds to go on, she was present at these
interviews.

Is there anything which resembles epilepsy;
she might have thought she was suffering from
epilepsy, and might have suffered from some-

thing else? – She might have suffered from syncope; but I examined her heart.

On Friday you examined her heart? – I did.

Was it all right then? – Yes. I found no evidence of valvular elision. She was rather agitated, certainly.

As far as you could see, was the husband doing all he could for her? – Yes.

At this point the husband burst into tears, and sobbed bitterly.

He was recalled and was asked where he wrote the note to the doctor.

Mr Williams, who had by then somewhat recovered his composure, said he came straight downstairs and wrote the note, thinking perhaps the doctor might not be in at the moment, and that when he did come in it would be given to him at once.

A Juror said he could see it was a very good method, for if the doctor was not in, the note would be given to him immediately.

Coroner: (to Dr French) You don't think a post-mortem examination necessary in this case? – No, sir.

After receiving a note from one of the jury, the Coroner asked the Doctor: After you got there at 8 o'clock, was the body still warm? – Yes.

How long did you think she had been in the bath? – I can't possibly say, sir. I can only say that rigor mortis had not set in.

When would that set in? – It commences about three or four hours after death. It would be pure speculation.

The Foreman said from the time Mr and Mrs Williams got up, and the husband went out and returned not a great deal had elapsed; certainly not enough to make such a quantity of water cold.

Dr French: Personally, I should say it was cold.

The Coroner asked the jury if they would like the case adjourned for a post-mortem examination.

After consultation, the Foreman said they would like to ask the doctor if a post-mortem examination would throw any further light on the case.

Coroner: I had better put the question to you. (To Dr French) Do you think the cause of death was due to anything else but drowning?

Dr French: I have no reason to suspect any other cause but drowning, sir.

The jury then said they did not wish for a post-mortem examination.

The Coroner then summed up and, referring to the evidence, said the theory put forward was that the deceased was drowned by having an epileptic seizure while she was in the bath and getting her head under water. That was by no means an improbable cause of death, because they knew epileptics had fits at all kinds of times, and it would be possible that when a person was washing he should fall down over a basin, and as the result of the seizure be drowned in a few inches of water. Still more was it possible for such a thing to happen to a lady in a bath. The evidence was reviewed in detail, and dealing with the discovery of the body the Coroner said he did not think any great importance attached to the time when the bath was filled. No doubt when it was filled it was a matter of time and trouble to the person who filled it. The evidence was not at all clear that it was anything but cold. At any rate the bath was three-quarters full, and this poor lady was found in the bath with her head under water. Assuming the husband was fond of his wife – and there was no evidence to the contrary, but a great deal of evidence that he was – it was a terrible plight. Probably the best thing to have done was to have got the water out of her at once. Instead of doing that he propped the head up in the bath the best way he could, placing the head over the side of the bath, went downstairs and hurriedly scribbled a note in pencil, saying he was afraid his wife was dead, and suggesting the doctor should come at once. With this he went to the doctor's house, three minutes walk away, and this letter was taken to the doctor by the doctor's servant. The doctor came at once, reaching the house almost as soon as the husband got there himself. Unfortunately, according to the evidence of the husband, the deceased's head had slipped down in the water. The doctor had the head raised out of the water, artificial respiration was tried, and water ran from the mouth and stomach, showing that death was due to drowning. The Coroner pointed out that this was not a natural death; it was a violent death. But they knew that persons were frequently drowned by accident, and not only by accident, by design.

This woman might have wanted to drown herself; but there was no evidence of that. Was she drowned by accident, or was she drowned by violence; that was the point. If she was drowned by violence they would have expected to find some evidence of a struggle, and they would not have expected to find a piece of soap in her right hand. To have the soap was a natural thing for anybody who was having a bath; but it would be a very unnatural circumstance with anybody who had been struggling in the water with someone else. They saw that although there was not clear evidence of epilepsy they found the doctor consulted, and it looked as if the husband were anxious about his wife, because he had been to the doctor early in the morning, and the doctor had come to attend his wife for epilepsy.

If they were of the opinion that she went into the bath herself, as the husband said she had the intention of doing, and while there had an epileptic seizure while in the bath, which caused her to fall into the water and to be drowned, then their verdict would be death by misadventure, which meant accidental death. He should like to say that although the husband did not do the most sensible thing, yet he really did not see any evidence on which to censure the husband at all.

He had taken very great care in taking these depositions, and had gone into the case with more than ordinary perspicacity, because he had a request from one of the relatives to do so, apparently from one who had never seen the husband at all, and it was obvious, reading between the lines, that the marriage was not popular with the relatives of the lady. A request had been made to him to have a post-mortem examination, and if he had had the request earlier he should, with an abundance of caution, have requested the doctor to make an examination; but looking at the facts, and they admitted death was due to misadventure – and there was abundant evidence that the deceased was drowned – he did not see how a post-mortem examination would help them arrive at their verdict. But he thought, having had the request, that he would put it to the jury. They told him they did not require such an examination, and their view corresponded with his own, though he did not tell them beforehand, as he wanted the jury to decide for themselves. They had gone into the matter very carefully, and he hoped the relatives would be told that the case had been thoroughly and carefully thrashed out.

The jury, after a few minutes' consultation, returned a verdict of "Death by Misadventure".

The enquiry lasted some considerable time, and at the close the husband was again very greatly distressed.

The Summer-House Killing
The Killing of Mrs CAROLINE LUARD
by an Unknown Assassin
on Monday the 24th of August 1908
at 'The Casa', Ightham

It would be difficult to picture a more comfortable couple than Major-General Charles Luard and his wife Caroline Mary. His ancestry was among the French Huguenot families who sought refuge in England from the religious persecutions of the late seventeenth century. He rose rapidly in the ranks of a chosen military career – a commission in the Royal Engineers at the age of seventeen; in 1882 appointed Lieutenant-Colonel, and after thirty years in the service retired in 1887 with the rank of Major-General. His marriage to the daughter of Thomas Huntly, a wealthy Cumberland landowner, took place in 1875, and the two sons of the match followed their father's military calling*.

---

*Charles Elmhurst Luard served with the Norfolk Regiment and was awarded the DSO at the battle of Abassi. Eric Luard distinguished himself with the Queen's Own during the South African War, and died of fever in Somaliland in 1903.

Major-General Luard and his wife had lived in the appropriately respectable area of the Kentish Weald between Sevenoaks and Wrotham for thirty years, when the uncharacteristic mystery occurred that was to cost Mrs Luard her life, and her husband his reputation and his life.

Luard had matured into a rather stuffy, though active, old gentleman, and at the age of sixty-nine was still paternally active in local community affairs – he had been a county councillor for Kent for fourteen years, and was the patron of a number of sports clubs in the area. Caroline Luard was an elegant, jolly "country-lover"; she was twelve years Luard's junior, and to use a quaint expression of which they would both have approved, was remarkably "well preserved" for her age. She too had made her modest but indelible mark on Ightham social life, and was highly regarded for her generosity. As a couple there was no doubt that they were as close as two individuals could get – more like young lovers, some said, than retired gentry.

The rambling red-brick Victorian manor-house in which the Luards lived, Ightham Knoll, was two miles from the village of Wrotham – which boasted the nearest railway station. Their nearest neighbour, a retired stockbroker named Horace Wilkinson, lived at Frankfield House, some half-mile away, though the well-wooded grounds of the two properties bordered each other.

It was in the early evening of August 24th 1908 that the peace of Horace Wilkinson's home was shattered by a distraught military figure screaming, "She's dead! she's dead!" at Mr Wickham, the coachman. Wickham in turn summoned Herbert Harding, the Wilkinson butler, who elicited that it was Mrs Luard who was dead, and that it had been the General who had discovered the corpse at the 'Casa' – a secluded summer-house about equidistant between the neighbours' houses which, though in Horace Wilkinson's Fish Ponds Woods, seems to have been generously offered for the use of the Luards.

While the coachman called the police and a doctor, the butler accompanied the unhappy Charles Luard back to the Casa, on the

Mrs Caroline Luard

veranda in front of which lay the motionless figure of Caroline Luard, her head in a pool of drying blood, her face being licked by the family's whimpering Irish terrier.

It had been at about 2.30pm on this sunny August afternoon that the General had decided to stroll over to the Wildernesse golf club at Godden Green. His purpose was to collect a set of clubs that he had left there, and needed for a weekend game elsewhere. He was accompanied by his dog, Scamp, and, for the first part of the journey by his wife. After about a half-mile Mrs Luard remarked that, as it was now three o'clock, and as she was expecting a visitor to tea at four, she would merely stroll on to the 'Casa', and then return to Ightham Knoll. They parted company, and the General continued on his way to Godden Green. At approximately 3.20pm he was seen by Thomas Durrant, a local brewer's manager. The General was then about a mile and a half from the 'Casa'. (This was to prove a significant sighting, as it was to be established that the shooting occurred at 3.15pm.) The golf club steward, Harry Kent, saw the General arrive at 3.30, and leave again ten minutes later; at the same time he was seen

Major-General Charles Luard

by a labourer named Ernest King, who also spoke to him.

General Luard returned by an alternative route through the village of Crown Point, where he met the Reverend Arthur B. Cotton, vicar of near-by Shipbourne, with a small party of ladies taking photographs in Seal Chart Wood. One of these ladies was later to remember timing an exposure with her watch, so placing the meeting exactly at 4.05pm. The vicar politely offered the old gentleman a lift in his car, which the latter refused. Ten minutes later the car overtook General Luard on the road, and this time the offer of a lift was accepted.

Dropped at the gates of Ightham Knoll at 4.30 the General was surprised to find that the expected visitor, a Mrs Stewart, wife of a local solicitor, was none too pleased to have been kept waiting since she arrived at 4.20 to find both the host and hostess absent.

Luard was much puzzled, and not a little anxious, about the non-return of his wife, but the habits of a lifetime prevailed, and he politely took tea with his guest. By the end of the refreshment, both were very much puzzled and more than a little anxious by Mrs Luard's non-return, and at Mrs Stewart's suggestion they set out, in company with the faithful dog, along the mistress's expected route home. After a short distance, as she had another appointment, Mrs Stewart excused herself and left man and dog to trek the path to the summer-house. It was 5.35pm.

As they approached the summer-house the dog ran ahead, then stopped, barking furiously on the veranda, leaving its master to bring up the rear to see the cause of the fuss lying there, her head in a pool of drying blood.

It was shortly after General Luard had returned to the terrible scene, in the company of Harding the butler, that authority arrived in the person of Dr Mansfield, whose practice was in Sevenoaks. Mansfield's preliminary inspection of the body revealed a bullet wound in the left cheek, and another behind the right ear; this latter he judged to have been fired from very close range by the powder burn around the wound. In addition there was a scalp wound which could have resulted equally from a blow or from a fall.

Next on the scene was Superintendent Taylor, of the Kent County Constabulary, who was able to contribute a possible motive for the crime – the glove on Mrs Luard's left hand had been pulled off and the rings she habitually wore were missing. The robbery theory was given additional strength by the observation that the lady's skirt pocket had been cut out, and the purse that she carried in it was also missing.

The inquest held by County Coroner Mr Thomas Buss opened in the very hall of the

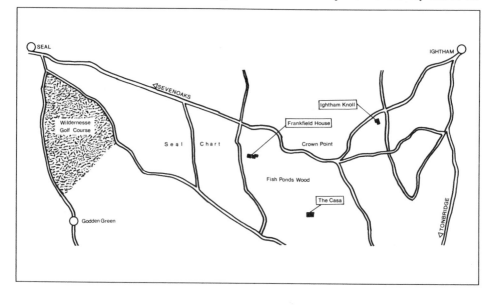

Luards' manor house, but later transferred to Ightham's *George and Dragon* inn. It revealed that there were, so to speak, "ear witnesses" to the tragedy; Mrs Annie Wickham, wife of the coachman, had been standing in the porch of her house with her daughter when they heard a single shot, followed by two further shots in quick succession. At the same time – close around 3.15pm – Daniel Kettle was labouring in Horace Wilkinson's garden; he also heard the three shots, which he recalled attributing to a farmer shooting squirrels. The third bullet, matching the two which had killed Mrs Luard, was found embedded in the path around the summer-house veranda.

The inquest then heard that the police had failed to find the murder weapon; London gunsmith and ballistics expert, Edward John Churchill, gave scientific evidence, and added that none of the General's three pistols could have fired the .320 calibre 'shorts' which had been recovered from the scene of the murder.

A timetable was compiled (see below) to re-establish General Luard's alibi for the time of the crime – a process which, for some reason, that gentleman bitterly resented – and then the inquest adjourned, leaving matters in the hands of the police.

2.30 General and Mrs Luard leave Ightham Knoll.
3.00 Mrs Luard takes off in direction of the 'Casa'; General Luard in the direction of the golf course.
3.15 Shots heard from the direction of the summer-house. Assumed to be the time of the murder.
3.20 General Luard is seen by Thomas Durrant.
3.30 Seen by both club steward Kent and labourer King at Wildernesse golf club.
3.40 Seen by same witnesses leaving the golf club.
4.05 Seen in Seal Chart Wood by Rev. Mr Cotton and his party.
4.15 (approx.) General Luard accepts a lift in the vicar's car.
4.30 Arrives at Ightham Knoll and meets Mrs Stewart.

After a while, however, it was apparent that, in this direction at least, the court was to be disappointed. Some sort of tramp, or itinerant labourer, who the police were convinced was the culprit, could not be linked to the time and location of Mrs Luard's death. The jewellery which they had assumed the "tramp" would immediately sell did not turn up despite extensive coverage of jewellers' shops and pawnbrokers. No fingerprints could be lifted from the scene of the crime; and police had still failed to turn up a murder weapon.

It had only been two years previously, in 1906, that provincial police chiefs had received Home Office permission to tap the vast reserves of experience and facilities of London's Scotland Yard. Unlike many of his colleagues, Kent's Chief Constable, Colonel Warde, was not too proud to realize that this was the very kind of assistance that he desperately needed – assistance that arrived in the persons of Chief Inspector Scott and Detective Sergeant Percy Savage.

Under Scott's experienced and cynical eye, the information to date was reassessed. In particular the detectives set about demolishing the "tramp" theory, which had already wasted so much police time. On his first visit Inspector Scott had noted the very significant fact that, located as it was in the midst of woodland, it was impossible to approach the summer-house without telegraphing the fact through the loud crackling of dry bracken surrounding it. Besides, the old exposed floorboards on the veranda creaked, and would have ensured that no unwelcome vagrant would have been able to approach Mrs Luard closely enough to shoot her in the back of the head at point-blank range. And, reasoned Scott, whoever heard of a tramp with a gun? A brick or a tree branch, a knife perhaps, but no vagrant in the Inspector's long experience would have anything as pre-eminently saleable as a gun in his possession. It was further unlikely that such a vagabond could resist the temptation of exchanging Mrs Luard's rings for a few pounds and a pawn ticket.

With much the same patient analysis, the greater part of the local police force's theories were eroded. Worse still, Inspector Scott had no theory of his own to replace them: the police, as they say, were baffled.

Up to this point the case was a puzzling one, but by no means unique in police history. It was not unknown for wealthy middle-aged ladies with no apparent enemy in the world to die at the hands of an assassin; not unheard of for the police to come up against a blank wall in their inquiries into that death. It is the bizarre and distasteful events that comprised the aftermath that were to lend the mysterious death of Caroline Luard its celebrity.

Every case of mysterious murder, of unsolved murder, carries in its tow a lunatic fringe who, for reasons best known to psychiatrists, confess to being the wanted killer. It was ever thus, but a masterpiece of the genre turned up during the search for Mrs Luard's murderer.

A keeper, patrolling Regent's Park in London stumbled across a brown coat, a hat, and a pair of shoes beside one of the ornamental lakes; there was no sign of an illicit bather, but in one of the coat pockets was a note. It was addressed "to Charles Francis Storm, Esq." and read:

My dear Father,
I can bear this suspense no longer. The Ightham affair has preyed on my mind. I fired the shots while the devil was in me. By the time you get this I shall be beyond human aid.
Your unfortunate son,
Jack Storm

Clearly this heavy-handed hint was designed to point at suicide, though there can be few who would attempt to drown themselves in four feet of water, even while "the devil" was in them. The police were obliged to drag the lake, though, and came away empty-handed. Indeed, as empty handed as the group of Lancashire dowsers who wandered about Ightham for a day brandishing their divining rods.

Enough of the bizarre. There was to be a further development which added mindless malice to the existing tragedy.

A series of rumours began to circulate in the area around Ightham. Now, it must be emphasized that there never was, still is not, the slightest reason to suspect Major-General Luard of involvement in his wife's death. Quite apart from the lack of motive, his cast-iron alibi makes it physically impossible for him to have been anywhere near the 'Casa' at the time of the murder.

But vicious gossip knows no such reason. It was not long before rumour not only had General Luard slaying his own wife, but also bribing witnesses and coroners' juries; even Scotland Yard was said to be engaged in the cover-up. The fact that all these accusations were transparently untrue did not stop them spreading, and when the distraught victim began to get hissed at and abused in the street, he went to ground; the General simply shut himself up in Ightham Knoll and refused to come out.

Next came the embellishments to the rumours. Additional sins compounded the already outrageous lies; that the General kept mistresses in London; that he was a mad sadist who regularly beat and tortured his wife. And the rumours began to be circulated by other means than wagging tongues – letters began to drop on to the desks of the investigating officers, at the homes of members of the coroner's jury, in General Luard's own sanctuary.

But while the police were busy ignoring this new development, Major-General Luard was quietly slipping into a state of total despair, total misery; a grief accentuated by a steady stream of scurrilous letters.

At the peak of his father's purgatory Captain Charles Luard wired to say that he was due to arrive from South Africa in two days. So black was the General's mood, that he could not face even his own son. He accepted instead the invitation of an old friend, Colonel C. E. Warde, MP (coincidentally, the brother of the Chief Constable of Kent), to spend the night of Thursday the 17th of September as a guest in his house, Barham Court, near Wateringbury.

On the following morning the General rose at eight o'clock, washed and dressed, and walked to the railway crossing at Teston, a quarter of a mile away. He waited patiently in a clump of bushes for the 9.09am from Maidstone West, and threw himself under the thundering wheels.

When the police began to collect the terribly mutilated body, they found pinned to the coat a neatly handwritten note – "Whoever finds me, take me to Colonel Warde".

It is doubtful whether his friend would have liked to see the unfortunate Luard as he was then, let alone have him delivered; but when the police searched the General's bedroom of the previous night, they found three letters, one addressed to his son Charles, another to his brother-in-law, and a third to Colonel Warde. This last read:

> My dear Warde,
> I am sorry to have to return your kindness and long friendship in this way, but I am satisfied it is best to join her in the second life at once as I can be of no further use to anyone in future in this world, of which I am tired and in which I do not wish to live any longer. I thought that my strength was sufficient to bear up against the horrible imputations and terrible letters which I have received since that awful crime was committed and which robbed me of my happiness. And so it was for long and the goodness, kindness and sympathy of so many friends kept me going. But somehow in the last day or two something seems to have snapped. The strength has left me and I care for nothing except to join her again. So good-bye, my dear friend, to both of us.
>
> Yours very affectionately,
> C.E.L.
>
> P.S. I shall be somewhere on the line of railway.

The following week the coroner's enquiry on Mrs Luard came to a close, and the coroner summed up, in part: "Never has there been a case in which the police have been so much in the dark, and unable to find any trace of the murderer, or any available clue as to who committed the crime . . ."

The jury added: "We wish to enter our most emphatic protest against those persons who have written or forwarded anonymous letters and postcards to various members of the jury, with the view to influencing their minds; and we shall hail with pleasure any action which may be taken to bring such persons to justice."

But there was no action; nobody was brought to justice. And anyway, it was too late. At least, it was too late for General Luard.

The verdict on Mrs Luard was "wilful murder against some person or persons unknown". And that is the stage at which it has remained ever since. Whether the police could have solved the crime at the time is arguable. Certainly there was a lot of woolly thinking and chasing of red herrings; probably the accusation of bungling could be upheld – at least up to the point where Scotland Yard became involved. But perhaps their greatest error was one of default; their seeming disinterest or inability to prevent a tragic, grief-stricken old man from being hounded to death in a trial by scandal.

General Luard (centre) at the funeral of his wife

The Misdeeds of a Lovely Boy

The Murder of Mrs ROSALINE FOX
by her Son SIDNEY HARRY FOX
on Wednesday October the 23rd 1929
at the Metropole Hotel (now demolished), Margate

Sidney Harry Fox was a blackguard, and a very successful blackguard at that. In fact he may have been born a crook – at least, if one believes that such traits are inherited – because his mother, Rosaline Fox, was known to travel a fairly crooked path herself.

Mrs Fox had been born at Great Fransham around the year 1866, the daughter of a Norfolk agricultural labourer. She married early to a railway signalman and bore him three sons before walking out of the matrimonial home to live on what wits and good looks nature had been kind enough to bestow on her. Rosaline soon took up with another railwayman, a porter this time (perhaps it was the uniform!), and the union was blessed in 1899 with little Sidney Harry.

Sidney grew apace, and before anyone had time to take breath he was starting his own career, supplementing his meagre income as a page boy with rather more profitable pickings from other people's pockets and houses. Like all beginners he made a few mistakes, and repaid his debt to society in the time-honoured way. By the outbreak of the Great War in 1914, with Sidney in his middle teens, he seemed to have life in the palm of his young hands. For a start, he had discovered that his brand of boyish charm and vivacity was attractive both to women and to men of a certain age and appetite; Sidney had discovered his homosexuality early, and took great pride in it. There was a phrase current in those days to describe just such a lad as Sidney; he was a 'lovely boy'. And when he was not being entertained by some generous host or hostess, he was being boarded by His Majesty's prison service.

A brief and undistinguished military career embraced a term of imprisonment for forgery and some time in the sick bay recovering from an epileptic fit. For these services to King and Country, Sidney was pensioned off with a weekly stipend of eight shillings. His not entirely unprofitable contribution to the war effort behind him, Sidney Fox went back to what he did best – living off people gullible enough to let him get away with it.

Time having taken its toll of Rosaline Fox's 'assets', mother and son formed a partnership that was to last until Sidney's decision to convert his mother into a *realizable* asset. Between them they travelled from town to town and from hotel to hotel the length and breadth of the country. The Foxes never stayed very long in one place – if they had it might have meant paying their bills, and that would have offended the family principles; they had plenty of cheques to spread around, but sadly no credit at the bank with which to honour them.

In 1928 Sidney engaged in a romantic encounter with a Mrs Morse, a lady who at the time of her infatuation with young Fox was involved in a divorce from her husband. In this Sidney was, however unwittingly, to make the only generous gesture in his life, he provided Captain Morse with a corespondent. In moved the Foxes to the Morse residence in Southsea; and they could almost certainly have ended their days there in comfort and tranquillity, but two circumstances mitigated against this sensible option. The first was Sidney's pride. The thought of a life fulfilling his sexual obligations to Mrs Morse offended, as he saw it, the dignity of his homosexuality. The second was the knowledge that the good lady had made a will of which Sidney Fox was the sole beneficiary; unfortunately it required that Mrs Morse should die first, and with commendable self-interest Sidney obliged as best he could. It was not his fault that the victim woke from her sleep before the open gas tap in her bedroom had done its worst. But Sidney's impatience also made him careless, and his subsequent blatant theft of Mrs Morse's jewellery earned him fifteen months in prison, and his white-haired old mother was removed to the work-house.

When Fox was released from gaol in March 1929 he rescued his mother from the care of the parish and together they went on the road again, scrounging and deceiving as of old. But time and illness had tired Mrs Fox, and she began to dwell on the happier world to come; she made her will on April 21st, leaving her worldly goods to her devoted son. To Sidney's chagrin he knew exactly how few those worldly goods were; but he was a resourceful young man, and as an investment for the future he took out a few thousand pounds' worth of accident insurance policies in his mother's name to supplement the worldly goods. Was it purely academic interest that caused Sidney to ask the insurance agent "Would this policy cover the case of drowning in the bath? Would it apply supposing a person was poisoned, say in a restaurant?"

During the following six months the Foxes travelled through London, Canterbury, and Folkestone, leaving in their wake a flurry of unpaid bills, stolen cheques, and unredeemed pawn tickets. When the pair arrived

Sidney Harry Fox

at the Metropole Hotel in Margate on October 16th 1929 they had no more than the clothes they stood up in, and a few solitary coins rattling in the corners of their pockets. Six days later Sidney borrowed the money for his fare to London and visited the insurance company; with his last few shillings he had the policies on his mother extended to midnight on the following day, October 23rd. Sidney Fox was about to realize his assets.

On the morning of the 23rd, Sidney announced to the hotel management that he and his mother would be checking out on the following day, and he would be obliged if his bill could be made up. That evening Mrs Fox and her son dined together in the hotel restaurant, and as a special treat Sidney ordered half a bottle of port for his mother as a nightcap.

Shortly before midnight Sidney Fox was rushing madly around the hotel corridors shouting "Fire!" Summoned to room 66, the manager was in time to see the partly clad body of its occupant being dragged from the smoky interior. Still hopping about in the background was the victim's son – Sidney Fox.

Police and medical assistance quickly

Rosaline Fox

arrived, the latter unable to render any assistance to the silent figure of Mrs Rosaline Fox. Dr Austin certified the cause of death to be shock and suffocation through smoke inhalation. On the following day a verdict of death by misadventure was returned at the coroner's inquest. Clutching an advance of £40 on his imminent insurance claim, Sidney accompanied the remains of his mother to their final resting place at Great Fransham. On the morning of the funeral Sidney was in negotiation with the manager of the Norwich branch of his insurance company. Three days later he was back in Margate in police custody – blackguard to the end, he had walked out of the Metropole without paying his bill.

But it was two months before Sidney was called to account for his greater crime. Police suspicion had resulted in a Scotland Yard presence, in the person of Chief Inspector Walter Hambrook, and a forensic presence, in the person of Sir Bernard

Room 66 in the Hotel Metropole showing the burnt armchair

Spilsbury, being dispatched to Great Frensham where an order for exhumation had been made. The conclusion of Spilsbury's examination was that Mrs Fox had not died from suffocation as had been supposed, but from manual strangulation; as the basis for this opinion he gave the small bruise at the back of the larynx. Unfortunately, the rapid decomposition that set in once the body had been exposed to the air rendered this telltale mark unrecognizable to later observers – a fact that was to have serious repercussions in court.

The trial of Sidney Harry Fox opened on March 12th 1930 before Mr Justice Rowlatt. The Attorney-General, Sir William Jowitt, led for the Crown and Mr J. D. Cassels had the difficult task of making Fox seem innocent.

Much of the early evidence concerned the fire itself, and the mysterious way in which everything pointed to the fire originating *beneath* a heavy armchair which stood between the gas fire (ostensibly the source of the blaze) and the bed on which Mrs Fox lay. In his evidence the Chief Officer of the Margate Fire Brigade testified that the only way in which he had been able to start a fire with similar characteristics was with petrol. Petrol like that in a bottle found in Sidney's room, which he claimed to have bought to clean his suit!

With the death occurring only minutes before Mrs Fox's accident policies ran out, and the ample proof of Fox's poverty, there was enough evidence of motive to convince the most stubborn of jurors.

But the prosecution did not have all its own way. When it came to refuting Spilsbury's medical testimony the defence was ready to fight back. As we have noted, the decomposition of the corpse of Mrs Fox had rendered Sir Bernard's strongest proof – the bruise to the larynx – unobservable to later examiners. Examiners like the great Professor Sydney Smith, a forensic pathologist every bit Spilsbury's equal in experience and reputation. It was Smith's contention that Mrs Fox had died of a heart attack, and that Spilsbury's 'bruise' was a sign of putrefaction: ". . . if there was a bruise there it should be there now; it should be there for ever". Unmoved, Sir Bernard maintained: "It was a bruise, and nothing else; there are no two opinions about it!"

On the seventh day of the trial Sidney Fox had the star billing; he was in the witness box for the greater part of the day, though he did himself little credit. His contribution to his own defence can be summed up in his answers to the Attorney-General on the subject of the night of the fire:

Sir William Jowitt: Did you realize when you opened the communciating door [between Fox's room and his mother's] that the atmosphere in the room was such as would probably suffocate anybody inside? – *Fox:* If I had stayed in three or four minutes, I should have been suffocated.

So that you must have been greatly apprehensive for your mother? – I was.

Fox, you closed that door? – It's quite possible I did.

Can you explain to me why it was that you closed the door, instead of flinging it wide open? – My explanation for that now is that the smoke should not spread into the hotel.

Rather that your mother should suffocate in that room than that smoke should get about in the hotel? – Most certainly not, sir.

Why, at the moment when you believed that your mother was in that room, did you trouble one twopenny bit about the smoke getting into the hotel? – I have not admitted that I did shut the door. I very much doubt that I did.

Does it not strike you now as an inconceivable thing to have done? – Not in the panic I was in; I don't think it was.

I suggest the communicating door was closed. You don't dispute that? – I don't know.

Before rushing down you closed the door of your room? – I don't remember closing the door.

And then you passed the door of No. 66? – I must have done so to get down.

Did you open that door? – Not then. What would have been the use?

Will you swear you did not? – Yes.

So that you left your mother, as you say, with the communicating door closed, and with the door of room 67 closed; you passed the door of No. 66, but you did not open that, and you knew that your mother was inside that room? – Yes, I did not stop to open the door. I rushed downstairs to get help, which I think is a reasonable explanation.

Don't you think that before rushing down for help you might have flung the doors open as wide as you could? – No, I don't.

Why not? – Because I wanted to get help as quickly as possible.

Do you say you do not remember whether you closed your mother's door? – I hardly know what I did. It is all very well to try to pin me down to details, but I don't hardly remember what I did do. I was agitated at discovering the hotel on fire.

Discovering the hotel on fire? That was what made you agitated was it? – Yes.

I should have thought that what would have made you agitated was your mother being in that room? – Certainly.

Which is it now? – I do not remember. You cannot pin me down to detail. I cannot remember all that happened that night.

I suggest that if you had wanted to preserve your mother's life you would have flung open the doors? – I tried to get in, and when I could not, I dashed downstairs.

There was one thing between. You closed the door? – I do not remember.

Sidney was found guilty of the murder of his mother and was sentenced to death. Although he consistently maintained his innocence he must have realized that the game was up; or perhaps it was just another example of his arrogance that he refused to apply to the Court of Criminal Appeal. Sidney Fox was hanged at Maidstone Prison on Tuesday April the 8th 1930; he was thirty-one years old.

The Pluckley Enigma
The murder of Miss GWENDOLINE MARSHALL
on Tuesday the 6th of October 1980
at her home, Enfield Lodge, Pluckley
and the Imprisonment of PETER LUCKHURST for the Killing

Until 1980 there was nothing to distinguish Pluckley from dozens of similar villages that dot the uneventful landscape of Kent. The population has risen steadily over the decades, and like many villages around which large towns have grown that population has diversified in recent years. The top of the village is much as it ever was, with its substantial houses and stone cottages clustering around the picture-postcard Norman church; it is the image that the mind's eye creates in response to the words 'country village'. But Pluckley has a newer, quite different, type of resident occupying the rather drab post-war council estate at the bottom of Forge Hill. It too is an archetype, representative of a rash of 1950s housing programmes.

Miss Gwendoline Marshall was a member of the 'upper' village class, though her spacious house, Enfield Lodge, stands at a distance from the main residential centre in its own six acres. A short, slight woman, Miss Marshall could also be said to be an archetype, for she typified that kind of elderly eccentric whose habits are rendered acceptable by their possession of money. A fiercely independent person, Gwendoline Marshall was a virtual recluse, rarely going out into the village and having what necessities she could not grow in her vegetable garden delivered, paying the bills by post. Her one regular outing was the weekly trip to London. The villagers speculated wildly about these visits, which were in fact to a property in Bloomsbury which had been left to her by her parents. Miss Marshall's art-student tenants there provided her with a comfortable income on which to live, and indulge her own hobby of painting. Enfield Lodge had also come to Miss Marshall from her father, who had built it in the 1930s.

Gwendoline Marshall encouraged only one visitor to the Lodge, young Peter Luckhurst from the council estate. Until her premature death from tuberculosis, Peter's mother had been Miss Marshall's only regular visitor in her capacity as cleaner. This meeting of distant generations seemed conspicuously successful – for Peter his elderly friend was like a mother-substitute, a sympathetic ear in to which he could tell his troubles; more practically, the boy was given the freedom of the orchard and, uniquely, the privilege of shooting rabbits on the six acres. From Miss Marshall's standpoint Peter was not only a lively young companion for whom she seemed to entertain a genuine affection, but was useful at light jobs around the house and gardens. All in all it was a more satisfactory relationship than many in the village would have thought.

But something was about to go terribly wrong.

At three o'clock on the afternoon of Tuesday October 7 1980, Miss Marshall's nearest neighbour, Mrs Lucy Wilson, was disturbed in her garden by a young woman in evident distress who begged her to come to Enfield Lodge. It transpired that the woman and her husband, Alan, had been given a rare invitation to pick apples in the Marshall orchard, and when they arrived could not raise the

mistress of the house to announce themselves. Now, led by Alan Dryland his wife and Mrs Wilson went round to the side of the house. Lucy Wilson called through the open kitchen door, and when there was no reply stepped into the room and called again. While wondering over Miss Marshall's unaccustomed absence the search party noticed a pool of fresh blood on the floor. They looked further and found another patch in the lounge; in the dining room Miss Marshall's ransacked handbag lay on the table. Nervously following the bloodstains upstairs Dryland and Mrs Wilson were horrified to see the trail lead from one room to another of the upper floor. Leaving the house in state of shock the party began a search of the grounds and outbuildings, all except for a garden shed which had been padlocked. Fearing the worst, Mrs Wilson summoned the police. When PC Coulson arrived it was apparant to his trained eye that this was no job for a village bobby, and he summoned the Ashford force.

As more police officers arrived a systematic search of the house and grounds was put under way in the hope of finding Miss Marshall – dead or alive. At around six o'clock in the evening Sergeant Eric Peacock approached the garden shed and ordered the padlock cut off . . .

. . . There on the floor lay the twisted body of Gwendoline Marshall, her hands tied tightly behind her back, her face and head terribly mutilated, her throat cut, and worst of all, a hay fork had been thrust through her neck, pinning her to the wooden floor.

Within the hour Detective Superintendent Earl Spencer, head of the East Kent CID, had taken charge and ordered immediate house-to-house inquiries. By eight o'clock detectives had spoken to a local ne'er-do-well named Nikki Mannouch about his activities that day. Mannouch claimed to have been in company with Peter Luckhurst, who he placed at the scene of the murder at 2.30 that day. On the following afternoon both Mannouch and Luckhurst were taken to Ashford for routine questioning; nobody could have anticipated the extraordinary statement that was about to be made by Peter Luckhurst. After initially denying that he was at the Lodge at all on the day of the murder, Peter simply looked up and in a quiet voice said: "I hit her with a log. I wanted some money. I had too much to drink." Later that day Peter Luckhurst wrote his statement:

> I had known Miss Marshall a long time but only through my mother. I left the *Spectre Inn* at around 2 o'clock. From there I went into my house got my bike and went to Enfield Lodge where I left my bike and entered the house. On entering I saw Miss Marshall and I grabbed a log and hit her. I asked have you got any money. She replied no. So I hit her again on the head trying to knock her out but failing this I got angry and forced her around upstairs and downstairs of the house, but I could find no money at all except a cheque book which was no use so I left it. I hit her again this time knocking out the lady. While unconscious I got her to the shed and tied her hands and pushed her on the floor and kicked her and I went all weird and started hitting her with a [garden] fork. On recovering from the funny turn locked the door and ran like hell. I got on my bike and went home and into my shed. From my shed I saw Nick Mannouch walking past. I asked him where he was going. He said up to the village so I went with him to get his bike which he'd left there and we then went back to my house where I ate my tea and then left for Smarden.

A subsequent search of the Luckhurst home was rewarded by the discovery, in a kitchen drawer, of a knife stained with blood of the same group as Miss Marshall. In addition, minute spots of blood were found on Peter's clothing, though it proved insufficient to provide an accurate match.

Peter Luckhurst's trial at Maidstone Crown Court in June 1981 was all but a formality. By now he had withdrawn his confession, which he claimed had been made under pressure. His defence was as predictable as it was unsuccessful; he had simply been visiting Miss Marshall, and found her already dead. His uncannily accurate description of the crime was simply conjecture. Why then, having stumbled innocently upon this ghastly scene, did he not immediately summon the police? Luckhurst's reply was hardly calculated to endear him to the jury: "I won't give them assistance for nothing!"

After a five-day trial and a two-hour jury retirement Mr Justice Stocker sentenced

Peter Luckhurst to be detained during Her Majesty's pleasure.

And there might have been the end of a tragic but by no means unique case.

But that would be to reckon without the good citizens of Pluckley – from both ends of the village. Peter, they had decided, was innocent. It wasn't that the boy was universally approved of – he had been a difficult youngster, particularly after the death of his mother; he rarely attended school and managed to get himself into more than the average number of scrapes – petty theft, vandalism, lying . . . But never, the village agreed as one, was there any hint of violence; indeed, quite the reverse.

The result of this overwhelming dissatisfaction with the outcome of the trial was the Peter Luckhurst Defence Committee, and under this umbrella new moves were made towards reassessing the evidence. The Committee appointed a solicitor to press for a revision of the case with a view to appeal; the main grounds for the Committee's unease could be resolved into a number of questions to which no satisfactory answer could be given.

1. Why, for example, in his crucial statement did he not make any mention of cutting Miss Marshall's throat? Which in turn exposes the enigma of the knife – would he really have been naive enough to leave the bloody weapon hanging around in the kitchen for his family to find? And how did he get it home without it staining his clothes?

2. There was never any question that the clothes in which Peter was picked up by the police were the same as he wore on the day of the murder; nor had there been any attempt to clean them. But despite the pathologist's stated opinion that the killer would have been "covered with blood", Peter's clothing was stained with so little that it was impossible to make a comparison with the victim's group.

3. How was it possible for Peter Luckhurst to carry out such an extended crime without leaving a single fingerprint? He denied wearing gloves, and this is consistent with the recollections of people who saw him that day.

4. In his interview with the police Peter gave

an accurate description of his tour around the house, pulling and shoving Miss Marshall with him – with one exception. He omitted the downstairs toilet; indeed, when questioned he had no knowledge of its existence. It was, however, smeared with the victim's blood.

All these points and more were to be welded into a case with which it was hoped to overturn Peter's conviction.

In addition, one of the *Kentish Express* journalists, Dudley Stephens, began a newspaper campaign under the headline 'The Unanswered Questions of the Pluckley Murder'. Even the lunatic fringe was represented in the person of Brian Ford, a private detective who had left his Hastings 'practice' to pursue his theory that Miss Marshall had been the victim of what he called "a Ritual Killing".

But Peter's case became the inevitable victim of fickle hearts and empty pockets as people lost interest and the solicitor's fees overstretched the modest Defence Fund. The appeal faded into memory, and while few villagers believe to this day that Peter is guilty, there the matter rests.

But if Peter Luckhurst did not kill Gwendoline Marshall, who did? And why did Peter confess; and how did he know so much about the crime and yet leave out crucial details that cast suspicion on that confession?

On the basis of their own first-hand researches Justine Picardie and Dorothy Wade advance a theory that offers so far the most plausible explanation of the unanswered questions:

Say Peter Luckhurst was not alone. Say he was merely an accomplice in Miss Marshall's murder, possibly even only a 'bystander'. This would explain how he knew so much about the crime, but had so little blood on his own clothes. It would explain the absence of fingerprints, and if he were not the protagonist himself, he could easily not have seen or registered the contact with the downstairs lavatory. Furthermore, if he ran away before the killer had completed his task Peter would have known nothing about the cutting of Miss Marshall's throat. But for this to be true it would mean that the murderer must be somebody that Peter knew well (and obviously feared, which accounts for his silence); and in a village community a stranger gets noticed, so the killer must have been known to a great many people – may be living at one end or the other of Pluckley to this day.

A footnote apropos of Peter Luckhurst's readiness to confess is the story that is told of the time that a car was vandalized in the village. Despite the fact that most of the villagers knew who the culprit was, a completely innocent Peter Luckhurst confessed to the crime, was taken before a juvenile court, and fined.

The Problem of the Uncooperative Victim
The Murder of Miss MARGERY WREN
by an Unknown Assailant
on Saturday the 20th of September 1930
in her shop at 2 Church Road, Ramsgate

On the evening of Saturday 20th September 1930, 82-year-old Miss Margery Wren was found, still alive but with fatal bludgeon wounds, on the floor of her Ramsgate shop. During the subsequent five days before she succumbed to her injuries Miss Wren made it quite apparent that she knew the identity of the person responsible for the attack, but was unwilling to name him.

Despite a number of seemingly relevant clues, and the services of one of Scotland Yard's most experienced detectives, the assailant was never brought to trial. The police had, it is true, a short-list of suspects – not uncommon in such a case – but what has given this crime its enduring mystery, and rarity, is the reluctance of the victim, even in the face of death, to cooperate in the apprehension of her attacker.

In his autobiography* Superintendent Hambrook states categorically "Owing to the fact that nobody had seen the murderer near the shop at the crucial time, I was unable to lay my hands on him; nor could I penetrate the strange mystery of why Miss Wren was apparently anxious to shield him". But does this mean that he had no idea of who the killer was or, as Browne and Tullett point out enigmatically in their biography of Bernard Spilsbury** "Superintendent Hambrook says that there were six suspects of whom A, B, and C were able to clear themselves [at the inquest]. One of the remaining three, D, E, or F was the murderer. Miss Wren knew which, and the police may know too. But it has never been possible to pin the crime on him."

The following notes are presented in such a way that all available details are given alongside a chronological schedule of events and eye-witness accounts. Your deduction, and conclusion, is as good as anyone else's – the Case File is open.

The Attack

Despite the conflicting accounts given by Miss Wren herself, it was fairly early established that a brutal attack had been made on the old lady's person. The accident explanation first given by the victim ("I came over giddy and down I went") was, however, not entirely discounted until the patholigst submitted his report; support for the theory rested on the testimony of a widowed cousin who recollected that Miss Wren's rather old-fashioned habit of wearing long skirts had often led to her tripping up. In addition, Margery Wren had fallen over some six months previously while trying to reach some boxes on a shelf in the shop; on that occasion she had quite badly injured her face.

When Sir Bernard Spilsbury performed his post-mortem he listed seven lacerations to the top of the head, and a further eight wounds and bruises on the face, consistent with having been inflicted by a pair of firetongs (such as was found close to Miss

*Hambrook of the Yard, Walter Hambrook. Pub: Robert Hale, London, 1937
**Bernard Spilsbury – His Life and Cases, Browne and Tullett. Pub: Harrap, London, 1951; reissued 1980

Wren's battered body) which anyway were found to have blood and hair from the victim's head stuck to them. There had also been an attempt at strangulation.

There is good reason to believe, apart from Miss Wren's suggestions, that her assailant was familiar with his victim and her habits, and was no stranger to the layout of the premises (indicated by the methodical way in which the building was searched by the killer). He appears to have left by the back entrance through the yard.

The Chief Constable of Ramsgate, Mr S. F. Butler, issued the following statement:

The police are now convinced beyond all doubt that Miss Margery Wren was the victim of a brutal and savage murder. This disposes of any theory that may still exist in the minds of the public to the effect that Miss Wren may have met her death by accident. I earnestly appeal to any person entering or leaving the shop between the hours of 2pm and 6pm on Saturday last, or to anyone who saw any person in the vicinity of the shop or entering or leaving the premises between these hours, to communicate with me at once.

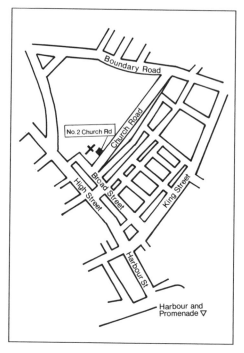

The Motive

Motive was always the controversial question; unlike most similar crimes there did not appear to have been a robbery associated with the attack. Of course, the assailant could have been disturbed before he had a chance to steal – but why, then, was the house methodically searched, but nothing of value taken from it; the signs pointed to the fact that the intruder had a definite plan in mind. For example, drawers had been removed from cupboards and examined – *carefully*. What was the purpose? What was more important than the money and valuables . . . and important enough to kill for? Perhaps, as Hargrave Lee Adam* suggests, it was a search for a document – but if so, what sort of a document? That the killer was not a criminal by 'profession' is at least partly justified by the fact that of the many fingerprints found where the murderer had been, none could be matched to a known villain.

It may be useful to consider the financial standing of Miss Wren.

For about fifty years, until two years before the murder, Margery Wren had lived in and run the little shop in Church Road, Ramsgate, with her maiden sister Jane. When the latter died, she left property valued at £921 12*s*. 7*d*. She appointed Mr Stewart Watson Oldershaw, solicitor of Lincoln's Inn, London and Mr Harry Jarralt of Picton Road, Ramsgate, to act as executors and trustees. Her furniture and personal effects she left to Margery; she also provided that her freehold shop and cottage, together with the goodwill of the business, should be held in trust – the income to be paid to Margery Wren. On Margery's death it was to pass to a cousin, Richard Archibald, of Chapel Place in Ramsgate.

In her own will, Margery Wren bequeathed most of her property to a cousin (probably Mrs Cook). In the meantime she lived frugally – not entirely of necessity, as she had made it known that she had some £1000 invested in Government Bonds, as well as various sums of money in tin boxes kept hidden about the house; (these last had not been looted by the attacker, despite his having found them). As with many elderly

Murder Most Mysterious, Hargrave Lee Adam. Pub: Sampson, Low, Marston, London, 1932

Miss Margery Wren

retiring eccentrics (she would, for example, plead poverty in order to get a free bowl of broth from a near-by soup kitchen) Miss Wren attracted a reputation as a miser who was hoarding a fabulous wealth. Did this play a part in the crime?

The Investigation

When Chief Inspector Hambrook and Detective Sergeant Carson arrived from Scotland Yard on September 24th, they found themselves faced with the unusual problem that not only was the victim unwilling to cooperate in the identification of her attacker but showed herself to be capable of deliberately misleading the enquiry by giving the names of several quite respectable and totally innocent local people. All these bogus clues had to be investigated as a matter of routine, and so added to the already difficult situation.

Aside from Miss Wren's own contribution to the confusion, the police had to deal with varying degrees of frustration as the result of other red herrings, One of these was a small linen handkerchief which was found in the shop, and thought to hold the key to the assailant's identity. The handkerchief bore a name in one corner, which eventually proved to belong to a ten-year-old pupil from St George's, the local school; it trans-

Margery Wren's shop in Church Street at the time of the attack

The shop, now a private residence, in 1987

pired that a set of half a dozen of them were given by an aunt to the boy and his brother, and to avoid squabbles over ownership their mother had marked the corners with their respective names. The object in question was almost certainly dropped by the lad on one of his after-school trips to the Wren tuck-shop.

Another, deliberate attempt to mislead the police was made by a young man who said that on the day of the murder he had taken a train from London that arrived at Ramsgate at about four o'clock in the afternoon; and he claimed that he had alighted at Dumpton Park station. He was subsequently forced to admit that fear of suspicion had led him to fabricate the story of getting off the train before Ramsgate. He had in fact travelled as far as that station, walking to his home past Miss Wren's shop in Church Road.

The coroner's inquest was unable to be more definite in their investigation. The coroner, summing up, reported "The fullest enquiries have been made into the circumstances, and if any real evidence had resulted from the inquiries it would have been brought before you." A verdict was returned of murder, by

"person or persons unknown".

The Statement of Ellen Marvell

Twelve-year-old Ellen Marvell, who alerted her parents and, ultimately the police to the attack on Miss Wren, gave this statement to the police concerning the events which followed her mother sending her to the shop to buy blancmange powder –

I went with Jessie Langton, who is fourteen years old. I tried to open the shop door, but found it locked. I can generally open the door, but as I could not do this I rattled it so as to ring a bell which hangs inside. I looked through the glass pane and saw Miss Wren sitting in a chair in the back room. Her hair was down her back, and she was not wearing the cap she usually wore. I rattled the door again, and then Miss Wren got up from her chair and came and unfastened the door. When she did so I saw blood running down her face, and there were bruises on her face. I said "whatever have you done, Miss Wren?" and she said "What do you want?" She could not speak very plainly;

[*concluded on page 90*]

CHRONOLOGICAL SEQUENCE OF EVENTS
ALSO GIVING THE CONFLICTING STATEMENTS OF THE VICTIM, MISS MARGERY WREN

Date and Time of Events	Miss Wren's Statements
Saturday 20 September 1930:	
3.30pm. Reuben Beer, a coal dealer, delivers ½cwt of coal.	
4.15pm. Miss Wren seen sweeping leaves away from the front of the shop.	
5.15pm. School children returning home from cinema see Miss Wren in her shop, handing something to a woman customer.	
5.35pm. One of the children, 12-year-old Ellen Marvell, arrives home – which is opposite Miss Wren's shop.	
6.05pm. Ellen Marvell sent by her mother to buy blancmange powder at the shop. Ellen finds the shop door locked and Miss Wren in a bloody state; she calls her father.	
app. 6.15pm. Mr Marvell arrives at the shop and sends Ellen to fetch Dr Archibald; Jessie Langton, a friend of Ellen, is sent for the police. On the way to the doctor, Ellen tells her mother the story and Mrs Marvell joins in helping Margery Wren.	In reply to Mr Marvell's questions, Miss Wren says she has "had a tumble . . . a quarter of an hour" earlier.
app. 6.30pm. Mrs Cook, Miss Wren's cousin arrives after having been sent for. Dr Archibald arrives.	Miss Wren tells the doctor that she tripped over some firetongs, and asks if she is going to die. She explains to PC Arthur that she has fallen over a poker.
Police Constable Arthur arrives.	
app. 6.45pm. Miss Wren taken to hospital where she is visited by Dr Archibald who asks her again to explain her injuries.	First she tells the doctor that she had a fall, then states that a man had caught her by the throat and then beat her with the tongs. She mentioned the names of several people (who were subsequently cleared by the police) and added "He has escaped, Doctor, and you will never get him".

Later that night Inspector Baldwin visits Miss Wren at the hospital.

Miss Wren makes the statement "I was sitting in the armchair in the back room opposite the shop door. I came over giddy and down I went. I tried to pull myself up with the chair. I managed to pull myself up and went to the shop. Nobody has been to upset me or knock me down. No strangers have called at the shop, and if anybody had called I should have seen him. After my accident I went and locked the door as I did not want anybody to see me in that state". Later she changed her story to "Yes. He suddenly seized me by the throat", but refused to name the assailant.

Sunday 21 September 1930:

A policewoman at Miss Wren's bedside renews the attempt to coax the name of the attacker out of her.

Miss Wren tells the policewoman several contradictory stories. "Nobody hit me as I have no enemies"; then "There were two of them set about me . . . if I had not had my cap on they would have smashed my brain-box. One said 'Now I have got you I'll do you in'. I was sitting in the armchair in the parlour when they came in. One of them grabbed me by the jaw from behind and then threw me down, and they both set about me. I did not really see them – only the wild eyes of one of them when he was smashing my head. There was a knocking at the door, and then they made their escape . . . He did it and I must suffer".

Monday 22 September 1930 and
Tuesday 23 September 1930:

Miss Wren, in an increasingly weak state in hospital, receives several personal and official visitors and makes further mysterious references to the crime.

During her stay in hospital Miss Wren made several further cryptic references to the attack:

"He tried to borrow £10"; and

"I don't know why he should have come into the shop then";

"Is the little black bag safe?"

(The bag was an item to which Miss Wren seemed to attach a lot of importance, and which she carried around with her. It did not, as some had conjectured, contain her fortune; indeed, it contained nothing of interest at all.)

Miss Wren continues, through confusion, malice or delirium, to point an accusing finger at several local citizens; these names were probably dropped as red herrings in order to divert police attention from the real killer.

Asked by the vicar if she had anything to say regarding the attack, Miss Wren declined with "I do not wish to make any statement". To Mrs Baldwin she said, with reference to the vicar's visit, "I did not tell him anything, see."

Magistrate fails to elicit any further information; Miss Wren deposes "I have seen my doctor and vicar. I have received communion. I know I am going home. I do not wish him to suffer. He must bear his sins. I do not wish to make a statement."

Miss Wren is visited by a vicar and a friend, Mrs Baldwin.

Wednesday 24 September 1930
Chief Inspector Hambrook and Detective Sergeant Carson arrive at Ramsgate from Scotland Yard to take charge of the investigation.

A magistrate arrives at the hospital to take Miss Wren's dying deposition.

Thursday 25 September 1930
Miss Margery Wren dies in hospital.

Friday 26 September 1930
Bernard Spilsbury performs the post-mortem on Miss Wren's body, and confirms the cause of death and the fact of murder.

[? Monday 29 September 1930]
The coroner sums up at the inquest; a verdict is returned of murder committed by "person or persons unknown".

she could only whisper. I told her I wanted blancmange powder. She did not seem to understand, and I tried to make her understand what kind of powder I wanted, but she kept asking me if it was raspberry. I told her several times I wanted vanilla, and she then went behind the counter and put four or five packets on the counter near the scales and said "Take the flavour you want". Then my father who had been waiting for me to return home, as he wanted to go to the pictures with my mother, called out, "Come on, Ellen; you are a long time". I shouted "Come and look at Miss Wren. Her face is covered with blood". My father came across and asked Miss Wren how long it had been done, and she said faintly, "A quarter of an hour". She also said she had had a tumble. My father told me to fetch Dr Archibald, and my friend Jessie Langton went for the police. I ran indoors first and told my mother, and then went for the doctor while my mother ran over to the shop and bathed Miss Wren's head.

You Should have Banged the Youth into Dumbness*

The Murder of RICHARD FAULKNER TAYLOR by JOHN ANY BIRD BELL

on Friday the 4th of March 1831 on the edge of Bridge Wood, near Strood

---

This malefactor, at the time of his execution, was only fourteen years of age. He was indicted at the Maidstone Assizes on Friday, the 29th of July, 1831, for the wilful murder of Richard F. Taylor, a boy aged only thirteen years, in a wood in the parish of Chatham.

From the evidence it appeared that Taylor was the son of a poor man, a tallow-chandler, who lived at Stroud

*William Shakespeare, *Twelfth Night*, iii.2.

[now Strood]. On Friday, the 4th of March, the little fellow, who was described as having been possessed of peculiar intelligence and an amiable disposition, was dispatched to Aylesford to receive a sum of nine shillings, the amount of a weekly parish allowance to his father. He was dressed at the time in a 'southwester', with a belcher handkerchief round his neck, blue jacket and waistcoat, brown trousers, and shoes and stockings; and his father, at his request,

James Bell   *John Any Bird Bell*

lent him a knife, with which he expressed the intention to cut a bow and arrow on his way home. The boy arrived safely at Aylesford, when Mr Cutbath, the relieving officer of the parish, gave him the usual amount of nine shillings. The boy had previously been instructed by his father as to the mode of carrying the money, and the little fellow had shown him how completely and how securely he could conceal it, by putting it into a little bag, which he could carry in the palm of his hand inside a mitten which he wore; and on this occasion he was observed to place the silver in the customary manner in his hand. He usually reached home at about three o'clock, but this afternoon he did not return. As night advanced his father became alarmed at his absence; and the next morning he determined to go himself to Aylesford, for the purpose of making enquiries for him. The fact of his having received the money was ascertained; but all search for him proved unavailing, and his parents were left in a most painful state of doubt as to the cause of his sudden disappearance.

It was not until the 11th of May that the real facts of the murder of the unhappy boy were discovered. On that day a man named Izzard was passing through a bypath in a wood situated at a distance of about two miles from Rochester, and about thirty rods [165 yards: about 151 metres] from the high road, when he found the body of a boy lying in a ditch. The mitten was cut from his left hand, and his clothes were disarranged as if there had been a scuffle. Although the body was so much decomposed as to prevent his being able to discover by what means death had been produced, the remains of blood upon the shirt, coat and neckerchief left no doubt of the dreadful death which the boy had suffered. He had died of a wound which had been inflicted in his throat with a sharp-pointed instrument, the mark of which was still visible, and which could not have been inflicted by the deceased himself.

A diligent search was immediately instituted for the purpose of endeavouring to find the instrument with which this terrible murder had been committed, and in a short time a common white, horn-

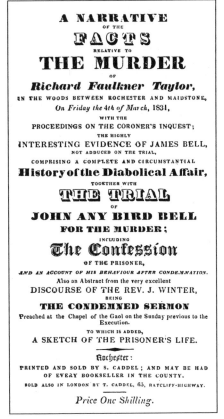

A NARRATIVE
OF THE
FACTS
RELATIVE TO
THE MURDER
OF
Richard Faulkner Taylor,
IN THE WOODS BETWEEN ROCHESTER AND MAIDSTONE,
On Friday the 4th of March, 1831,
WITH THE
PROCEEDINGS ON THE CORONER'S INQUEST;
THE HIGHLY
INTERESTING EVIDENCE OF JAMES BELL,
NOT ADDUCED ON THE TRIAL,
COMPRISING A COMPLETE AND CIRCUMSTANTIAL
History of the Diabolical Affair,
TOGETHER WITH
THE TRIAL
OF
JOHN ANY BIRD BELL
FOR THE MURDER;
INCLUDING
The Confession
OF THE PRISONER,
AND AN ACCOUNT OF HIS BEHAVIOUR AFTER CONDEMNATION.
Also an Abstract from the very excellent
DISCOURSE OF THE REV. J. WINTER,
BEING
THE CONDEMNED SERMON
Preached at the Chapel of the Gaol on the Sunday previous to the Execution.
TO WHICH IS ADDED,
A SKETCH OF THE PRISONER'S LIFE.

Rochester:
PRINTED AND SOLD BY S. CADDEL; AND MAY BE HAD OF EVERY BOOKSELLER IN THE COUNTY.
SOLD ALSO IN LONDON BY T. CADDEL, 65, RATCLIFF-HIGHWAY.

Price One Shilling.

handled knife was found, corroded with rust, which had every appearance of being the weapon that had been used by the murderer. The discovery of this weapon afforded some clue to the parties implicated in the transaction, and a man named Bell, and his two sons, John Any Bird Bell and James Bell, respectively of the ages of fourteen and eleven years, were taken into custody. These persons lived in the poorhouse adjoining the spot where the murder was committed; and the information obtained by the constable, by which the knife that had been found was discovered to have belonged to the boy John Bell, afforded conclusive testimony of one at least of them having been concerned in the foul deed.

An investigation into the circumstances of the murder took place before the magistrates at Rochester, the result of which was that convincing proof was obtained of the implication of the two boys. During this inquiry it became necessary that the body of the deceased be exhumed – it had been buried immediately after it had been discovered and the coroner's jury had sat – in order that the person of the boy might be searched – an operation which had been previously unaccountably omitted. When this examination was made, the two younger prisoners were taken to the graveyard for the purpose of observing the effect of the proceeding upon them. The elder boy, John, maintained throughout a sullen silence; but his brother James, on being desired to enter the grave and search the pockets of the clothes of the deceased, which had been buried on his person, cheerfully complied, and brought forth the knife which the father of the unhappy lad had lent him on his setting out for Aylesford. This was the only article found upon him, and robbery, therefore, it was at once seen, had been the object of his murderer.

The prisoners after this underwent another examination before the magistrates; and upon their being again remanded, the younger boy confessed that he and his brother had committed the murder – that his brother had waylaid the deceased in the wood, while he had remained at its outskirts to keep watch. Upon this the evidence of the younger boy was accepted. The father having been discharged from custody, although strong suspicion had been felt of his having been an accessory after the commission of the crime, the prisoner, John Any Bird Bell, was committed for trial. The statement of the younger boy exhibited a remarkable degree of depravity in the conduct of his brother and himself. He said that they had long contemplated the murder of their wretched victim, as they had learned from him the errand upon which he so frequently travelled from Stroud to Aylesford and back; but various circumstances had prevented the completion of their design until the 4th of March, when it was carried out by John, who afterwards gave him one shilling and sixpence as his share of the proceeds of the transaction.

On the way to Maidstone the prisoner acknowledged the truth of his brother's statement, and pointed out a pond where he had washed the blood of his victim off his hands on his way home after the murder. He also pointed to the opening which led to the spot where the murder was committed, and said to the officer: "That's where I killed the poor boy." Then he added: "He is better off than I am now: do you not think he is, sir?" – an observation to which the constable assented.

At the trial the prisoner exhibited the utmost indifference to his fate, and appeared to entertain no fear for the consequences of his guilt. He maintained his firmness throughout a most feeling address by the learned judge, in which he was sentenced to death, but exhibited some emotion when he was informed that a part of the sentence was that his body should be given over to surgeons to be dissected. At half-past eleven o'clock on Monday morning the wretched malefactor ceased to exist, and his body was given to the surgeons of Rochester for dissection.

The Mystery of Brompton Road
The Murder of ELLEN ANN SYMES
by REGINALD SIDNEY BUCKFIELD
on Friday the 9th of October 1942
in Brompton Farm Road, Strood

If it were appropriate to apply the terminology of connoisseurship to the "craft" of murder, then Reginald Buckfield's crime would rate very lowly indeed; it was a murder as colourless as it was without purpose. What has made it unique among

[1] 'Thames Mount', home to Ellen Symes and her family

[2] The home of Ellen's parents at 39 Dickens Terrace

[3] The Symeses would have been familiar with this car park sign if not with the modern rebuilt Institute behind

[4] On the left the former 'Valhalla'

the crimes of the century is a document that Buckfield penned while in police custody; a text, in the form of a fictitious short story, that was at one and the same time a confession and an alibi. In order to see the relevance of this extraordinary composition, we must first sketch in the landscape, and introduce the characters in the real-life "Mystery of Brompton Road".

(Numbers in square brackets – [5] – refer to similarly marked points on the map and to photographs of the locations as they appear today.)

The victim was Ellen Ann Symes, a woman in her mid-thirties; Ellen was married to Alfred James Symes, a joiner, presently seconded to the night shift of a local munitions factory. The family was further enriched by a four-year-old-son, and for five months Mrs Symes had been anticipating a second happy event. The Symeses were resident at Thames Mount, a house in the Brompton Farm Road, Strood [1].

To alleviate the inevitable loneliness of a

"night-work widow", Ellen Symes had slipped into the routine of spending Friday evenings with her parents at their house in not-too-distant Dickens Terrace [2]. The evening of 9th October 1942 was no exception, and after occupying the hours up to 9.30pm in comfortable family pursuits, Mrs Symes and her son accompanied the old couple to the Wainscott Workers Institute [3] where she parted to turn along Hollywood Road (now Hollywood Lane) towards home.

At about 9.40 the occupant of the ambitiously named 'Valhalla' [4] was in the rear garden when he heard what might have been the call of a screech owl, or could have been a human scream. As he was pondering this puzzle the scream was succeeded by a thud, as though something had fallen heavily against the fence at the front of his house. To Mr Pattenden's understandable horror, he quickly discovered that the heavy "something" was the body of a woman, now lying on the ground bleeding profusely. The push-chair in which her boy was being transported lay overturned beside the woman, its occupant unhurt but clearly very frightened.

By the time medical help arrived, in the person of Dr Charles William Greene, Ellen Symes was in no need of it; her life-blood had escaped through a savage stab wound in the front of her neck. Following a trail of blood, it was obvious that Mrs Symes had been attacked some thirty yards back down the road, and had been desperately trying to reach home.

Nine o'clock the following morning, the police had begun their routine questioning of all persons known to have been in the vicinity of 'Valhalla' on the previous day. Mrs Symes's son had already offered the information that his mother's attacker was in soldier's uniform, and it fell the lot of Henry

Giles, War Reserve Policeman No. 13, to encounter a chirpy little artillery gunner, 3969722 Buckfield. Reginald Sidney Buckfield, nicknamed "Smiler" for the disarming physical characteristic of always appearing to be smiling, had been a labourer in civilian life hailing from Houghton, near Mansfield, where he lived with his wife and three children. Buckfield had enlisted in June 1940, and had served in Africa before being stationed with 542 Heavy Anti-Aircraft Battery at Oak Street Camp [5], a short walk from Brompton Farm Road. On September 26th, Reginald Buckfield had gone absent without leave from the camp, supporting himself by casual fruit-picking in the neighbourhood.

The Gunner's manner, and responses to

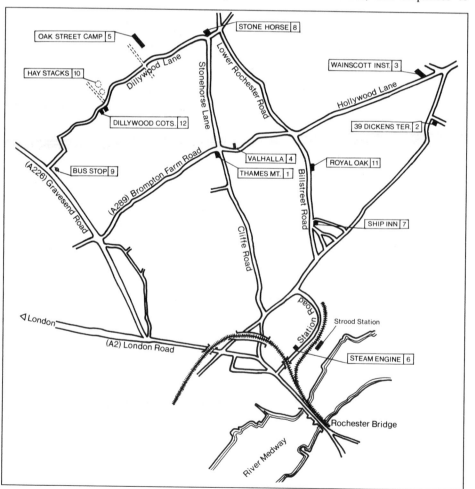

questioning, at the police station alerted officers to the likelihood that Buckfield was more than a mere army absentee. In the course of interrogation the prisoner had already confided the information that he had been questioned in previous years on three further cases of murder.

While he was in custody, Buckfield gave the following account of his movements on the evening of the murder, an account which is significant when read in the light of his subsequent literary pretensions:

On Friday, 9th October, 1942, I worked at Robertson's Farm from 10.30am to 6.00pm, then I got a lift into Rochester and went to the cafe opposite the Majestic [cinema] at about 6.35pm. I had a meal and bought 20 cigarettes, Player's Weights. I left there at about 7.00pm and went to the Seamen's Institute where I had a wash. I then went back to Strood and went to the *Steam Engine* [now *Steam Packet*] public house [6], where I stopped until 8.10pm. I made the habit of going into this public house every night. I then walked to the *Ship Inn* [now *The Ship*] at Frindsbury [7]. I went into the public bar and had a pint of beer and a meat pie. I left there at about 8.55pm and walked down Bill Street Road. I did not go into any other public house. I crossed over Brompton Farm Road and turned left at the *Stone Horse* [8]. I carried on up Dillywood Lane and went to its junction with Gravesend Road where I stopped [9]. I saw a bus for Gravesend stop near me at about 9.35pm. A sailor and a civilian girl got off and went down Dillywood Lane. Just before 10.00pm Bombardier Parrett spoke to me where I stood on the corner. He asked me for a light off my cigarette. He left me and went down Dillywood Lane after we had a short conversation. Shortly afterwards, the 10.00pm bus from Strood came along. Six A.T.S. girls got off including Bombardier Beach, Margery Verrall, and all I said to them was Good night. You girls had better hurry up or you'll be late again and get another 14 days C.B. I followed the girls along Dillywood Lane and went to the [hay] stacks [10] and went to sleep. The next morning I was arrested.

Reginald Buckfield was then confronted with a bone-handled table knife, sharpened

[5] After more than forty years, the Gunner's old battery station has become Pocock's Garden Centre; but the concrete bunkers and gun emplacements remain

[6] Sidney Buckfield's 'Steam Engine'

[7] The Ship Inn, now simply The Ship

to a point; this he strenuously denied ever having seen before. It was the murder weapon which had been found close to the scene of the crime.

Returned to the cells, "Smiler" Buckfield set to work on the document which elevated his

[8] The Stone Horse

[9] The bus stop at the end of Dillywood Lane

[10] The footpath remains; the hay stacks long since gone

case from the merely futile to the positively interesting. The unfinished short story "The Mystery of Brompton Road" extends to some 7000 words of narrative, written in the first person of Buckfield himself – sometimes called "Smiler", and sometimes, more mysteriously, Gunner X – and relating to the crime with which he would be charged. It is a rambling, disjointed, and in parts incomprehensible text, but it contains such information as only the killer would have had.

The trial of Reginald Sidney Buckfield at the Old Bailey began on Wednesday 20th January 1943 before Mr Justice Hallett; Mr L.A. Byrne appeared for the prosecution, and the defence of Buckfield's life was entrusted to Mr Hector Hughes KC. The following extract from the transcript of the trial is representative of the wholly farcical defence offered by the prisoner to refute the evidence of his short story:

Mr Justice Hallett: . . . You were asked why you headed the first sheet not "A Mystery", but "The Mystery of Brompton Road"? – *Buckfield:* Well, I was thinking of London at the time, my Lord, of Brompton Road.

The second batch, as I have it, is also headed "Mystery of Brompton Road Murder". You say "when I headed those two sheets 'Mystery of Brompton Road' I was thinking of Brompton Road in London". Is that right? – That is so.

Then the fact that the murder had taken place in Brompton Farm Road near Strood was a mere coincidence? – That is so, my Lord.

A very disastrous thing, was it not, that you should have, out of all the tens of thousands of roads in London, selected the one road that happened to have the same name as the road where the murder had happened? – Well, it seems that way, my Lord, yes.

The jury occupied their retiring room for only one hour; and even so, some cynics expressed wonder at what they could have been doing for so long. Their verdict could have surprised nobody, and when Mr Justice Hallett passed sentence of death on Buckfield he was still smiling. Still smiling, no doubt, when the customary medical investigation assessed his sanity. Still smiling when he was found to be insane; and still smiling his way through life in Broadmoor.

The original manuscript of Buckfield's "The Mystery of Brompton Road" gives a strong indication of an author only semi-literate. Punctuation, when it exists – which is not often – is misleading and frequently incorrect. It is often difficult to ascribe dialogue to a specific person and, further, it would appear that details of the other three murders for which Buckfield had been picked up and questioned may have been sprinkled into the narrative. The version which follows has been edited from the text which was read verbatim from his manuscript at the Gunner's trial. Punctuation and spelling have been inserted or corrected, and linking words have been added where these are necessary to the sense of the story.

In order to relate the fiction to the fact, this version has been annotated with comparisons between the story of "Gunner X" and the murder of Ellen Ann Symes. Finally, very little has changed in the couple of square miles which constitute the location of the Brompton Road Murder, and the geographical references, indicated in the text by numbers (see also introductory paragraphs), can be traced on the sketch-map and from the recently taken photographs.

THE MYSTERY OF BROMPTON ROAD

By Gunner Buckfield

Chapter One

"Hello, Smiler."

"What a bloody night!"

"Not so bad," Bert replied.

Smiler: "You coming to get a drink?"

"Well, I don't mind if I do; get out of this wind and darkness."

"What's yours?" said Smiler, as they entered the bar.

"Well, I dunno," said Bert. "I fink I'll have a pig's ear."

"O.K., two pints of nine, guvnor."

"Coming up, Smiler. What's the weather like outside?" the barman asked as he handed the drinks over and took the money.

"Bloody cold and dark," the two cockneys said at once. And a remark was passed by a Cheekie Chappie that it was "a luverly night for a murder, guvnor."

Laughter.

"You know, my old china plate, there is many a word said in jest that comes true. Ain't that right, Smiler?"

"Yes, I suppose so."

Now let's weigh these two men up. Start with Bert,[1] so called. He's a married man, got a wife and one daughter; his job is doing night work round Strood or Rochester. Happy-go-lucky sort of guy, cares for nothing, lives along the Brompton Road somewhere, or shall we say near it. His wife and child are happy-go-lucky, so that makes the merry-go-round.

Now we will drop Bert for a while and go on to Smiler,[2] a soldier in an R.A. station somewhere in England but . . . at the time an absentee, unbeknown . . . to . . . more than half a dozen people, including an A.T.S. from 542 Battery; her name for the time being is Miss X. The ways of Smiler were happy-go-lucky, full of life and laughter; his build about 5ft.8in. to 8½in., fair hair, blue eyes, and a scar on the bridge of his nose. One would say he wasn't the type of man that girls will go crazy over, but wait and see; as this story carries on, you will be surprised that he turned out to be a real Bluebeard.[3]

"Come on, Smiler, you are slow in drinking. Whatcha finking about? The wife or the little A.T.S. girl?"

"Turn it in now, Bert. I don't want everybody to know I'm messing about with an A.T.S.; same as usual."

By the way, Smiler's been fruit-picking today.

"What are you thinking about, guvnor?" asked Smiler.

"You know, you're a bit of a mystery. How is it you get out every day?"

"Ah," said Smiler. "That's my business."

---

[1] It is clear that, apart from the fact that the latter had a small son not a daughter, Bert's is a description of Alfred Symes.

[2] A fairly accurate, if idealized, portrait of the author himself.

[3] The promise is unfulfilled, perhaps because the story is unfinished. The worst that can be levelled against Gunner X – according to the text – is a rather callous reaction to A.T.S girl Miss X's state of impending motherhood. 'Bluebeard' is more likely a reference to the guilt of the story's author.

"Good luck if you can get away with it," replied Bert.

"Hello, Bert! Hiya, Smiler!" This came from a person unknown by name to the two men,[4] but in a pub one gets known within a short time. (You will see who the stranger was in the closing Chapter of this story.[5]) "How's your wife?"

"She's not bad."

"Ain't she with you?"

"No," replied Bert. "I think she's up her mother's or somewhere around, what with baby and all. She's nearly always out up there."[6]

"My," said the Stranger, "If that was my wife, I should be a bit worried over her whereabouts, wouldn't you, Smiler?"

"No, I don't think so," replied Smiler. "If my wife went out on her own, she could come back on her own for me."

Bert: "Funny you saying that, Smiler; she always do. Her mother and father see her to the bottom and the rest of the way she comes home on her own."

"Well," said the Stranger, "and I suppose you stop here till turn-out time?"

"Not me," said Bert. "I'm on night work. Besides, the wife always gets in just before 10pm or 9.30pm."

"Well, let's forget about women. You going to have another drink before you go, Bert? How about you, sir? You want a drink?"

"Well, I don't mind."

"What is it?"

"Brown."

"Two pints and a brown, guvnor. Thanks. How much? Two and tuppence? Blimey, that's dear."

Bert: "I didn't want a big one, chum."

"Go on, drink the b------ stuff. It's there."

"Well, Smiler, I'm off. See you tomorrow night."

"Yus, I s'pose so. Good night."

"Well, Smiler, I suppose you will soon make tracks towards home."

"Yus, mustn't be late."

---

[4] This mysterious 'Stranger' is the first indication that Buckfield has begun to work out a line of defence.

[5] Another unfulfilled promise.

[6] Subsequently found to be true. But how did Buckfield know so much about the Symes family, particularly the details which follow of Mrs Symes's movements on the night of the murder?

"Where you say you are stationed?"

"At Oak Street, Dillywood Lane," said Smiler.

"I know," replied the Stranger, "That's the Battery just above the *Stone Horse*."

"Well," said Smiler, "I don't know you, only by sight, but tell me, how did you get to know my pal and myself?"

Stranger: "Well, to tell you the truth, I've seen you every night going that way; you cross over by Brompton crossroads."

"That's right," said Smiler.

Stranger: "Don't you think it's quicker going along Brompton Road as far as the buses stop to go back into Strood; there's a turning brings you smack bang to the *Stone Horse*, which is right on Dillywood."

"No," said Smiler, "I much prefer the way I go – straight down the Cliffe road, that's better. By the way, talking about women not so long ago, you gave me the idea you knew Bert's wife. If you're a stranger to Bert, how do you know his wife, or where they live?"

Said the Stranger: "I've seen her and him together many a time, but not at night, in daytime. She dresses very select."

"What d'you mean," said Smiler, "select?"

"Well, a pair of high heeled shoes, a turban sort of thing, and light blue coat."

"Blimey, you seem to know a lot about people, guvnor."

All this conversation was taking place in a public house called the *Steam Engine*.

"Is that the right time, guv?"

"No, Smiler, ten minutes fast; 8.10pm's the right time."

"Thanks. Good night, I'll be getting back." These were Smiler's words as he departed.

Chapter Two

BEER TALKS

The following day was much better so Smiler, getting up, went on his daily round which, starting from the straw-stack above Oak Street Camp, Dillywood, came down to Strood, which was as far as he'd go in the morning, have breakfast at a little cafe and get cleaned up at the barber's facing; when finished, he made his way back to the farm where he stopped for the rest of the day fruit-picking. Now this had been going on for a fortnight. It is said that the world is small and, after seeing this woman picking fruit in the same orchard, I agree with the saying.

So once again the conversation opens with "Didn't I see you at Strood the other night?"[7]

"I don't know," was Smiler's answer. "Maybe you did."

"I know it was you, because I followed you into the *Steam Engine*. You were talking to Bert what's-his-name – lives at or near Brompton Road."

"That's right," said Smiler. "Come to think of it, that was you in the corner."

"That's right," says he. "What's happened to the little A.T.S. who you were with last Sunday?"

"What A.T.S.?" asked Smiler.

"You know who I mean. The one you were with at the *Stone Horse* – with dark hair; looks like an Italian."

"Oh, her! I still see her at nights," replied Smiler. "By the way, how do you know about me and her?"

"Smiler," was the reply, "beer talks!"

With that the conversation ended.

Chapter Three

THE MYSTERY OF MISS X

"Hello, Smiler, am I late?"

Answer: "It will be the day when you get here on time. I am getting fed up hanging around for you. It looks bad."

"Never mind, my Darling. It's a pity you had to wait for me," said Miss X.

"Don't worry yourself," said Smiler. "No more [after] tonight."

"But Smiler, you can't leave me. If you do, I will commit suicide. I won't be disgraced in front of my friends."

"What's the matter?" asked Smiler.

"You know what."

"Now listen here. You have been out without me quite a lot, with sailors and soldiers down Chatham, and if you think you're going to take me for a ride forget it, you might get hurt."

Miss X: "You will regret the day you ever knew me and went absent; and Dillywood Lane will be your downfall."

"Meaning what?" said Smiler.

"Never mind. One of these mornings before long you want to get a paper. You'll

most probably find that someone's been killed."

"Don't be silly," said Smiler, "you have not got the guts."

"I did not say it would be me, my Darling," said Miss X.

Laughter.

"You mean me?"

"Yes, my dear, I could kill you when you tease me about other women."

"That would be nice. What would you get out of it? The rope?"

Miss X: "If I had a knife now, I would kill you."

"That's the worst of you Italians; you remember the night you threw a knife at me, and the time I smacked your face for coming behind me with one."

"When I was shouted at! Look, Smiler, what happened . . ."

We both forgot it on account of trouble brewing.

Chapter Four

THE WEEK-END AT STROOD

"Well, Ann, and how are you today?"

"Not so bad. Same as usual, Smiler?"

"Yes, cup of tea and a sandwich. Well, no work today; I think I'll go to the pictures."

This was while having tea in the cafe in Strood facing the barber's. Now the time I left would be about 9.30; then went up to see the P.N. boys who have such a thing as smokescreens; had dinner in their mess, also tea; after that went to the Invicta [cinema], saw Gene Autry in *South of the Border*, came out 8pm to *Steam Engine* pub.

Did the same thing the following day. Once more the Stranger was there [in the pub]. On seeing him I went around to where the piano was, which is at the back of the room for women and children. To my surprise he came round and asked me if I wanted a drink. I had a pint off him, and after I tasted it I began to play the piano. I think the time would be 9.30 when I noticed a lady get up with a child and, after saying goodnight went out. Now the funny part about it, as much as I can remember, [is that] the Stranger, within two or three minutes, followed her out.[8]

That was nothing to go by; it is the usual

---

[7] This is probably the mysterious 'Stranger' in conversation with Smiler.

[8] We are already beginning to get a sinister picture of the Stranger in connection with a woman and a small child at 9.30 at night.

thing. But what did make me think was that the other woman in the place told me the man that treated me had been following her all the evening, and that the woman lived my way, or near my Battery and, on their behalf, asked me to follow the lady as they feared something would happen to her and the child.

I then asked where was her husband. The reply was, "Out East somewhere."

With that I came straight out, walking fast. I thought I would pick her up, but was disappointed; I never saw anyone.

That ended my week-end.

Chapter Five

THE MESSAGE FROM MISS X

"Now, Smiler, how about coming to our dance at Cliffe on Friday?"

"I think I will, but it will be late by the time I get home and clean up; getting on for seven."

"Never mind, the dance don't finish till 11.30pm."

This again was asked of me by the lady I'd seen at Strood, who also lived at Cliffe. Well I didn't say no more or think about it till I got down to Strood. After a clean up I went to the pub. To my surprise, once more the Stranger was there – dressed in uniform. I asked him where he was stationed. He said, "At Lower Hope, Cliffe," and that there was a dance on at Strood; would I go?

I was a bit doubtful about going, till in walked a fellow from 542, a pal of mine but only a bit of a kid.

"Ah," he said as he approached, "here's a letter for you from Miss X. She told me where I would find you, and to give you it."

I looked at the time, which was 8.35pm, opened the letter and read, "Darling, can't get out tonight to see you at [straw] stack, so go to the dance at Cliffe."

I was puzzled over the dance part, because I had not seen her to tell her I was going. The woman in the orchard had not, so I wondered how she got to know. I put the letter in my pocket without another thought, and made up my mind all of a sudden to go to the Cliffe dance with the Stranger. We caught the five to 9pm bus from Strood, landed about 9.25pm, had a drink in a pub, finished up at the dance. Won Spot Prize for waltz; came out 11.30pm. Slept two to three hundred yards from Globe Cinema. That

was the beginning of the end [at] Cliffe.

Chapter Six

MY LAST WEEK OF FREEDOM

"Hello, Pop, is there any fruit-picking being done round here?"

"Yes, son," replied the old boy. "Go to Benuncles Farm, or Robertson's; you will get a job there."

"Thanks," said Smiler.

Now the farms I'd been working on were Whitbread at Wainscott and Brice on Cliffe Road and, owing to the job getting near the end, I started out for [Robertson's at Hoo]. When arriving there, I was asked if I was on leave.

I said, "Yes, forty-eight hours."

With that no more was said till my forty-eight hours expired. I was then asked again how I managed to get out so much.

I replied, "By framing sergeants."

That went off, so I stopped there till Friday. After 6pm, I left the farm and got a lift to Rochester, to the cafe facing the Majestic; had tea, cleaned up and went to the pub once more. All the time I was working I was being watched. It did not worry me.

[11] The Royal Oak

I made tracks out of the pub just at 8.10pm, reached another called the *Ship Inn* at 8.30 or 8.35pm,[9] stopped till 8.50 to 8.55pm, made tracks towards Dillywood, got settled down after all these little things were done by me at 10.15pm. The little things mentioned are: I stopped and asked for a light below the *Royal Oak* [11], which would be 9.05pm, off a civilian with a cycle;

---

[9] Attention to detail in the matter of time now becomes obsessive, and clearly represents an attempt by Buckfield the author to work out an alibi for 'Smiler'; that is, himself.

he never had such; walked on towards 542 by *Stone Horse* on Cliffe road; looked in *Stone Horse*, carried on to outside Battery gate. Stopped there for five or ten minutes, time being 9.20 or 9.25. Knowing Miss X was out, decided to wait for her at bottom to come off bus; got to bottom at 9.30, saw bus. Sailor and civilian girl turned down Dillywood. Didn't move till asked for a light by a Bombardier from 542 Battery. (How I came with a light? On the inside of my battle blouse, I found two pockets; I found a red-top match in the corner.) After a short conversation Bombardier left, asked time – 9.55pm. Bombardier just round corner, bus came down 10.00pm, girls jumped off. Six of them passed me; said "Good night" to them all, also mostly Miss X, but did not get no reply. Gave about five minutes for woman, then started back, reached straw stack 10.15pm. That ended Friday.[10]

Now read on.

Saturday 10th – Accused of murder.

[*This ends the first part of the manuscript. Following the more specific title of "Mystery of Brompton Road Murders", Buckfield enlarges on the activities of the Friday, penning in a more detailed account of Smiler's movements*]

MYSTERY OF BROMPTON ROAD MURDERS

by Gunner Buckfield

The Last Chapter
SMILER ACCUSED TURNS DETECTIVE

"What a terrible night to be out," thought Gunner X to himself as he came out of the pub called the *Steam Engine* at about 8.10pm to start back on his way to his rough sleeping quarters, which was a rough old straw stack. "Still, never mind," thought him to himself, "being an absentee from the Army you have got to sleep somewhere out of the police's way."

So with no more ado he made tracks. After walking about ten or fifteen minutes he came to another pub, which is on a corner of a street or road called Bingham; the name of the pub is the *Ship Inn*. Being cold and browned off, Gunner X decided to get another drink before he laid down for the

night, so he entered the side being the public bar. What he had there was a pint and a pie. Now the time when he entered would be about 8.25; seeing the time was young, he decided to stop there for a while. He did so. He noticed the time when he came out, which was 8.50 or 8.55pm. Now, while walking towards his sleeping quarters he had to pass two more pubs, which were, as it happened, on the same side as the *Ship Inn*; these he did not go in. So whilst carrying on he pulled a cig from his pocket, which he bought down at Rochester in a cafe facing the Majestic, to take his mind off the weather. On searching his pockets for a match he found he never had one. So, disappointed, he put the fag back in his pocket. But about a hundred yards below the *Royal Oak* he banged into a fellow with a cycle. So, taking cig out of pocket, he went across and asked for a light. Once again disappointed; the fellow never had such a thing. Taking no notice, he proceeded down the road.

Now just below where the man was standing is the crossroads – one road on the left is Brompton [Farm] Road, which takes you out to the Gravesend road; straight over takes you to Cliffe. So, as we go along with this story, I should like anyone whom it may concern to time Gunner X after leaving the *Ship Inn* till the time he got to his destination, which was a straw stack just above 542 Battery, which is on the right-hand side of Dillywood Lane. Before we forget this, there are three ways to the place stated above. They are from Strood straight along on the Cliffe road; the next is along the Gravesend road; and third is the crossroads what is mentioned in the early part of this story – by turning left along Brompton Road and right when you come as far as the buses stop to go to Strood, it will bring you right on to the *Stone Horse*, which is at the bottom of Dillywood. Now, let's get back to where he left off. From the *Ship Inn* to the *Royal Oak* takes about five minutes which, as I said he came out of the pub at 8.55pm – around about that, we will say – it would make it 9.00pm; a few minutes whilst asking the fellow for a light would make it about 9.05pm. Now from there straight across the crossroads on Cliffe road, which Gunner X said he took to 542 Battery, would take a good walker ten to fifteen minutes at least. We will say for the time being it took ten

---

[10] This Friday is important, it is the Friday on which, in real life, Ellen Symes was murdered.

minutes. That would bring the time to 9.15pm.

Now, whilst he was near the Battery gates, he decided he would wait and see a young lady who he had become very friendly with whilst stationed in the Battery who, being in the A.T.S., we will call her 'Miss X'. (The reason for this? You will see why Gunner X does not want her name mentioned.) On knowing her so much and her days out, he found that, being Friday, she would be out for the day; so, after about ten minutes, he decided to walk down to the bottom of the road to where the buses came from Strood and Gravesend. That would take about five to ten minutes. When at the bottom a bus came along, which would be about 9.30 or 9.35. You will notice the time corresponds with the time of the distance covered with the time of the bus near enough. Off the bus, about fifty yards from where Gunner X was standing, two people made tracks towards the corner. On passing, Gunner X noticed it was a sailor and a civilian girl; the way which they turned was down Dillywood. Now from 9.35 till 10.00pm he did not move off the corner till about ten minutes to 10pm.

His reason for moving then was that a Bombardier from 542 asked X for a light. Before we go any further, I will tell you how Gunner X managed to get a light. On the inside of a battle blouse you will find, if you look into it, two pockets; in the corner of one of these he came across a red-top match. That is how he was able to supply a light. Now this Bombardier did not jump off the bus; he walked down and, having a torch to show him his whereabouts, he was roughly 700 to 800 yards away coming from Strood – so Gunner X estimated. As he left, the 10pm bus came along on time. He noticed this because the Bombardier was just around the bend when the bus pulled up. It did not stop on the corner, but several yards up the road. Gunner X knew that the girl friend of his would be on it. He was right; there was six came down, of which he knew at least three but, owing [to the fact] that he did not get no answer when saying "Good night" [to the one] who he thought would be Miss X, he is not sure that she was with them. So, after giving the girls about five minutes' start, he made tracks towards his resting place, which was a straw-stack, as mentioned; the time being, when he settled down, about 10.15.

[12] The group of cottages facing the hay stacks where Buckfield slept. He had asked for a light for his cigarette at the cottage just befor his arrest

Saturday, October 10th, 8.25am. Went to house facing stack [12], asked for match. After getting a light I started walking towards the top of the road. I was walking for about fifteen minutes when, just above Brompton Road, I was stopped by a police constable, who asked me where I came from.

Reply was: "542, Dillywood Lane."

Then asked to show my book. He knew that I was Gunner X, who they have been looking for. We done no more, but made tracks for the police station, which is somewhere in Strood. On arriving, the sergeant in charge got on the phone to another place, somewhere in Rochester. Ten minutes had gone when I was ordered into a car: three minutes in that brought me to police headquarters. After waiting for about fifteen minutes, I was shown into a room, which is known as C.I.D.; was then told to take my clothing off, which I did, and was glad to do so. I was then asked my whereabouts and what I'd been doing since being absent and where I'd been sleeping and eating.

I replied to these questions that I'd been working on farms fruit-picking, eating in cafes, getting shaved by a barber at Strood, named Bates. After a long wait I was then taken out again by car to show the driver the way I went to my sleeping quarters after leaving the *Steam Engine*. This I did, the same way as stated in the first part of my story.

On arriving at destination, I was asked to show the spot where I slept. On doing so, the police gave it the once-over. They came back to me with a question, something like this: "Where or what have you done with your knife?"

Now Gunner X, knowing what he was in for by saying "I sold it," stands in for another charge, which is 'selling Government property'; but he did not care, for the truth is much easier to speak than lies. Now Gunner X, after having these questions shot at him, thought it funny that they should make him go to all that trouble. "After all," he told them, "I'm only an absentee from the Army."

Still he was not told what it was all about. The next move of the police was making inquiry at 542, he still not knowing what it was all about.

Well, that ended for Saturday. Taken back to Police Headquarters, fingerprints taken, cup of tea, cheese sandwich, wrote two letters, and put in a cell for the rest of the day.

Once again we start.

Sunday, 11th. Questioned again. "Where is my wife living? Am I paying separation allowance?" This got me wild, because I have never left my wife, but I did not show it. The next was, "What do you mean when you said you were accused of the same thing before at Kettering?"

"Well," said Gunner X, "the last time I went absent I was picked up for the murder in Southport and three in London. I think," said Gunner X, "that the police have got a liking for me."

"Well," said the Chief, "How long ago was that?"

Reply: "Six, seven months. I was stationed at Bold Hotel, Southport, Lancs."

I was beginning to get fed up; knowing I was just an absentee, I thought I was entitled to an explanation. I told the Chief so. To my surprise he came straight out and told me. His words were: "Three hundred yards from where you slept, Gunner X, a woman was found murdered, and the funny part about it is that you were in the vicinity at the time it was committed."

"It certainly looks bad for you," said the Chief. Did I know it!

So once again we started questions. While talking, a knife was produced from a box, which would be about eighteen inches in length, three to four inches wide; handle, sort of orange with a bit of red worked in. Anyhow, I was asked if I had ever seen it before.

Answer: "Never in my life."

Well, that went by. Then we came back on the subject about Miss X being in trouble, meaning pregnancy. Well, the same as I have stated and which has been proved by all the women, it was over her I was on the road at the time. I know it looks black for me concerning her, but I would rather have that trouble than be classed as a murderer. With this, after signing my name to a statement with a few more little details, I was sent back to my cell.

This, my dear friends, ends Part One of this Mystery.

GUNNER TURNS DETECTIVE[11]

Now we will get at a few facts.

Say for one minute I am the murderer. All right! What and when can these questions be answered?

No. 1: From 9.05pm when I left man with cycle, I had got to walk to the cross-roads; say I turned up Brompton Road – that would at least be ten minutes; so I've got from 9.05pm till 9.30 when I see the bus come in. So, taking from 9.15pm, I have got to see the woman, kill her – that's putting it blunt – and walk about half a mile down the road. Is it possible it could be done? 9.15 murder and half-mile walk in fifteen minutes? I think I should want a Spitfire.

No. 2: Say the first could be done. Alright. Now the knife that was shown me I think had something to do with the crime. Well, if I was a murderer, do you think I should leave the knife hanging around? Not on your life, boy. That thing itself is good enough to convict a man.

No. 3: Now why should a murderer, after committing a crime, hang about a straw-stack all night with the body three hundred yards away (so I'm told). Don't you think that would be foolish of him? I know that I wouldn't have done.

Now, say I'm Chief Inspector of the City Police; I can just imagine that! But anyhow, I am, so we will take as what the police call 'motive' for the murder that she is a married woman, so they say, with a baby son or daughter; a habit of hers was walking along the road nearly the same time every night. Right! If on Friday she was with her people, which I am told, and left them on the corner,

---

[11] In which Reginald Buckfield puts Gunner X on trial, and defends him. The author reveals a suspiciously detailed knowledge of the crime and of the movements of Ellen Symes.

why is it that her people never came any further with her?

Or, having a baby with her, what was the cause of her being out so late with the child? Or at what time did her husband go to night work? Did he leave her and her people? Was there any time he had come to meet her and found out a few things?

It is funny for a mother and son or daughter to go out without father. At the present state of affairs anything could have come between man and wife. If so, jealousy would be the motive. On the other hand, say the lady, for instance, got to know friends; as you know yourself, it could happen that a married woman falls in love with a soldier; then, say, if so, after a few weeks it would wear off, the woman being afraid of her husband finding out. The soldier's part is getting a raw deal from the woman; also afraid of [the husband], that he has been out with his wife. What would happen? Murder may be in two men's heart, and the cause would be jealousy and being taken for a ride.[12]

(I hope you will not be offended with what's down here, as it's only something I have wrote while being detained. It is not the first time I, Gunner X, have been questioned on murder.)

Just one more thing. If the mother was killed, why wasn't the child? Also who found the baby? How and when did the child get back home? Why did the child leave it till morning before telling its father? Where was the father at the time of the crime? He could have done these two things: left home to go to work, as I'm given to understand, checked in, showing himself openly; could have returned back after, him thinking his mates had seen him at work for an alibi, and waited; or probably he needn't have gone till late, with plenty of excuses about one thing and another.

Now we will go over the course. First, a man on a cycle, or with one, about, we will say, one hundred to one hundred and fifty yards from the cross-roads. At 9.05pm Gunner X walks right over the cross-roads to Dillywood; following up behind is a soldier who has come from the blue, unknown to Gunner X and don't come from 542 Battery.

Now, thinking it was an officer, Gunner X darted for cover, and to his surprise the Unknown did not come no further but turned around and went back, not at the time thinking anything wrong. Proceeded on journey. Now the last man to be seen is a Bombardier walking from that direction. Now we will take the man with the cycle. He could have waited till I was out of sight, which would only have been a few seconds, left his cycle and walked to the corner of the road or along the road; he could know the woman coming along and could have committed the crime and away on the cycle. The soldier could have been hiding on the corner waiting for her; on seeing me pass in soldier's clothes, he could have killed her, timed me walking from the cross-roads to the *Stone Horse,* could have come down the road what runs right bang into the *Stone Horse,* where he could have followed me unknown in what direction he came. Gunner X would be lost to think which way he did come from, because he sort of came from the blue half-way along Dillywood Lane, and I think it would take a clever man to solve that one.

That brings two [more] men in that could have had time to commit the crime. While Gunner X was walking to Oak Street Camp, now Number 3 had, say, from 9.30pm to five to ten, which is twenty-five minutes. Now we come from Strood, leave there, say, on the bus which would be around 9.20pm from Strood, stopping place Brompton Road, which is out of sight from Dillywood Lane. It is easy for a man to jump off the bus at 9.30pm at the road named, commit the crime, and walk from Brompton Road to where Gunner X was standing in five to ten minutes. Take note of the time: it leaves fifteen minutes to play around in. That makes Number 3 involved.

I am not accusing anybody, but for something to do I thought I would try and be a bit of a detective.

Notice that the four men was in the radius of the crime, and all near enough near the same place between nine and ten pm. It is a coincidence that, according to Smiler's story (who calls himself Gunner X) that there were four men in the vicinity of the crime within three hundred yards; yet not one of them, we hope, heard or knew there was murder on the night of Friday, October 9th, 1942.

---

[12] Could we be getting close to Buckfield's real motive for the crime? A 'close' acquaintance with Mrs Symes would certainly account for his familiarity with her family life.

That, my dear friends, brings it to "girl murdered by person unknown." We hope the police succeed in their duty to find the murderer, so as to clear myself, Gunner Buckfield. This is a partly true story and partly fiction, showing how easy it is for an innocent man to be convicted of crime, and what can really happen.

Gunner Reginald Sidney Buckfield

MURDER IN CAMP
Gnr. R. S. Buckfield

SECOND MURDER
(Miss X, A.T.S. girl, name Kay Harmer)

"Good morning, Captain."

"Good morning. What can I do for you?"

"I'm a Police Inspector from Scotland Yard; there's my card. What I want to see you about is, you remember, the girl and the Gunner that was involved with the murder at Brompton Road but were found innocent. I would like to see them for a few minutes."

"Bombardier, tell Miss X and Gunner X the Captain wants to see them."

Five minutes later:

"Good morning, sir."

"Good morning, Gunner. Just a few questions I want to ask you and your lady friend, Miss X. You remember the killing at Brompton?"

"Yes, sir."

"And the Stranger also?"

"I do."

"Tell me this," said the C.I.D., "How many times in the eighteen days you were absent then did you see Bert or the Stranger?"

"Saw Bert once, and the Stranger three times."

"Sorry, sir, but I can't find Miss X."

"Isn't she on duty?"

"No, sir. Checked out last night at 6.30pm; hasn't been seen since."

"Did the guards check her in?"

"No, sir. Marked absent."

"Thank you, Bombardier. Gunner X, were you with Miss X last night?"

"Yes, sir."

"What time?"

"From seven to eight pm. She then left me, stating she had a headache and that she was going back to camp to bed."

"What did you do afterwards?"

"Stayed in the *Stone Horse*."

"That'll be all for now."

"Excuse me, sir. I'm a War Reserve Policeman. Been sent here to find you."

"Yes, what is it?"

"One A.T.S. girl, sir, found dead with a knife in her back."

"Just a minute, Gunner X. You say you saw Miss X seven to eight pm?"

"I did, sir."

"Constable, where was the girl found, and what time?"

"Place found, sir, Brompton Road, top part. Time: 8.15."

Captain: "What's wrong?"

C.I.D.: "I would like to take Gunner X down to the station, sir."

"Right-o; as you like."

DOWN AT THE MORGUE[13]

"Hello, you again?"

"Yes, that's me."

"What's it for this time?"

---

[13] The original title of this Chapter was 'Down at the Station'.

"Just want you to answer a few questions."

"O.K., what are they?"

"Seen this knife before?"

"Yes, I think so, once."

"When was that?"

"The last time I was here; absent."

"You sure?"

"I think so."

"Car's ready, Inspector."

"Right! Put your hat on, Sonny, you're coming with us."

In three minutes landed outside Morgue.

"Alright, take the sheet off. Now have a good look. Do you know the lady?"

"Yes, sir, that's Miss X."

"You sure?"

"Yes, I ought to know. I've been a friend of hers for twelve to fourteen weeks."

"That's all."

"Why, hello Bert, what are you doing here?"

"Found the body, Smiler, with the police constable."

"O, like that? Sad about your wife, Bert. Haven't got the killer yet?"

"No, but they will get him in time."

"I hope so. Blimey, Bert, if it isn't the Stranger we treated, the week your wife got done in. Well, I'm blowed! What's he doing here?"

"Witness, Smiler, against you."

"What do you mean?"

"Said he saw you and the victim on the night of the crime."

"Come on, Tommy, jump in."

With that return to Police Headquarters.

THE RETURN BACK TO CAMP

"Pull up, driver. Don't go right in."

"Ay, ay, sir."

"Right, Gunner X, come with me."

[Captain:] "Back again. What is it this time?"

"Sorry to inform you, sir, that the lady in question this morning was found with a knife in her back."

"Good gracious! Suicide?"

"No, murder! I would like to have a look round camp, sir; also I should like to see her friends that saw her yesterday."

"Do as you wish. Gunner X knows all her friends."

"Thanks. Good morning."

"Ditto."

"Bombardier Beach."

"Yes, sir."

"When working with Miss X yesterday, did she look worried or mention where she was going in the evening, or who with?"

"Not to my knowledge, sir."

"You sure?"

"Well, she did say she was meeting Gunner X."

"Was she worried about seeing him?"

"Well, in a way, yes."

"How? Describe to the best of your ability."

"Well, every time the two were together, it always ended up in a wicked argument."

"Why did she carry on meeting him, if [it was] like that?"

"Well, sir, what I think is, the girl was in trouble, and she swore she would never let Gunner X off, and if it came to a parting for good, she said she would take her own life."

"Did she know that Gunner X was married?"

"No, sir."

"Hadn't he told her?"

"So I was told by Miss X, that he had a daughter."

"Thank you."

SEARCH OF BILLETS

"Now, Gunner X, which is your billet?"

"That one on the right, sir. Right near the fence."

"Lucky, ain't you?"

"What do you mean, Cop?"

"Well, you could get out from here without anyone seeing you, also get back. Five minutes and you're at the *Stone Horse*."

"Yes, it could be done."

"Where is your bed?"

"In the corner."

"Nice place; right near the door. Hello, mate of yours?"

"Yes."

"Tell me, Gunner, were you in here last night between eight and eight fifteen?"

"No, sir, I was in the canteen."

"Was there anybody you know [in here]?"

"No, sir, not as I know of. Three on leave, two on guard, rest of us in the canteen."

"You never saw X here from the time he went out till he came in?"

"No, sir."

"Thank you."

IN A TOUGH SPOT

"Well, Cop, what news?"

"Nothing for the time being. Wait a minute, I was asking you about how many times you had seen Bert and the Stranger, so called."

"I told you. Once Bert; three times Stranger."

"Did you notice how the Stranger behaved when he heard of the murder?"

"Yes, sir, I would say he was quite normal."

"He was? You notice any marks on his body?"

"No, sir, but he had a very peculiar way of taking a cigarette and lighting it."

"Can you show me the way he did it?"

"I think so."

"Here, have one of mine."

"Thank you, sir. Player's? A nice cig."

"Yes, what kind do you smoke?"

"Any kind, as long as it's a smoke."

"But which is your favourite cigarette?"

"Player's Weights."

"That's a mighty queer way of taking a cigarette. Right thumb and little finger."

"That's what I thought."

"Well, I might want to see you again, Gunner X, so be around when I come."

"I will, don't worry."

With that the Cop left.

A LETTER FROM A CORPSE

"Letter for you, Gunner X."

"Thanks. Who's it from?"

"I don't know, but it looks like Miss X's writing."

"I wish it was," said Gunner X, and after a few seconds opened the letter.

This is how it read: "Darling, do not worry over me, as I'm still alive and well. So sorry to hear the police have seen you and questioned you on what they think is me, Miss X. Don't let it fool you, my dear, as the person is none other than my twin sister. Owing to the state I'm in, I found it would be better to quit the Army till the trouble's over."

[*End of manuscript*]

The Terrible Tragedy at Tonbridge
The Murder of FRANCES ELIZA O'ROURKE
by HAROLD AMOS APTED
on Tuesday the 31st of December 1901
in Vanshall Lane, near Tonbridge

Nobody had ever seen a murderer – and everybody felt instinctively that he *was* a murderer – simulate innocence as well as the man in the dock. The man who had assented, in his quiet voice, that he was Harold Amos Apted. Neither in his clear voice, his boyish, open countenance, his placid yet serious demeanour, and his respectful behaviour towards the court was it possible to detect the slightest sign of guilt, the least lack of candour, the faintest indication of fear, the remotest approach to remorse . . . The evidence of your ears convinced you of his guilt; the testimony of your eyes made you doubt the question.

This brutal murderer of a little child, this lurer of innocence to shame and death, left no actual confession to the crime, but it is quite certain that in spite of his assumption of injured innocence Harold Apted killed little Frances Eliza O'Rourke. It was a base and cowardly crime, and the perpetrator well deserves a niche beside such monstrous child-slayers as Fish, of Blackburn; Baker, of Alton [see this volume]; Coates, of Dartford; Pavey, of Acton; and many others whose foul lustful passions ultimately made of them murderers. There have been, to our national shame, an extraordinary number of crimes of this character – i.e., the outraging and murder of little girls, in this country. No nation can show so many instances, not even France – popularly presumed to be so much less moral than our immaculate selves. This is true – and the fact can easily be verified – though it is a pity indeed, that it is true. Of murderers of this type, Harold Amos Apted

– this smart-looking youth of twenty – was undeniably the worst.

The murder of Frances Eliza O'Rourke, on the afternoon of December the 31st, 1901, created the greatest consternation and excitement throughout the districts of Tunbridge Wells, Southborough and Tonbridge. Its circumstances were so peculiar and sensational that public attention was at once focused upon so unusual and terrible an event. Imagination revolted at the idea of a young child, merely a well-developed baby, being induced to accompany a driver of a van, being outraged in the vehicle, being driven, unconscious, or possibly dead, towards a pond, and being thrown therein, half stripped, and with the deadly weapon which had done the deed still environed by the dead child's hair. This was the nature of the discoveries made by the police in the course of the few days which followed the original finding of the maltreated body in a shallow pond. The place of the discovery was a lonely and secluded one, near Vanshall Farm, about a mile from the outskirts of Tonbridge. A labourer passing that way early on the morning of New Year's Day observed, in a rank and shallow duck-pond, separated from the road by a fence, the body of a female child. It was floating on the top, and was almost in a nude condition. The finder did not then make any attempt to secure the corpse, but hurried to a public house at Pembury, known as the *Vanshall Inn*, and reported the discovery to the landlord. That person immediately hurried to the spot, and, with assistance the poor little body was recovered, brought to the bank, and reverently carried to the parlour of the inn. The landlord, aware that a horrid crime had been committed, lost no time in sending for a medical man, who stated that the child had been outraged, and that her throat had then been cut, the left jugular vein being severed.

After this the most important question was that of identity. There resided at that time at 4 Elm Road, Southborough, a tailor named John O'Rourke. It was the custom of this tradesman to dispatch his little daughter, Frances Eliza, aged seven and a half years, to another tailor – for who he worked – two or three times a week. Her mission was to take and deliver a bundle of clothing to Mr Jenkinson at Tunbridge Wells, the distance

being at least three miles each way. This journey strikes one as rather an undertaking for a child of seven, but it must be said that little Frances was a big girl for her age and remarkably forward and intelligent. About four o'clock on the afternoon of December 31st – a Tuesday – This little girl was sent the usual journey with a bundle of clothing. She accomplished her errand, and left on the return journey. Night came on, and as she did not return, and no tidings reached them concerning her, the parents became greatly alarmed, and made inquiries in all directions without result. At about eleven at night the local police were informed of the fact of the child's disappearance, and very shortly after the recovery of the body the bereaved father was called to identify his poor little girl, his grief and rage against the murderer being terrible to witness. As soon as possible after the discovery of the body information was given to the authorities at Maidstone, as well as to the Tonbridge and Southborough police, and early on Wednesday detectives arrived from the county town, and a thorough investigation was begun. Fortunately for the end of justice, the police were soon in possession of a first-class clue. Entwined in the girl's hair was a blood-stained knife. Its larger blade was half open, and the hair had become twisted round the angles made by the steel and the bone handle. It seemed safe to conjecture that the most recent possessor of the knife was the murderer.

A complete search was made of the spot where the body was found and of its environs. No footprints were visible, but the police expressed their conviction that a cart or van had been driven close to the fence which divided the road from the pond, that the occupant had descended with the corpse in his arms, had scaled the hedge or fence, and had thrown the body into the stagnant water. On the Wednesday night the remainder of the girl's clothing was found in a remote field about two miles from the pond in question. It had been strewn, rather than hidden, amid some brambles near a wood. Most of the garments, the underclothing in particular, were stained with blood.

A number of persons now came forward to declare that they had seen little Eliza O'Rourke sitting beside the driver of a van not far from the scene of the murder on the afternoon of December 31st. At least, they

said, if the child was not Eliza it was someone dressed similarly and about her age. It
appeared that she was actually last seen
about half-past four on the Tuesday afternoon in St John's Road, Tunbridge Wells,
and at that time she was sitting next to the
driver in a dark coloured van, pulled by a
brown horse. In consequence of this information, which was strongly corroborated,
the police directed all their energies towards
the discovery of this van and of its driver.
Certain facts engendered a more or less
general suspicion of one Harold Apted, who
was known to drive a van, and had been seen
therein by various people close to the scene
of the crime on the afternoon in question.
The police went to interview this youth, and
his answers to certain questions, though
given without any apparent hesitation, could
not be accepted as altogether satisfactory.
His own account of his movements on that
day was vague and suspicious, and his statements were either uncorroborated or absolutely refuted when inquiry into them was
made. The detectives began to entertain a
strong suspicion of young Harold Apted;
nevertheless his arrest was not considered
advisable until January 3rd, he being in the
meanwhile strictly watched.

What manner of man was this Harold
Apted? To begin with, he was only twenty
years old. His appearance was decidedly
superior, and he was attired always in a style
above his station. He drove a van for a local
butcher, but he looked rather like a young
clerk, and his general aspect was mild and
respectable. He was a member of the local
Bible class, he sang in the church choir, and
was everywhere regarded as a quiet, well-
ordered, inoffensive young fellow. He had
never displayed any great partiality for the
society of young women – it would, perhaps,
have been better for him if he had – though
he occasionally 'walked out' with a pretty
girl in the neighbourhood, with whom he
went for a walk, it is said, on the night of the
murder. Apted lived with his parents in the
Tonbridge district, and had several brothers
and sisters, to whom he was a shining light
rather than otherwise. Occasionally he was
seen in the local public-houses – he called in
one at least about a quarter to half-past five
on the night of the murder – but usually he
was remarkably abstemious and appeared to
have all his passions well under control.

The theory of the police was – and everything points to it having been the correct one
– that the murder was committed in the field
or the wood in which were found the blood-
stained garments of the unfortunate child.
There the poor little mite, lured to the spot
on some pretence, and trusting to her devil-
ish guide, was barbarously outraged. Her
screams and cries probably alarmed her
assailant, who decided – as usual in such
cases – to augment his crime with that of
murder. He cut her throat with relentless
savagery, and the child died almost instantly. Then he placed the body again in his
van, drove to the pond, the situation of
which was well known to him – and threw
the corpse, mangled, bloody, and half nude,
into the pond. It was a dastardly deed,
worthy of the devil himself, and one rejoices
to know that, unlike some others, it was not
destined to go unpunished.

On the Saturday after the discovery, at the
Tonbridge police-court, Harold Apted, described as the son of a coal merchant, was put
in the dock, charged on suspicion with the
murder of Frances Eliza O'Rourke. The
building was besieged with a curious crowd,
who evinced the utmost animosity towards
the accused man, of whose guilt most of the
populace seemed already to have satisfied
themselves.

Detective-Sergeant Fowle, of the Kent Constabulary, stated that at six o'clock on the

Friday evening he arrested the prisoner at his residence, Woodside Road, Tonbridge. At the police-station he told him he would charge him with suspicion of wilfully murdering Frances Eliza O'Rourke by stabbing her in the neck in Vanshall Lane, and he replied, "I never came home that way. I know nothing about it." Upon examining the clothes the accused wore on the night of the murder, witness found stains which appeared to be of blood. He also examined the van which the accused was in charge of on the night in question, and upon it he found what appeared to be bloodstains. There were some stains on the body of the van and some on the straw lying within it. There were also marks of blood underneath the cart, where it had apparently been washed through. In further evidence the detective declared positively that the cart had been washed, and Apted said, "I deny that. Do you say the blood had soaked through the wood of the van?"

Witness: "Yes, I do."
Prisoner: "I deny that."

After other evidence had been given, the prisoner again said that he knew nothing at all about it, and was remanded until the following Tuesday. Ultimately he was fully committed for trial, and was sent to Tunbridge Wells, and then to Maidstone Gaol, there to await the judicial inquiry. He conducted himself with much decorum in the meantime, ate and slept well, and actually gained a few pounds in weight during his incarceration.

The trial took place on Tuesday and Wednesday, February 27 and 28, 1902, at the Maidstone Assizes. Mr Justice Wright presided, and the prosecution was conducted by Mr Gill and Mr T. Mathew, the defence being entrusted to Mr Hohler and Mr Pitman. The court and its precincts were crowded when proceedings were opened. The prisoner, who pleaded "Not Guilty," in a loud, firm voice, was rather a good-looking young fellow of average height. He was slightly built, clean-shaven, and rather dark, with somewhat close-cropped hair. He was attired in a neat suit of blue serge and carried a bowler hat. He bowed politely to the court, and then took his seat in the chair provided for him, folding his arms and preparing himself to give full attention to the opening address by the counsel for the Crown.

The father of the poor little victim was the first witness. He stated that the deceased was tall for her age, and looked more than seven years and six months. For the last two years his child had taken his tailoring work from Southborough to a shop at Tunbridge Wells. When she did not return home on the night of the murder he gave information to the police, and next morning was informed of the discovery in Vanshall Lane. He was not acquainted with the prisoner.

Thomas Jeffrey, landlord of the *Vanshall Inn* at Pembury, was informed by a labourer named Challis that he had just seen the body of a child in the pond. He procured assistance and went to pull her out. He saw that the throat was cut and that a knife, with the big blade open, was twisted in her hair. He left it exactly as he found it. The body was removed to his inn and a doctor sent for. A policeman found the marks of wheels within three feet of the pond. The cart must have been taken quite close to the fence.

Dr Watts, of Tonbridge, was the medical gentleman who first inspected the body. He stated that he found a deep wound in the left side of the neck, caused by a stab rather than a cut. The knife found in the child's hair probably, he thought almost certainly, occasioned that wound. There was a bruise below the stab, and great violence had been used. Portions of the underclothing still adhered to the corpse, and these were much torn and bloodstained. The deceased had been outraged. She must have bled to death after the stab, which divided the carotid artery, in little more than a minute. Both the stab and the bruise had been administered by a person standing opposite to her and using the right hand. Then followed witnesses whose testimony was of the utmost importance. Ethel Muggeridge, aged 15, resident at Southborough, saw the child on December the 31st on her way home from Tunbridge Wells. She knew Frances O'Rourke to speak to. She observed about the same time a van come along the road, a young man being inside. The van stopped. The little girl, who was carrying a black bundle, got in and the young man drove off. This was in the afternoon, between half-past four and a quarter to five. She had been taken – I mean the witness – to the police-station, but had failed to point out Apted as the driver of the van. It was getting dark when she saw the deceased.

Another girl, Julia Holloway, also observed a dark-coloured van about 4.30 to 4.40 on the last day of the year. The horse was a brown one. She saw a little girl sitting within by the side of the driver. She wore a brown ulster and a white sailor straw hat. A young man, clean-shaven, had been driving. Rosa Dupont, aged thirteen, also saw the deceased being driven by a young man in a van, but this witness – it was elicited in cross-examination – had failed to identify either van or prisoner.

W. Emery next stated that he had assisted to load the van which Apted drove with calves on December 31st. A cord required shortening, and the prisoner produced a knife and cut it. The duty of the accused was to take the calves to market. This witness denied there was any mess in the cart through a calf bleeding, though the prisoner had attempted to account for the blood in this way.

Conrad Smith, a carrier, had passed the accused driving an open van that day. He noticed something by the side of the prisoner which looked like a child. He would not like to swear that it was a child on the seat with Apted, but that was his impression.

T. Hankins identified the knife found in the child's hair as his own property, but he lent it to the prisoner three weeks before to kill rabbits. (Apted admitted that this witness had once lent him a knife, but declared that this was at least seven months before the murder, and that the one found with the deceased was not the same. The defence laboured this point, but Hankins always insisted that the knife was his and that Apted had never returned it.) He had, he declared, picked the knife out from ten others shown him by police.

Police Sergeant Fowle called on the prisoner at the house of his parents on the day after the crime. He asked Apted what had induced him to come home from Tunbridge Wells that way. The prisoner replied: "To call for a Christmas-box." The witness asked for and received the clothes worn by Apted on the previous day. There were distinct traces of blood on the shoulder of the coat, which the accused said "came from the slaughter-house." He also remarked, "I have never had a knife in my life. I did not

come that way, and I know nothing about it." On January 3rd he arrested him.

Dr Stevenson found mammalian blood on the floor of the van, but preferred not to say positively that it was that of a human being. He had also found blood on the prisoner's clothing, and it had soaked through the lining of his coat.

Statements made by the prisoner at various times were put in and read. In all Apted protested his innocence. He declared that the knife found in the child's hair had never been lent to him. He said again and again, "Many an innocent man has been sent to the gallows." He made certain allusions to his movements, but two witnesses on whom he said he had called on the afternoon of the 31st denied that they had seen him that day.

The defence was earnest and painstaking, and several witnesses were called to prove that Apted had been seen at several places a little after five o'clock, the idea being to establish an alibi. The prisoner's aged father declared that his son had returned home about ten minutes to six, that there was nothing unusual in his manner, and that he had sat down and eaten a good tea. He had washed his hands but had not changed his coat.

The judge summed up with strict impartiality, and the jury retired to consider their verdict at about five o'clock. They were not long in coming to a decision, and returned with a verdict of "Guilty"; the prisoner, however, being recommended to mercy on account of his youth. The judge expressed his concurrence in the verdict, but held out little hope of a reprieve.

The execution was fixed to take place on March 18th. The prisoner remained at Maidstone Gaol, and was there visited by his parents on two occasions, the last being on the day before the end. During the evening prior to the execution Apted wrote letters to many of his relatives, most of them teeming with scriptural allusion, but expressive of no regret for his abominable crime. He had eaten very little since he had learnt that the Home Secretary had declined to interfere with the sentence of death, but summoned to arise about six o'clock on the morning of the last day, he made a fairly good breakfast. At half-past seven he received the Holy Sacrament. He was pinioned by the brothers

Billington, and the procession formed at three minutes to eight. The convict walked without any assistance and evinced the utmost fortitude. Death was instantaneous.

Maidstone Gaol, above in 1829, below in 1988

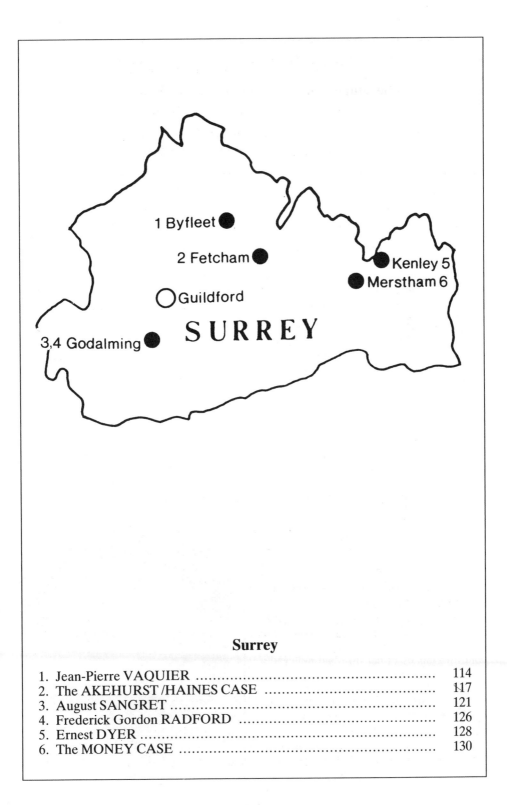

1 Byfleet

2 Fetcham

Kenley 5
Merstham 6

Guildford

SURREY

3,4 Godalming

Surrey

Mr Jones's Liquid Breakfast

The Murder of ALFRED POYNTER JONES
by JEAN-PIERRE VAQUIER
on Saturday March the 29th 1924
at the *Blue Anchor Hotel,* Byfleet

One of the most striking characteristics of the eternal triangle is the great difference in personality and social stature displayed by the two male sides of the figure. Whether in age, temperament, outlook, or material or spiritual accomplishment, the lover is generally to be found at the opposite extreme to the spouse. The triangle, if one may be indulged in pursuing the geometry, is never an equilateral one; if it were it would never have developed its third side. This fundamental truth was never more apparent than in the *affaire de coeur* between Mabel Jones and Jean-Pierre Vaquier, and in the consequent murder of Mabel's husband Alfred.

———————

Vaquier was a French Basque, born in Niort in the Department of Aude, and displaying all the striking features of temperament and dark good looks of that most aristocratic race. At the time he met Mabel Jones he was forty-five years old and using his expertise with the newly invented radio – or 'wireless' – in keeping in working order the set proudly installed in the Hotel Victoria, Biarritz for the entertainment of its guests. The Frenchman cut a most dashing figure in his elegant dress and his immaculately shaped beard and moustaches combed flamboyantly outwards.

Mabel Jones was very much the English rose. She was married with two children, but was nevertheless of an independent spirit, and with money of her own had indulged a string of business ventures with no very marked success. It is characteristic of 'Mabs' Jones that her remedy for impending bankruptcy was to seek the comfort and luxury of the Victoria Hotel, Biarritz.

Here they met. Vaquier had no English, Mabel no French, but through the intermediary of a French-English dictionary they conducted an affair whose passion would have been the envy of any linguist. That the situation was not without humour was shown at Vaquier's subsequent trial. Mrs Jones described to the court how she and her lover had been interrupted by the chambermaid in his hotel bedroom on their return to England:

"I told him [Vaquier] he had put me in a nice plight."
Judge: "Did you say that in English?"
"Yes."
"By that time he was understanding?"
"No; he simply got the dictionary."

Good things coming to an end as they often do, the dream was broken by Mabel's husband insisting she return home.

Mabel's husband: Alfred Poynter Jones, aged thirty-seven, married to Mabel in 1906. He had purchased the *Blue Anchor Hotel* in Byfleet, Surrey (with his wife's money, it is said), which must have been a great convenience – for Alfred liked nothing better than

to spend his days drinking. In fact he did very little else, and life became a monotonous cycle of heavy-drinking, deep alcoholic slumbers, and monstrous hangovers.

When Mabel Jones returned from France at the beginning of February she did so in a very leisurely way via Bordeaux and Paris, with Vaquier as her devoted travelling companion. On England's shore the Frenchman booked himself into the Russell Hotel in London while Mrs Jones made her way out to Surrey. Within a week Vaquier had booked himself into the hotel *Blue Anchor* at Byfleet as an unpaying guest of the landlord's wife. Whether Jones knew of the liaison – or cared if he did – is uncertain; he may well have approved of Mabel's 'distraction' as a way of giving himself more drinking time. Certainly Jean-Pierre at the end of six weeks had become as familiar to him as the hotel's beer pumps. An interesting postscript is that unlike Mabel, Alfred Jones was very competent in Vaquier's native French. It is a postcript because very soon the triangle is to lose one of its sides.

Jean-Pierre Vaquier

On the evening of March 28th 1924 the *Blue Anchor* was host to a big party at which there was a great deal of drinking done, not least by Alfred Jones, and it was well past midnight before the inebriated landlord lurched unsteadily to his bed.

Despite a massive hangover (which anyway must by now have become part of life's grey pattern for Jones), he was up and slouching about the bar before nine the next morning. There in the bar parlour sat Jean-Pierre Vaquier, always an early riser, sipping his coffee. There on the mantelshelf sat Mr Jones's invariable apéritif to the day – a bottle of bromo-salts. Closely watched by Vaquier, Jones staggered to the bar, mixed his seltzer and downed it in one long gulp. "My God", he shouted, "that's bitter!" It was one of the last coherent things that he uttered: by the time Dr Carle arrived the unhappy man was already going home; lying in agonized convulsions on his bed, he was dead by 11.30am.

The doctor was in no doubt that Alfred Jones had been poisoned, and from his experience a poison not unlike strychnine was the cause. After establishing that the victim had 'breakfasted' solely on bromo-

salts he sought out the bottle, which he observed with mounting suspicion had been thoroughly washed out and dried. The cover-up was by no means thorough enough to deter Carle, however, and from the sediment in the glass from which Jones had drunk the fatal draught, and from some crystals scraped from the floor of the bar parlour, the doctor was able to salvage sufficient to enable him to establish beyond doubt that the poison in Alfred Jones's stomach and small intestine originated in the glass, which had contained a cocktail of bromo-salts and strychnine.

The police investigation was already under way, though it was to be three weeks before Superintendent Boshier of the Woking force felt confident enough to arrest Vaquier and his mistress. On his apprehension Vaquier claimed: "I will make known tomorrow who administered the poison". In fact the disclosure was not made until the Frenchman stood in the dock at Guildford Assizes six weeks later charged with Jones's murder. In the meantime Jean-Pierre had been busy exposing his enormous conceit to the hungry lenses of the press photographers – as it turned out, very much to his disadvantage. On April 16th the photograph of Vaquier in one of the newspapers caught the eye of a man named Bland. And Mr Bland had a most interesting story to tell.

During the early part of March, Vaquier, who had returned to London for a few days, had cultivated the good will of a neighbour-

The Blue Anchor, Byfleet

ing pharmacist – Mr Bland – who just happened to speak fluent French. Vaquier had paid several visits to Mr Bland's shop to purchase small amounts of various innocuous chemicals which he claimed to require for experiments into a new type of radio receiver. So Mr Bland was less surprised than he might have been when his French customer's next shopping list included 20 grammes of perchloride of mercury and .12 of a gramme of strychnine hydrochloride. Both were deadly poisons, and Bland had never heard of their use in connection with radio, but who was he to dispute the word of this international expert? Vaquier signed the poisons register with the name "J. Wanker" (pronounced "Vanker") and he was not seen by the pharmicist again until he identified him in court as one and the same as Jean-Pierre Vaquier.

The trial opened at Surrey's Summer Assizes at Guildford on July 2nd 1929 before Mr Justive Avory. The Attorney-General (on this occasion Sir Patrick Hastings KC) led for the Crown (as is the custom in all poisoning cases) assisted by Sir Edward Marshall Hall KC, in an unfamiliar prosecution role. Vaquier's defence was in the capable hands of Sir Henry Curtis-Bennett KC.

Vaquier, quite naturally, was his own star witness – a role which he accepted with enthusiasm. Now was the time to make known who administered the poison – or at least who had ordered its purchase. (Vaquier had reluctantly accepted the futility of denying that it was he who bought the strychnine, and had devised a story implicating Mabel Jones's solicitor who, he insisted, needed it to put down a dog!) The following extract from the Attorney-General's cross-examination of the prisoner reveals more than a trace of eccentricity:

Sir Patrick Hastings: Do you know what strychnine is? – *Vaquier:* I knew it was a deadly poison.

Has anybody ever asked you before to buy dangerous poisons for them? – Nobody.

Was it only the second time that you had seen the solicitor of Mrs Jones that he asked you to buy strychnine? – Yes.

So the person who asked you to buy the strychnine was somebody to whom you had never spoken before? – I had never spoken to him before.

Did you know of any reason why he could not buy the poison for himself? – He told me he was very busy and had not time to buy it.

He gave you a sovereign for the purchase? – A pound note.

Did that strike you as a large sum of money to buy enough strychnine for one dog? – Perhaps he had no change.

Did you ever give him the change you must have got from buying the strychnine? – No, he never asked me.

[The prisoner is shown the poison-book signed by him]

Is that your usual signature? – No.

What is the name you have written there? – Wanker.

You knew, then, that you were putting a false name to the poison-book. Why did you not put your real name? – Because I had been told that when you buy poison you never sign your own name.

Who told you that? – The solicitor.

Did the gentleman who asked you to buy the poison tell you to sign a false name? – Yes.

Did it strike you as odd that a complete stranger who wanted to poison a dog was telling you to sign a false name? – No.

In the end, Vaquier fooled nobody. The court had listened with commendable patience to his rambling defence translated into and out of French by the court interpreter and had decided against him. The jury after an absence of two hours, brought in the anticipated verdict of guilty; it was not a popular one with M. Vaquier, whose abusive oaths were unnecessary to translate. His appeal dismissed, the flamboyant Frenchman bowed out at Wandsworth Prison on August 12th 1924.

"They haven't done it themselves..."
The Murder of JOHN AKEHURST and ELIZABETH HAINES
by an Unknown Killer
on Saturday the 14th of Ocober 1826
at their home in Fetcham

Leading from the peaceful village of Fetcham, bordered by orchard, garden and cornfield, runs a little lane, almost a by-way, down the hill to the tiny river Mole, and so into Leatherhead. And if you ask the natives of the place what that lane is called they will tell you that it is Murder Lane. Truly a dreadful name for such a pretty thoroughfare in such pastoral country! How did it come by its sinister title? Of what dreadful crime is the name a perpetual memento?

Let us go back to the year 1826 and recall the incident which is thus immortalized.

In that year there was living in a tiny cottage in Fetcham, at the top of Murder Lane (then a by-way without any title whatsover) an old man named John Akehurst. He had long passed the normal span of life, for at the time of which we write he wanted but four years to attain the dignity of a centenarian. He was not a feeble old fellow for all that, and his faculties were singularly clear. With him lived an aged woman, Elizabeth Haines, who acted as his housekeeper. Of course, to

Mr Akehurst Elizabeth was a mere child, being only seventy-four years of age.

On October 13th, 1826, a labourer named Thomas Brown, who worked for Akehurst keeping his little place tidy and generally doing odd jobs, called at the cottage about eleven in the morning and saw his master. An hour later Elizabeth Haines came to Brown's cottage to pay him his weekly wages of four shillings.

Two days later, on October 15th, Brown returned to the cottage at half past six in the morning to fetch a basket. The front door was open and he looked in. Seeing nobody about he called out to the housekeeper, but received no reply. Then Brown looked round the cottage, and noticed that a pane of glass had been smashed in the window of the wash-house, and that an iron bar which fastened the window of the lower room had been removed. Again he called out, shouting "Mrs Haines! Mrs Haines!" but he could get no answer.

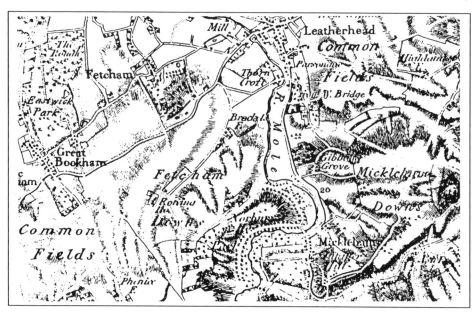

This alarmed him for he fancied that the old people had possibly been seized with some sudden illness, so he went and fetched his mother. Elizabeth Bennett, and she accompanied him back to the cottage. Again they shouted, and then Mrs Bennett said that she would go upstairs and see if the old woman was in bed. She went gingerly up the narrow stairs, and the next instant rushed down again, shrieking out that Mrs Haines had been murdered. Brown hesitated a moment. Should he go upstairs? Then fear seized him, and he went off as fast as he could to a neighbouring farmer, named Gibbs, and begged him to come and investigate with him. Farmer Gibbs came to the cottage and then the two men went upstairs. On entering the room occupied by Mr Akehurst a terrible sight was presented to them: lying on her back on the floor with her head in pool of coagulated blood was the body of old Mrs Haines. The men bent over her, but it only took them a second to realize that she was dead and had been so for some time. Leaving her exactly where she was they went over to the bed, on which a pile of clothes was heaped, and on removing these they found the body of the ancient Akehurst, also saturated with blood and stiff and cold. His head was terribly battered about and the flesh torn as if by blows from some heavy weapon.

In great alarm the two men went off and fetched one of the local justices of the peace, and that worthy magistrate, delighted at having something to do, went to the cottage, looked at the corpses, scratched his brown bobwig, and coughed. Then he delivered himself of the weighty statement: "They haven't done it themselves: they've been murdered!"

The fact that murder had been committed having now received the official sanction of the squire (for he was the magistrate) the news flew round the village and across the stream into Leatherhead, and soon a crowd of yokels was gathered outside the cottage, among the apple trees, discussing the crime. Unfortunately, no one seems to have had a good word to say for the old man, who was declared to have had a lot of money, but to have been a miser; and the general opinion was that he had been murdered for his wealth.

As soon as the ferment had cooled down a little, and when the crowd had dispersed, the coroner was notified, and an inquest was held at the *Bell Tavern*, Fetcham. The first witness called was the labourer Thomas Brown, who described how he had found the cottage open, and how he had previously seen both the deceased in good health. From inquiries made it seemed certain that that was the last time the old couple were seen alive.

118

Mrs Bennett was then called, and she told the jury how she went upstairs, and on opening the door saw the figure of a woman lying there on the ground. She was greatly alarmed and rushed downstairs again; she saw the boxes and chests of drawers in both the upstairs rooms had been ransacked and the contents tumbled about. She knew that Mr Akehurst was reputed to be a miser, and had heard him say that he had made a will. But she had also heard him say that he would have to mortgage his property if he lived another twelve months, for he would then have got to the end of his tether. She had never seen the poor old fellow with any money, and she did not think that he was possessed of any or was a miser.

The Leatherhead surgeon, Mr James Bright, was then examined. He said that he had been called out of bed at nine o'clock in the morning to examine the corpses. The head of Mrs Haines had been cracked open by a violent blow to the back of the skull. This was the actual cause of death. There were marks on the old woman's throat as if someone had caught her by the neck to prevent her crying out, but he was convinced she had not died from strangulation. Her skull was badly fractured, and there was an ugly wound at the back of her head. As for Mr Akehurst, his injuries were more extensive. His skull was badly battered in, and his lower jaw was smashed on the right side. He must have died rather slowly. Questioned as to how long the deceased had been dead when he was called to see them. Mr James Bright replied that he could not say within an hour or two. The murder might have been committed about one in the morning, or it might have been committed on the previous day. Certainly at least five hours had elapsed since death when he was called.

That was all the evidence that was offered to the jury at the inquest, and of course a verdict of "Wilful murder against some person or persons unknown" was returned. Then the primitive police of Leatherhead took the matter in hand, and set about making arrests.

First of all their suspicions fell on a tramp named Jones. It was rumoured about the village of Fetcham that this man had said that the person who had committed the murder had only got twenty-five shillings for his trouble. How did he know? Of course, he was speaking the truth, and of course he was the guilty party, argued the police. So Mr Jones, tramp and tinker, was arrested and searched. He had a bundle of new clothes under his arm when apprehended, which he said had cost him seventeen shillings, and in his pockets were eight shillings, so making twenty-five shillings in all. Therefore he was the murderer, said the police. But unfortunately it was proved that Mr Jones had ordered those clothes on the day of the Leatherhead Fair, four days before the murder, and had then paid for them. He also declared that he had found the money at the fair, where it had probably been dropped by some drunken person. The more the police inquired, the more they felt convinced that they had made a mistake; especially as Jones was able to prove every one of his movements since the day of the fair: so he was released. Then he went about saying the old people had been knocked on the head with a hammer, and suspicion was again directed to him, but when threatened with arrest for a second time he avowed that he only guessed from the nature of the wounds that that was how Akehurst and Haines had been killed. Then it was remembered that Akehurst had a daughter named Ayres and three grandchildren resident at Oxshott, and that John Ayres, one of the grandsons, had visited Fetcham a month before the murder. Mary Ayres was a thoroughly bad lot and lived with a man named Page. They were disreputable, dissolute folk, who had sunk from bad to worse, and at last became tramps. While the police were hunting for these two – who, by the way, they eventually found living at the *Bell Tavern* in Fetcham itself – they made another arrest which proved to be a false one. A certain George Armstrong, of Little Princess Street, Marylebone, was taken into custody. He said that he was a casual labourer, and had been into Kent for the hopping. When walking about four miles from Esher he overtook a travelling tinker named William Hayward; then a gypsy joined the party. The gypsy had had two donkeys, and told the tinker he would part with them and get a pony. Then, pointing to a cottage, which was the one in which Akehurst lived, he said: "George, there's a d----d old miser living over that way. He has a pony. Let's go and fetch it." Then Armstrong said: "Don't you think he has anyone to look after him?" To which the

An Affecting Account of a
CRUEL AND HORRIBLE MURDER
Committed on the Bodies of
JOHN AKEHURST and ELIZABETH HAINES

Here is a black and horrid deed,
  Will fill you with affright,
Committed was near Leatherhead
  Upon last Thursday [sic] night,
O weep for this poor aged pair,
  Lament their cruel fate,
You need not blush to shed a tear
  While I this deed relate.

John Arkhurst [sic] and Elizabeth Haines
  For them I now deplore.
He nears a hundred years of age
  And she was seventy-four.
Confined to bed for many years
  This aged man did lie:
O cruel fate that he beneath
  A murderer's knife should die.

Last Thursday at the midnight hour,
  When all lay fast asleep.
Some murderous fiends by artful means
  Into the house did get.
Then to the room where Arkhurst lay,
  These monsters did repair,
Where he with feeble voice did pray
  His aged life to spare.

But they intent on deeds of blood
  Were deaf to all his cries.
None but a fiend could have withstood
  His tears, his groans, his sighs.
He raised his hands to ward the blows
  And mercy did implore.
The few grey hairs that crown'd his head
  Were soaked in his gore.

With cuts and wounds they mangled sure
  His poor and aged frame,
His nurse the noise did overhear,
  To his assistance came.
But O alas! With grief I tell,
  What all must now deplore.
All bath'd in blood, she quickly fell
  A corpse upon the floor.

Next morning by the dawn of day
  A lad who lived near,
Unto the cottage took his way –
  He often worked there.
He found the door was open wide,
  Which fill'd him with surprise.
On Mrs Haines he loudly cried
  Then for assistance hies.

The neighbours came – O such a sight
  They quickly did behold,
Their blood was chilled with affright
  They could not tears withold.
To see these bleeding aged frames,
  In such a mangled state:
While crimson gore the bed-clothes stain'd,
  Display'd their cruel fate.

O earth hide not their innocent blood –
  To Heaven it loud doth cry,
For vengeance on the Murderer's head –
  Where'er those blood-hounds fly.
May Justice soon them overtake,
  And punished may they be,
All for the harmless couple's sake
  They slew so cruelly.

tinker replied: "No, nobody but a stout boy to do the odd jobs and a dog." Armstrong then left the pair and turned off towards Leatherhead.

His tale was found to be accurate as far as his own movements were concerned, so he was liberated on the distinct understanding that he should keep the police informed of his whereabouts in case he was wanted to give evidence later on.

It was at this juncture that Grassmith, the Leatherhead constable, thought of looking at Fetcham for Page and Mary Ayres, and as we know found them at the *Bell Tavern*. He said that he would have to search them, and also examine their baggage. Page objected strongly to this course, and said that it was very hard lines on him to have his things pulled about by a policeman. However, the constable stuck to the point, and searched the couple. On Page was found a watch which was later identified as having belonged to the old man. Then he and his mistress were taken off to Horsemonger Lane Gaol, and there detained.

They made their first appearance before the bench on December 8th, 1826, when no evidence was offered, and they were remanded. Two days later they were again brought up, and then Richard Mitchell, a Greenwich Pensioner, said that he had known Page since the previous July, and they had gone hop-picking together. He had repeatedly heard Page threaten to "do for" Mary Ayres's old father. Then on another occasion he heard Mary Ayres say that she had been to see the old man, and had got some watches from him. That was some time before the murder, and the witness had

actually seen Mary pass several watches to Page. One of them was the watch found on the prisoner.

Cross-examined, Mitchell repeated his statement that he had heard Page say that they must get old Akehurst out of the light, and added that after Mary Ayres had returned from visiting her father she said that he had a very comfortable place which would suit her and Page very well when the old man was "put out".

In answer to this, Mary Ayres said that she had met a man named Pigg and another man, a gypsy or tinker, with him. They both said they should do something between then and Michaelmas as they were in great need of money. She thought they meant they would rob her father.

The magistrate declared that these people must be found and brought before him, and to that Ayres said it would be almost impossible to find them as they were tramps, like themselves. However, the case was adjourned from week to week, and after a long time the men were found. Then the case broke down hopelessly, for the testimony of the tinker proved that they and Ayres and Page were miles away at the very time the old people were murdered, and so of course they could not have committed the deed, however much they might have intended to.

After this the police lost heart and abandoned the hunt for the murderer of old Mr Akehurst and his housekeeper; and but for the people having named the lane in which the victims lived Murder Lane, the crime would have been forgotten.

The Wigwam Murder

The Murder of JOAN PEARL WOLFE
by AUGUST SANGRET
on or around Sunday the 13th of September 1942
on Hankley Common, Thursley, near Godalming

It might have passed through William Moore's mind on that early October morning that this was taking war games a bit too far. With a colleague, Marine Moore was taking part in an Army exercise over the

realistically battle-scarred terrain of Hankley Common, near Godalming. Keeping low to the ground in the chilly early light, the two camouflaged commandos skirted a broad expanse of heather and took cover in the tangled roots. Then Bill Moore saw the hand, brown and shrivelled, sticking up out of the ground in front of his nose; he had just recovered some of his composure when he saw part of a leg.

That was enough for the two squaddies, battle orders or no; they were back to base as fast as their legs would carry them. There would be plenty enough dead bodies when they got on active service; this one was for the law. Within hours police officers had been summoned by field telephone, and a cordon of military police had been placed on guard over the body on the Common.

By noon the following day, October 8th, 1942, the forensic scientists were beginning the grisly prologue to their work: Professor Keith Simpson, pathologist to the Home Office, and senior lecturer in forensic medicine at Guy's Hospital, London, and his long-time friend Dr Eric Gardner, consulting pathologist at Weybridge Hospital, here working on instruction from the coroner. These two familiar figures were soon to be joined by another legend – Detective Chief Inspector Edward Greeno of the Scotland Yard's Murder Squad, in company this trip with Detective Sergeant Fred Hodge.

In his own account of the medical aspects of the case*, Simpson recalled the terrible condition of the body; it had clearly been dead for several weeks (subsequent examination indicated about four), and the nature of the burial – barely a covering – had resulted in considerable activity by rats, who had destroyed much of the skull, and eaten several fingers off at the roots. Decomposition was causing the remains to disintegrate rapidly, and the smell, the flies, and the maggots that crawled in clusters on the putrefied flesh completed the charnel-house atmosphere.

Despite these obstacles, Simpson and Gardner were able to supply the detectives with some preliminary information. The corpse was almost certainly female; at least, the clothing gave this indication – a rotting green and white summer frock with an imitation lace collar, underclothes soiled by exposure, but with none of the disarrangement associated with sexual assault, a scarf knotted round the neck (but too loosely to have any connection with death), and red and blue

---

* *Forty Years of Murder*, Professor Keith Simpson. Harrap, London, 1978.

socks with no shoes. From what the vermin had left of the head, it was evident that it had suffered a severe bludgeoning from a heavy blunt instrument – Simpson took a guess at an iron bar, or wooden post. The position of the body and the minor lacerations on the ankles and feet allowed the pathologist to make one more deduction: "I think she was dragged here, head first, probably by her right arm. I suppose her shoes fell off on the way."

When Greeno arrived and had digested this initial estimate, he first mobilized a team of sixty men to search the common surrounding the body: he badly needed two clues – a murder weapon, and some means of identifying his victim.

Meanwhile, the unidentified remains were taken to Guy's Hospital mortuary, where a strong carbolic bath disposed of most of the maggots that infested its every cavity. In the comparative comfort of his own laboratory Professor Simpson set about filling in some of the details on his portrait of the dead woman: from her bones and teeth, age could be placed as accurately as between nineteen and twenty years: height 5ft. 4in. Her hair had been a fine texture, naturally sandy brown, but recently bleached. More perti-

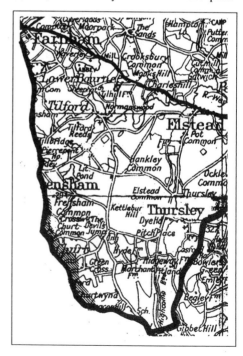

The half-buried corpse on Hankley Common

nent to the attack, Simpson found that, in addition to the obvious bludgeoning, there were a number of direct stab wounds to the head, and a further seven wounds on the right forearm and hand, clearly sustained by the unfortunate woman in trying to protect herself. Wounds can be read like a code by the skilled forensic pathlogist, and those in question had their own distinction – the wound in the right forearm had a small strand of muscle 'hooked' out of the cut, and a tendon was similarly protruding from a wound in the palm of the right hand. Simpson was able to tell the police that they were looking for a stabbing instrument, such as a knife, which had a 'hook', "like a parrot's beak" at the point.

Dr Gardner had also been hard at work in the laboratory. With the speed and confidence of experience, he had reassembled the dead woman's skull from the 40-odd fragments found in the locality of the body; it was complete but for the hole, $1\frac{3}{4}$ inches wide at the back, where the death-dealing blow had been struck.

Back at Hankley Common, Greeno's dragnet had produced results; a shoe had been found at a distance of 350 yards from the interment, its twin was picked up thirty yards farther on. In roughly the same location – the stretch of common known as Houndown Wood – a heavy birchwood stake was found; at one end it had been split, as if by a blow, and in the cracks of the impacted bark were eight hairs; human hairs; human hairs which, the microscope revealed, had come from the head of the victim. Greeno now had one of the murder weapons. He also had something else; he had the successful detective's ability to get the best out of the people around him. He turned now to the local police, men who if they were up to their job would have far more of a feel for local matters; and Ted Greeno was not disappointed. PC Tim Halloran, stationed at Godalming, was just such an observant policeman. He remembered an incident the previous July involving a young woman matching the Chief's description. She had been picked up for vagrancy after being found living rough in a shelter made of branches and leaves out on the Common. The woman had been cohabiting there with her boy-friend, a soldier stationed at a local camp, and both of them were taken to the police station for questioning. The carefully filed documents which recorded the incident revealed that the girl's name had been given as Joan Pearl Wolfe, the big French-Canadian half-breed Indian who was her consort had identified himself as August Sangret of the nearby Jasper Army Camp.

This was just the kind of information that Ted Greeno had been hoping for. His next obvious step was to find the man Sangret. The detective visited the Jasper Camp and spoke to the commanding officer. Yes, he remembered Joan Wolfe, she had been one of those pathetic figures who seemed always to be hanging around on the fringes of Army camps. She had, he told Greeno, nowhere else to go. He had been aware, too, that she had taken up with Sangret and that they were sharing a wigwam which he had fashioned after the model of his Cree Indian ancestors, out of beech stakes, heather and leaves, in the middle of Hankley Common. Indeed, Sangret had spoken to his commanding officer of marriage to Joan, but things had never been pursued as far as an official request. So for three months the couple had shared this bizarre al fresco love affair; he joining her in the wigwam when he had a leave pass (and sometimes when he had not). She devotedly playing the role of housewife, though the role may have become a little too realistic for comfort when Joan informed Sangret that she was expecting to add 'mother' to her duties.

Sangret, the Chief Inspector decided, must be seen without delay, not least because the soldier had already been booked down for leave and was off to Glasgow in a couple of days. If he got wind of any suspicion the rabbit warren of the city's back streets could hide him for ever.

Accordingly, on the day that he collected his pay and his leave pass, August Sangret was asked to wait in the guardroom for a few minutes as some people wanted to have a word with him. Those people were Edward Greeno, DS Hodge, and Superintendent Webb of the Surrey police, who escorted Sangret to the police station. In his autobiography*, Ted Greeno recalled his first impression of the suspect Sangret: "He was a handsome brute, stocky, not more than five feet seven inches tall, with a deep chest and massive shoulders tapering to a ballet dancer's waist. His hair was oily black and his

*War on the Underworld, Edward Greeno. John Long, London, 1960.

face lean and swarthy."

The soldier was shown some of the sad remnants of the dead girl's clothes, which he identified impassively, and without hesitation, as Joan's. According to his statement, Sangret had met Joan Wolfe in a pub in Godalming where she was drowning the sorrow of her soldier boy-friend's recent return to Canada. With the desperation of loneliness she quite readily substituted this strange half-breed Indian with the same homeland, and shared a life that alternated between wigwams in the woods and a derelict cricket pavilion. He had last seen Joan, Sangret claimed, on September 14th, when she had transferred her affections to another soldier. The statement turned out to be a marathon for the unlucky Fred Hodge, who over a period of five solid hours took down more than 17,000 words – and not one of those words in any way incriminated Sangret, an uncanny achievement that must have given Greeno many moments of doubt.

As he signed the statement, Sangret said, "I guess you have found her; I guess I shall get the blame."

"Yes, she is dead," replied Greeno.

"She might have killed herself", suggested the soldier.

But while this was taking place in Godalming police station, the searchers on Hankley Common had been turning up more tangible elements in the Case of the Wigwam Murder. Behind the cricket pavilion (by now a burnt-out ruin), which had served as a temporary home for Sangret and Joan Wolfe, police had found a pair of stockings and a knitting book; near by, a white-metal lucky charm in the shape of an elephant was picked up. This had been bought for Joan by her mother on a trip to Hastings, and was later tearfully identified by that lady. With the charm was a faded letter written by Joan to Sangret during her stay in hospital – a letter that proved an indispensable link in understanding the brutal fate of its writer. It informed Sangret of the pregnancy; it also hinted at marriage. Finally, although it had suffered badly from exposure to the elements, there was an Identity Card – the name on it was Joan Pearl Wolfe.

At the same time, some of Sangret's kit had been taken from the Camp, along with his bedding, to the laboratory of the Home Office analyst, the redoubtable Dr Roche

Lynch. One of the blankets had been recently washed, but the cleaning had failed to remove three small stains which, though Roche Lynch would not testify to it in court, Greeno was convinced were bloodstains.

For DCI Edward Greeno there passed a frustrating couple of weeks. He had established, beyond all legal doubt, the identity of the victim: Joan Pearl Wolfe. He had a suspect – in Greeno's eyes, *the* suspect: August Sangret. If Joan had been blackmailing him into marriage over the baby, there was a motive. Police had the instrument which crushed the back of the unhappy Miss Wolfe's skull. But Ted Greeno desperately needed the knife; the knife with the "parrot's beak" tip. And he desperately needed to prove a link between it and his suspect.

It was on Friday, November 27th, that Ted Greeno received the telephone call from Provost-Sergeant Wade at Jasper Camp: "I've got something that might interest you." And interest him it certainly did! Wade presented him with an Army jack-knife; it had a black bone handle and, more significantly, a curious hooked tip to the blade. The knife had been the cause of a blockage in the wastepipe of the camp's guardroom, and the shrewd Wade had remembered back to the day, some weeks before, when Sangret had been kept in the guardroom awaiting transfer to the police station. He had distinctly remembered Sangret asking to use the washroom.

Subsequent tests by Dr Gardner on Joan Wolfe's skull established conclusively that this was the knife used to inflict the terrible injuries on her. But proving that it belonged to Sangret – that was another problem.

However, in yet one more of this case's lucky happenstances, a member of the camp's Military Police named Crowle chanced to recognize the knife; and he too had a conveniently good memory. Convenient, that is, for Edward Greeno; less convenient for Private August Sangret. It was on August 20th, the MP recalled; he had been on patrol around the camp and came upon Sangret and Joan Wolfe shacked up in their wigwam. Stuck into a tree outside was a knife. It had a black bone handle, and on its removal from the tree, a strange beak-shaped blade. August Sangret was almost in the net.

Or rather, he wasn't. During the time that the investigation had taken August Sangret had left Godalming and, via Glasgow, was now stationed at Aldershot, where Greeno eventually found him flat on his back in the military hospital suffering from a virus infection. It seemed a prosaic end to a dramatic story; even so, Ted Greeno was well aware that he had not won yet. What if Sangret simply denied all knowledge of the knife? There was nothing but an MP's memory to connect the two. Everything depended on the right line of questioning. The detective began by setting his quarry at ease with a few innocent questions about his previous statement; a bit of friendly chit-chat; then: "The MPs at the Camp say there was a black handled knife stuck in a tree outside the wigwam, and that you said it was yours." "No, the knife was Joan's. I forgot to tell you about the knife before . . . I never thought about it . . . Joan used to carry it in her handbag." Sangret had been hooked and landed. With his customary verbosity, the soldier went on to make a second lengthy statement, describing how the knife had become an important part of their domestic activity, and was always left stuck in the tree for easy location. As soon as the statement had been signed August Sangret was arrested for Joan's murder. He responded simply. "I didn't do it. Someone did, but I'll have to take the rap."

At Sangret's trial at Kingston Assizes five months later, this same knife, along with poor Joan's skull, was taken into court to prove to the jury that *only one* knife could have caused the brutal stab wounds on the victim's head – Sangret's black-handled jack-knife; the one with the parrot's-beak tip.

Clutching the knife and skull, the foreman led his jury to their retirement, emerging some two hours later with the predicted verdict of "Guilty": unpredictably, they added a strong recommendation to mercy. Perhaps they saw Sangret as a noble example of our allied troops, whose task it was to fight for the world's freedom, being led astray by an immoral floozie with a tendency to prey on soldiers. At any rate, the Home Secretary and his legal advisers held no such sentimental views, and Joan Wolfe's killer was hanged at Wandsworth Prison on Thursday, April 29th, 1943.

A spoonful of poison helps the medicine go down

The Murder of MARGERY RADFORD
by her Husband FREDERICK GORDON RADFORD

on Tuesday the 12th of April 1949
at the Milford Sanatorium, near Godalming

Mrs Margery Radford had suffered from pulmonary tuberculosis for seven years. By 1949 she was terminally ill and had become a resident at the Milford Sanatorium, near Godalming in Surrey. Pulmonary tuberculosis is an especially distressing disease in its later stages; Mrs Radford was pale and emaciated, weighing less than five stones as she approached death, and her frail frame was convulsed by violent fits of coughing. Frederick, her husband, worked as a laboratory technician at St Thomas's Hospital, Godalming, about a mile from the sanatorium, an occupation which gave him a certain amount of medical insight into his wife's condition. He was, however, neither a devoted nor a caring spouse. He rarely visited his wife, and was rumoured to be having an affair with another woman. His one apparent concession was to send special food to the sanatorium to supplement his wife's diet.

On Wednesday the 6th of April, 1949, Mrs Radford became even more ill and vomited several times after eating jelly and some plums which had been provided by her husband. Later that day she was visited by a close personal friend, a Mrs Formby. Margery told Mrs Formby that she suspected her husband was trying to poison her. She then gave her friend a large part of a fruit pie which her father, Mr Kite, had brought in for her from her husband a few days previously and asked her to send it to Scotland Yard to be analysed. Mrs Formby was naturally very concerned, but was also a little worried that her sick friend might be exaggerating or imagining things. When she got home, she discussed the dilemma with her husband and decided to take a slightly less drastic course. She wrapped the pie in brown paper and posted the parcel to the Superintendent of the Milford Sanatorium. She wrote him a separate covering letter explaining Mrs Radford's grave suspicions.

The parcel and the covering letter arrived at the sanatorium on Saturday the 9th of April. The parcel was placed on the Superintendent's desk and the letter in his secretary's in-tray. The Superintendent popped into his office at around teatime. As his secretary was not at work on a Saturday, and the fruit pie was there on his desk with no obvious explanation, he assumed that it had been left by a friend as a present, and took it home with him. That evening he ate a small slice, about a sixth of the pie, and was immediately seized with stomach pains and a strong desire to be sick, though he could bring up nothing. He went upstairs to bed and, during the night, retched so violently that he burst the tiny blood-vessels in his eyes. In fact, he nearly died.

On Monday the Superintendent was still feeling distinctly off colour and rather queasy, but decided nevertheless to fulfil his obligations and go into work. When he

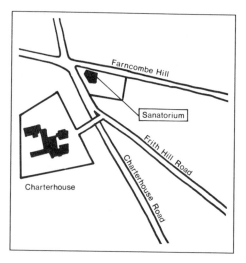

arrived he was handed the letter from Mrs Formby with his post, and the reason for his unpleasant weekend became fairly evident. He took the remains of the fruit pie to Mrs Radford to identify, and then, consulting her case records, noted that she had vomited three or four times on the day that the pie had been delivered by her father. He decided that it was time to call the Surrey police.

The next day, Tuesday the 12th of April, the remains of the fruit pie were sent to Dr G. E. Turfitt, the analyst at the Scotland Yard Laboratories; the pie was found to contain 3.25 grains of potassium arsenate. Chief Superintendent T. A. Roberts, head of Surrey CID, was placed in charge of the inquiry.

On the very same day, Margery Radford died in the sanatorium. The Police were now faced with a case of suspected murder. The post-mortem on Mrs Radford's body was carried out by Dr Keith Simpson, Medico-Legal Adviser to the Surrey Constabulary, with Dr Turfitt in attendance. The body weighed only 4 stones 13 pounds, yet it was found to contain 6.5 grains of potassium arsenate, over three times the amount necessary to kill a normal, fit human being. There were 2.75 grains in the liver alone. Traces of arsenic were detected as far as 5 centimetres from the roots of her hair, which indicated that Mrs Radford had been systematically poisoned for a period of between a hundred and a hundred and twenty days. It had been a highly calculated and singularly cold-blooded plan which had brought about Mrs Radford's premature demise.

The obvious course for the police was to interview Frederick Radford, and he was accordingly brought into Godalming Police Station for questioning. When Chief Superintendent Roberts faced Radford with the results of the autopsy and tests on the fruit pie he sat looking shattered, with his head in his hands. "I don't know anything about it", he replied. "That means murder. I know it looks black against me. I admit I bought the pies and gave them to Mr Kite to take to my wife. Why should I want to kill my wife? I knew she was going to die anyway! I would not be such a fool as to use arsenic with my experience, as I know the police could find it easily enough. If you think I did it, charge me and let a judge and jury decide."

The police were pretty sure they had their man, but there were still some residual doubts. After all, as Radford himself had pointed out, his wife would have died anyway, so why had he bothered to take such a perilous course of action? It was also true that he must have known how easily traceable arsenic is, though the symptoms of the poison were similar enough to the debilitating side effects of her tuberculosis to have gone unnoticed, but for Mrs Radford's suspicions and the unfortunate accident to the Superintendent of the Sanatorium. Chief Superintendent Roberts decided to be cautious and let Radford sweat for a while. He was driven back to his house in a police car, on the understanding that he would return to Godalming police station the next day to attend the inquest on Mrs Radford; when the police car dropped him at his door, Radford invited the policemen in for a cup of tea, which they judiciously declined.

The next morning Frederick Radford was discovered dead in his bed. His body was already cold. He had been more concerned for his own pain than he had ever been for his miserable and defenceless wife, dying slowly of tuberculosis and cumulative arsenical poisoning in a sanatorium. For himself he had chosen a dose of nearly instantaneous prussic acid.

There have been reliable methods of identifying even the smallest trace of arsenic in the body for almost 150 years, so it is not only incomprehensible that Frederick Radford should choose this method of murder, but astonishing that he was almost successful. By 1949 a lot had been learned about arsenic.

One of the most potentially useful discoveries made by forensic researchers was that arsenic leaves a continuous trace in the hair. So, in cases of slow poisoning, it is possible to determine for how long the poison has been administered. Given that the hair grows at the rate of approximately 0.44 millimetres in a day, and as Mrs Radford had arsenic traces for a distance of five centimetres from the root, it was possible to calculate that her first dose of poison was ingested between 100 and 120 days before her death.

"I had a dream which was not all a dream"*
The Murder of ERIC GORDON TOMBE
by ERNEST DYER
in the month of April 1921
at 'The Welcomes', Kenley

When they left the Service at the end of the First World War, the two young Army officers remained close friends – like many whose relationships had been cemented by the mutual hardships of active service in a war notable for its privations. It was to prove the great irony that one of these young men was to achieve what the Kaiser's army could not – the shooting of his friend.

For 25-year-old Eric Tombe and 27-year-old Ernest Dyer the world made free by the blood of their comrades was their oyster. Tombe had a healthy bank balance, and Dyer knew some ways to manipulate it. Their first business partnership – a motoring venture – quickly ran into difficulties as did a second attempt to make a fortune from the new mode of transport. Learning from this, they exchanged four-wheeled vehicles for four-legged ones, and in 1920 Eric's money

*Lord Byron, *Darkness*.

bought them a racing stable and stud farm at Kenley, in Surrey. The farmhouse had been called 'The Welcomes', a name Ernest Dyer clearly took to heart when he moved in with his wife and children.

The proposition was no great success, in a large part due to Dyer's preference for backing horses over breeding them; and it was no doubt this financial instability that was responsible for the mysterious fire which damaged 'The Welcomes' in April 1921. Dyer's claim for £12,000 on the insurance was instantly rejected by the insurers, and he prudently let the matter drop. But it could be no curb to Ernest's passion for spending money – he had already been borrowing heavily from Tombe, and now began to forge the young man's signature on cheques. Not unreasonably, Eric saw this as a decidedly unfriendly gesture, if not treacherous, and consequent unfriendly words were exchanged. They may well have been the last

'The Welcomes' farmhouse

words the unlucky Eric Tombe ever uttered; certainly it was the last time he was remembered to have been seen alive.

Although not an intimate family, the Tombes had always enjoyed each other's company and confidence. Tombe senior was a clergyman, and both he and Eric's mother were of those advancing years when the presence of a son can be a great comfort. The sort of parents to fret when filial duty

Tombe recalled a letter from his son in which he mentioned his hairdresser, who operated in an establishment in London's fashionable Haymarket. Yes, the barber remembered Eric, he had been a regular, though not seen for some months now. The man also remembered Eric's pal – Dwyer was it, Eric called him? Lived somewhere down in Surrey – 'The Welcomes'.

Dyer was not at home when the old clergy-

Ernest Dyer

Eric Gordon Tombe

was not felt to be done. And when Eric seemed to have disappeared out of their, and everybody else's, life without leaving any word of explanation, the family was rightly worried. The 10 weeks dragged into months, and still there was no word from the errant son. A man of action, however eccentric, the Reverend Gordon Tombe began to insert a series of advertisements into the personal columns of newspapers – "Anyone knowing the whereabouts . . . " etc. When these did not produce the result so anxiously awaited by the distressed parents, Tombe came himself to London and scoured the West End haunts so familiar to Eric and Ernest, the two young men-about-town; but with no conspicuous success. Then Gordon

man called, but his wife was able to shed some light on the disappearance of his son. Mrs Dyer remembered her husband saying he had received a telegram from Eric, excusing his absence – "Sorry to disappoint. Have been called overseas."

The Rev. Tombe next thought he might benefit from an interview with young Eric's bank manager, and that gentleman received him with courtesy, and sympathy for the old fellow's evident anxiety. Anxiety which, the manager told him, he could rid him of that very instant. Eric Tombe had been in regular contact with the bank by correspondence, and a letter had only recently been received instructing them to allow power of attorney

129

to his partner Ernest Dyer. The old man's relief lasted no longer than it took to reach the bottom of the page: "But this is not my son's signature, this is a forgery." And the bank's file on the Tombe account revealed a whole series of such forgeries – one, for example, had transferred a sum in excess of £1,000 to a Paris bank "for the use of Ernest Dyer". Indeed, the man Dyer seemed to have quite cleaned out the account – and more besides. That he had fleeced his son was bad enough, but it began to occur to the tenacious old clergyman that Dyer might also be privy to his son's disappearance. But where *was* Ernest Dyer? He seemed to have vanished as completely as Eric Tombe.

It was not until many months later, in November 1922, that that question was answered; and then only by the intervention of chance. A man calling himself Fitzsimmons had been advertising in the local Scarborough newspaper, up in Yorkshire. It was one of the oldest confidence tricks in the book – "Contact advertiser for employment with outstanding prospects; small financial investment asked" – and the district police force had tracked Fitzsimmons to the Bar Hotel, Scarborough. On November 16th, a detective entered the hotel and asked to see Mr Fitzsimmons; as the man in question was escorting the policeman up to the room he occupied on an upper floor he made a movement which looked very like, in the words so beloved of the motion pictures, "going for

his gun". The officer lunged at him, there was a struggle, the gun went off and, true to the movie scenario, Fitzsimmons went limp . . .

But he wasn't Fitzsimmons after all. He was Dyer; and a search of his room revealed a treasure trove of incriminating evidence; not least among which were a pile of cheques bearing the forged signature E. Tombe, and a suitcase bearing the initials E.T.

And what of Eric Tombe? We might suppose that the one key to his whereabouts was now beneath six feet of earth. But that would be to reckon without the supernatural: to ignore those powers which are neither explicable nor controllable, the unknown secrets of the mind. Mrs Tombe, until now but a sad and silent bystander in this family tragedy, began to dream. She dreamed such nightmares as to wake her shouting and shivering with fear. The dream was always the same, always she saw the dead body of her son lying at the bottom of a well.

It was some days before the persistence of Gordon Tombe succeeded in persuading the hard-headed Francis Carlin of Scotland Yard's Murder Squad to take the dreams seriously. But after he and his handful of diggers arrived at 'The Welcomes', they had to take them very seriously indeed; at the bottom of a well, beneath stones and rubble, was the body of Eric Tombe, the back of his head removed by the blast of a shotgun.

The Merstham Tunnel Mystery
The Murder of Miss MARY SOPHIA MONEY
by an Unknown Killer
on Sunday September the 24th 1905
on a Train passing through the Merstham Tunnel

The railway line that runs between London and the south-coast resort of Brighton was already notorious as the location of the brutal slaying of Mr Frederick Gold by Percy Mapleton in 1881 [see this volume]. On the same line, almost a quarter of a century later, a second black spot was added.

At 10.55 on the night of Sunday September 24th 1905, Sub-Inspector William Peacock

and a railway work gang arrived at the Merstham Tunnel to continue essential repair work. Four hundred yards inside the tunnel the beam of Peacock's lamp picked out a large bundle by the side of the track. Further investigation revealed that the bundle was in reality the badly mutilated body of a young woman. When the police arrived to take charge of the matter the body was removed to the nearby *Feathers Hotel*

Mary Sophie Money

to await the inquest, and the forces of law and order set about assembling the available facts and theories.

First the victim: despite the terrible mutilation that had rendered her face unrecognizable, it could be seen that she had been a strongly built woman, aged about thirty-five, five feet two inches tall, with dark brown hair. A description was made of her clothing with a view to possible identification. She had been wearing a black voile dress and a hat trimmed with flowers and a pink bow. She had on a pair of scuffed patent-leather shoes with rubber heels, and wore several rings and a gold locket around her neck.

A suggestion that they might be dealing with a suicide was quicky dismissed by the discovery that the woman's own scarf had been forced into her mouth as a gag. Furthermore, the long horizontal scratches on the sooty walls of the tunnel indicated that the girl had been thrown (or possibly fallen) from the left-hand side of a train on the down-line – that is, coming from London.

It took less time than expected for the publicity to result in an identification, for on the following day the girl's brother was talking to the police. Robert Henry Money was a farmer in Kingston; he identified the dead woman as Mary Sophia Money.

It transpired that Mary Money had been only twenty-two years old, and had been employed as a book-keeper in the accounts department of Messrs Bridger and Company, dairymen, of 245 Lavender Hill, Clapham, where she herself lived. On the day on which she met her death Mary had been at her place of work with another girl named Emma Hone. At seven in the evening Mary announced that she was going for "a little walk"; she never returned. Emma Hone waited up for her in the house until one o'clock in the morning, and then retired to bed assuming that her friend had missed the train and stayed over with friends – though it must be said that she never had before.

Subsequent investigation placed Mary Money shortly after 7pm in the sweet-shop owned by Miss Frances Golding, situated on the station approach at Clapham Junction. Mary had purchased some chocolates, and mentioned in passing that she was going to Victoria; and there is no reason to suppose that she would lie gratuitously to the shop-keeper. In fact it seems certain that Mary did go to Victoria because a ticket-collector remembered her checking the platform number with him.

For what purpose Mary Money journeyed to Victoria station we will never know; the shops would all have been closed, and it was uncommon for girls in those days to go alone to places of entertainment. It was most likely she went to meet somebody, probably a man, and quite possibly her killer.

What happened between the time she would have got to Victoria – say around 7.45pm – and the time that she was found lying in the Merstham Tunnel is anybody's guess. However, a study of the railway timetable for that Sunday reveals that since the body was still warm when William Peacock discovered it, the most likely train from which Mary was launched was the 9.33 from London Bridge which passed through Croydon and reached the Merstham Tunnel at 9.55 before stopping at Redhill a few minutes later. Checking this reconstruction, the police were lucky to find in the guard on that train a perceptive man. He could clearly recall that at East Croydon he had looked into one of the first-class compartments and seen a woman dressed in dark clothes and accompanied by a man. His description of the woman fitted Mary Money though that of her companion, despite being fairly full, was too vague for identification. A little farther down the line at South Croydon the guard again noticed the couple in carriage 508, and he formed a distinct impression of furtiveness, of their trying to avoid being seen. When the train stopped at Redhill the guard saw the door of the couple's compartment was open and found it empty; looking down the platform, he saw the man, alone, walking towards the ticket barrier.

A signalman at Purley Oaks distinctly remembered seeing a man and a woman in a first class compartment of the south-bound train "struggling" – the man appearing to push his companion down on to the seat.

The conclusions to be drawn seem clear if we assume that these sightings were indeed of Mary Money and an unknown man friend. Perhaps he had started off gallantly escorting Mary back to Croydon after having a couple of drinks; perhaps Mary had got involved in the excitement of it all and agreed to go a few stops further down the line for a last kiss and cuddle. Perhaps, around Purley, the young man started to demand more than Mary was prepared to give, they struggle, she screams, he forces her scarf into her mouth to keep her quiet. It would be interesting to know whether there was any evidence of recent sexual assault on the body of Mary Money; whether the man got as far as this is or not he would clearly be very worried by the possible consequences of his passion. So worried that he bundled poor Mary, alive and struggling, out of the train window to be smashed by the walls of the tunnel and the wheels of the train. Or perhaps it happened differently . . .

THE ENIGMA OF ROBERT MONEY

There is an extraordinary postscript to the mysterious death of Mary Money which concerns her brother Robert.

Robert was what could be described as a thoroughly bad lot. It may be said in his defence that he almost certainly suffered from some mental instability which might account for his constant unnecessary lying – lies which during the investigation into his sister's death positively hindered the police inquiry. But Robert was also a double-dealer, a man who believed in spreading his affections as liberally as possible. At first to a woman with whom he lived under the name of Murray in Clapham, and to whom he gave two children; then he ran off with the woman's sister and married her; between them they produced another child. Tiring perhaps of stability, or just fancying a change, 'Murray' returned to his Clapham family, leaving them shortly afterwards in favour of his wife. And so back and forth until August 1912; in that month he rented a house at Eastbourne in the name C. R. Mackie. Having persuaded the whole of his ménage (none of whom were remotely aware of the existence of the others) into the seaside retreat he shot them, soaked their bodies in petrol, and set fire to the house, finally shooting himself. From the carnage one of the women survived.

As soon as it was realized that the aliases under which he had been living at the time – 'Captain' Murray and C. R. Mackie – masked the identity of Mr Robert Money, there was widespread, but inconclusive, speculation over his possible involvement in his sister's murder.

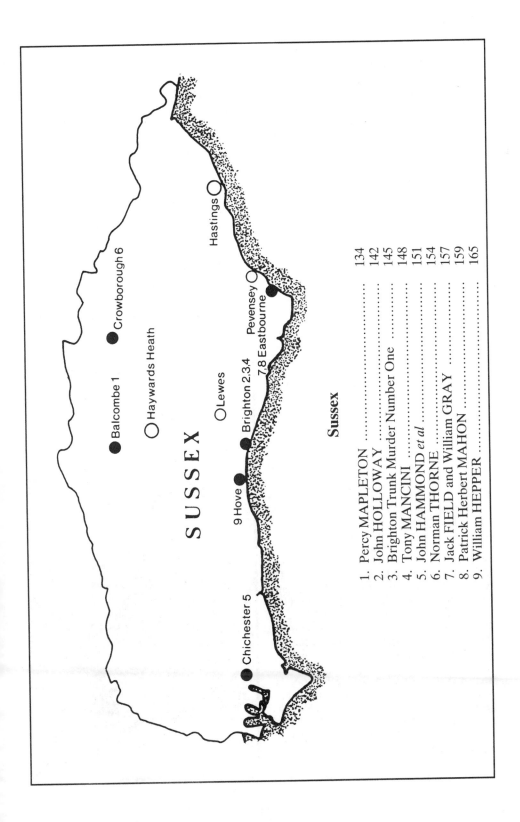

SUSSEX

Balcombe 1

Crowborough 6

○ Haywards Heath

○ Lewes

Brighton 2,3,4

Hastings ○

Pevensey ○

7,8 Eastbourne

9 Hove

Chichester 5

Sussex

Dark Deeds in a Railway Tunnel
The Murder of Mr ISAAC FREDERICK GOLD
by PERCY MAPLETON (alias LEFROY)
on Monday the 27th of June 1881
aboard a Railway Train near the entrance to Balcombe Tunnel

Percy Mapleton was a young man of twenty-two with a most distinctive appearance. Short in stature, he was rather thin and emaciated, with a prominent, beaky nose and a receeding chin, which latter were emphasized by his dapper dark moustache. He was also most vain and particular in his dress, sporting an evening frock coat and a black, low-brimmed hat, which he wore for effect, regardless of the time of day.

As a youth Percy had been rather shy and had suffered from somewhat delicate health, which had been a constant source of worry to his family. He was a romantic soul, and spent much of his time buried in books, later developing an equal passion for the theatre. This had led to literary ambitions of his own. He had written several plays, none of which had actually been produced, though he had penned a number of sentimental short stories which had been published in small magazines.

Unfortunately, Percy could not support himself from his literary efforts and was forced to work as a clerk. Even this was not sufficient to maintain the kind of life-style to which he aspired, and he was constantly short of funds; this lack of money caused young Percy considerable frustration. On Monday June the 27th 1881 he awoke early and resolved to be done with his problem whatever the consequences. Firstly, he redeemed from the pawnbrokers a revolver, which he had previously pledged for the sum of five shillings under the name William Lee; and then with the last of his money bought a train ticket at London Bridge Station. He walked up and down the platform in the hope of coming upon a respectable lady alone in a compartment, who might be easily relieved of her valuables by threats and the waving of his revolver. In this he had no luck, and eventually joined a First Class Smoking compartment whose only other occupant was an elderly prosperous-looking gentleman.

This gentleman was 64-year-old Mr Isaac Frederick Gold, a retired businessman who lived in Preston Park, outside Brighton. Mr Gold had retained an interest in one shop when he retired and was in the habit of travelling up to London each Monday to collect from his manager, a Mr Cross, the profits for the past week.

This he had done earlier that morning, carrying £38 5s 6d directly to his London bankers, where he had banked £38, before proceeding to the railway station to catch the two o'clock train.

The train passed as far as East Croydon, and slightly beyond, without incident. Eight miles beyond Croydon is the Merstham Tunnel, which is about a mile in length. As the train entered the tunnel a chemist by the name of Gibson, who was a passenger in another compartment, heard four sharp explosions, which he took at the time to be fog signals. When the train passed through Horley, farther down the line, a Mrs Brown and her daughter who were standing outside their cottage saw two figures struggling in one of the compartments as the train sped by.

Seven miles farther on, the train passed through the Balcombe Tunnel, and beyond that came a halt at Preston Park Station, just a mile from the end of the line at Brighton. The attention of the ticket-collector was immediately drawn to the dishevelled and bloodstained passenger in one of the compartments. He had a nasty-looking head wound, was minus his collar and the compartment in which he was slumped was liberally spattered with blood. The passenger claimed that his name was Percy Lefroy, and asked for a policeman to be called. The story he had to tell was as dramatic as it was unlikely. He claimed that he had begun the journey from London in the company of two fellow-passengers, an elderly man and a rural gentleman of about fifty. As the train entered the Merstham Tunnel, he continued, he had been attacked by the elderly man and rendered unconscious. He had come to his senses, alone in the compartment, and in his present state, just before the train arrived at Preston Park. He knew no more of what had happened than that. As Percy was helped from the carriage somebody noticed a watch chain dangling from,

of all places, his shoe. Inside the shoe was a pocket watch, which Percy claimed was his; it had been stashed in this unlikely hiding-place for safety. He was allowed to retain possession of the timepiece, and taken by the policeman to Brighton Town Hall to make a proper statement. From there he was removed to hospital, where he remained for some time having his wound attended to, two policemen keeping him company.

A search of the railway compartment had revealed three Hanoverian medals, which friends were later to claim they had often seen in Percy's possession, though he denied any knowledge of them. At five past three a hat was discovered on the up-line at Burgess Hill. At Hassock's Gate an umbrella, later identified as belonging to Mr Gold, was discovered by a young woman a few yards from the railway line. At a quarter to four a platelayer came upon the body of Mr Gold, a few yards from the entrance to the Balcombe Tunnel. A bullet had entered his neck and the multiple knife wounds which disfigured his body bore witness to the tenacious struggle he had put up to repel his attacker. At a quarter-past five another platelayer discovered a shirt collar on the railway line nearer to Brighton.

Discharged from the hospital, Percy Mapleton was permitted to visit a shop to purchase a new collar, and then, still accompanied by the two policemen, put on to the train going back up the line to East Croydon, en route for his lodgings in Wallington. During one of the stops on the journey an official of the railway company related the news, within Percy's hearing, that a body had been discovered near the Balcombe Tunnel. On reaching the house in Wallington, Number 4 Cathcart (now Clarendon) Road, which was the home of his second cousin, Percy left the two policemen waiting on the doorstep. Telling the servant inside that he was just popping out to visit a surgeon in the neighbourhood, he disappeared out of the back door with all the haste of a very guilty man.

Percy, now on the run, surfaced in Stepney on Thursday, the 30th of June, renting a room from a Mrs Vickers in Smith Street under an assumed name. For the next week, he stayed indoors most of the time, keeping himself to himself. He was, however, eventually forced by shortage of money to take a big risk. He sent a rather enigmatic telegram in the name of Clarke to his former employer, Mr Seal, in Gresham Street: "Please send me my wages tonight without fail about eight o'clock. Flour to-morrow. Not 33." That very evening two policemen, one of them Inspector Swanson, appeared at the house in Smith Street and took Percy Mapleton into custody. In his room they found a false beard.

During his imprisonment awaiting trial, Percy's ludicrous penchant for romance and drama again got the better of him. He managed to get a quite extraordinary letter, addressed to a girl-friend, smuggled out of the prison.

Monday, Oct 17
My Darling Annie
I am getting this posted secretly by a true and kind friend, and I trust you implicitly to do as I ask you. Dearest, should God permit a verdict of Guilty to be returned, you know what my fate must be unless you prevent it, which you can do by assisting me in this way. Send me (concealed in a common meat pie, made in an oblong tin cheap dish) [a] saw file, six inches or so long, without a handle; place this at bottom of pie, embedded in under crust and gravy. And now, dearest, for the greater favour of the two. Send me, in centre of a small cake, like your half-crown one, a tiny bottle of prussic acid, the smaller the better; this last you could, I believe, obtain from either Drs Green or Cressy for destroying a favourite cat. My darling, believe me when I say, as I hope for salvation, that this last should only be used the last night allowed me by the law to live, if it comes to that last extremity. Never, while a chance of life remained, would I use it, but only as a last recourse. It would be no suicide in God's sight, I am sure. Dearest, I trust this matter to you to aid me. I will face my trial as an innocent man should, and I believe God will restore me to you once more after this fearful lesson; but should He not, the file would give me a chance of escaping with life, while if both failed, I should still save myself from dying a felon's death undeserved. By packing these, as I say, carefully, sending with them a tin of milk, etc, no risk will be incurred, as my things are, comparatively speaking, never examined. Get them yourself soon, and — [an indistinct word]

and direct them in a feigned hand, without any accompanying note. If you receive this safely, and will aid me, by return send a postcard, saying: "Dear P., Captain Lefroy has returned." Send them by Friday morning at latest.

If not P.A., get arsenic powder from Hart or other (or through Mrs B.); wrap up in three or four pieces of paper.

God bless you, darling. I trust you trust me. I can conceal several small things about me in safety.

Fortunately for her, though replying in the most adoring terms, the girl in question did not meet Percy's eccentric demands.

Percy Mapleton appeared at the Magistrates' Court at Cuckfield and was committed for trial for the murder of Mr Isaac Gold at the Autumn Assizes in Maidstone.

The trial at Maidstone opened on the 5th day of November 1881, before the Lord Chief Justice, Sir John Coleridge. The prosecution was led by the Attorney-General, Sir Henry James QC, MP, with Mr Harry Poland and Mr A. L. Smith. The defence was headed by Montagu Williams QC, with Mr Forrest Fulton and Mr Kisch.

When Percy appeared in the dock, he was immaculately dressed in a tightly buttoned black frock coat, a low stand-up collar and a dark cravat. In his hand he held a new silk hat which had been purchased for him by friends. Yet even this was a disappointment to the young dandy, who had pleaded with the police to reclaim his famous dress coat, which he had been forced to pawn during his desperate period on the run. His vanity further revealed itself in his self-conscious striking of poses in the dock for the court artists. It was evident, however, that he was also very nervous, continually fidgeting in his seat and answering the charge with a barely audible whisper of "I am not guilty." Later he appeared to be dozing in his seat as the evidence was presented.

The trial had the appearance of going quite well for the defence. Although the Crown evidence was strong, it was all circumstantial and the prosecution case was presented in an unemotional, slightly pedantic, manner. At the close of the third day Percy himself was confident of success. As he quitted the dock he commented to the gaoler, "When I

am acquitted, I hope I shan't be mobbed."

The next morning the Lord Chief Justice began his summing up. It lasted until a quarter to three in the afternoon, and his tone was far from sympathetic. It took the jury little time to find Percy Mapleton guilty. As he was being taken from the dock Percy turned to the jury with his right arm out-stretched and declared dramatically, "Some day you will learn, when too late, that you have murdered me."

A few short days before his execution, Percy Mapleton wrote a letter to a close relative making a complete confession to the robbery and murder of Mr Gold. He was hanged on the 29th of November, 1881.

TWO BOXING NIGHTS
by
PERCY MAPLETON

Christmas time! There was no doubt about it. Everything and everybody savoured of it. The light of Christmas fires shone through and gleamed behind closely-curtained windows, with merry leaps, sending showers of golden sparks up dark chimneys, to emerge more bright and dazzling than ever in the clear, frosty air, like fleeting souls hastening through the gloom and cares of life to shine in higher regions.

"Christmas!" cried the bells, as they pealed softly through the still night air; "Christmas! merry Christmas! – Christmas! merry Christmas!" so merrily and cheerily that he must have been a man of stony heart who did not echo it, too, from sheer sympathy. Christmas! murmured the dark river, as it lapped against the buttresses of the old stone bridge, and then sped away with many a secret in its gloomy bosom to the sea, where, in company with many others of its race, it murmured still of Christmas; and "Christmas time!" pleaded the inebriated gentlemen when questioned by a stern policeman as to why they were sitting in frozen gutters at midnight. For that one day a sort of universal truce seemed to be established. Creditors forgot their debtors, debtors forgot their creditors; wives forgot to scold, husbands to abuse, and young husbands forgot their mothers-in-law, which was, perhaps, hardest of all. Conservatives and Liberals, Churchmen and Dissenters, "old boy'd" and "old fellow'd" each other to their heart's content, and the plea for all was – Christmas! But when the world got up next day, what a change was to be seen! Closed blinds, no church bells, shops shut – just as if every one was ashamed of his or her last night's festivity.

There wasn't much going on indoors today, for it was Boxing Day – that day sacred to Christmas boxes, bills, and last, but by no means least, pantomimes. And to go to one of these last the children were mad with hope long deferred. Papa and mamma affected not to like or care for such trivial amusements at all, but the children – sly dogs, those children! – knew that when once within the cosy recesses of that lovely private box no one would cry "bravo" more loudly, or clap his hands more vehemently, than papa. And what a lot of pantomimes there were, too! Just look at all the various hoardings: Robinson Crusoe, Jack the Giant-killer, Aladdin, and many other well-known stories had been made to contribute to the common good. But first and foremost among the brightly-coloured bills was the one that informed the reader "that on Boxing Night would be produced at the Rotunda Theatre" the grand Christmas pantomime, Jack and the Beanstalk. Then followed the list of characters, scenery, etc., and at the end, in large letters, "Clown – Jolly Joe Jeffs".

The Rotunda must have been a well-known theatre for pantomime, for that night it was crammed from floor to ceiling. Everything had gone off without a hitch. The music was pretty, the scenery magnificent, and the grand ballet had been pronounced by the crutch-and-toothpick genius in the stalls to be "splendid", and by an old lady in the pit to be "beastly".

And now, out of breath with honest laughter, warm, thirsty, and packed like sardines in a box, the great audience sat anxiously waiting for the "grandest transformation scene ever attempted at the Rotunda", vide bills. If there was excitement in front, so there was behind. Every one busy, excited, and nervous, the manager and stage-manager not being by any means in that happy condition described by the immortal Mrs Jarley as "Cool, calm, and classical."

Inside one of the principal dressing rooms was a man, clad in a clown's dress, pacing moodily up and down, and listening with feverish impatience for a footstep which never came. It was Joe Jeffs, and the person he was waiting for was his wife. And she was a wife worth waiting for, too. Young, pretty, and loving. Nellie Raynor, then only – and indeed, up to within a week or so of the present time – a ballet girl at a West End theatre, had brought some new joy and life to honest, hard-working Joe Jeffs, who, though nearly fifteen years her senior, loved her with a strong and passionate love, and would cheerfully have laid down his life if it had been necessary to save her from harm. And this winter, when Nellie, through her husband's influence, got engaged at the Rotunda as columbine, Joe Jeffs thought that his cup of happiness was full to the brim.

A knock at the door. "Come in," cried the clown. Mr Flies, the stage-manager entered. Flies was a little short man, with a round red face, with very short black hair, so short that it always stood on end, as if each hair was desirous of looking over its neighbour's head.

"I'm very sorry, Mr Flies," said the clown, humbly, "very sorry; but Nellie told me tonight she wasn't well, and would lie down for a bit, and would come later on. I sent a boy to our place some time ago, and she must be here in a minute."

"Minute!" roared Mr Flies, "what's the good of a minute? I – who the devil's that?" as a hand was laid on his arm.

It was the harlequin, in the bills Roberto Taylori, out of them, Bob Taylor, an old friend of the clown's.

"I've got an idea," said the harlequin, giving a kindly unseen nod to his friend. "Say a few words to the public, and let my girl Bella go on for the part tonight; she's about Mrs Jeffs' size, and I've taught her the trip long ago."

Miss Bella Taylori was in the front row of the ballet, consequently could dance well and look pretty; but, best of all, was there on the spot, so to speak. The stage-manager didn't take long to make up his mind.

"Bob," he said to the harlequin, "You're a brick. The very thing. Get the girl dressed at once, and I'll get the guv'nor to speak to them." Them being the audience, who were now in a state of noisy impatience. Mr Flies hurried off.

"Tell your missus it's all right old man," said the friendly harlequin, as he hurried away.

The clown was about to reply, when a light footstep was heard approaching. A happy smile lighted up his face. "At last," he said, with a sigh of relief, as the footsteps neared the door. Quickly he turned the handle and threw it wide open, but only to start back with a cry of disappointment, for the newcomer was not his wife, but the boy he had sent an hour previously. "Well," cried the clown, "what did she say?"

The boy shook his head stolidly.

"I didn't see her, sir," he said; "only the landlady, and she give me this." The clown held out his hand, and into it the boy put a tiny note, on which was written, in a woman's hand, "To be given to my husband."

"You can go," said Joe Jeffs in a voice which was so hoarse and strange that for a moment it startled the lad. When the door was again closed, the clown looked at the tiny missive. Was she frightened that he would be angry with her for remaining so long behind the time, and so did not care to come at all, but wrote instead? That must be it. With trembling hands he hastily tore it open, and read: "Husband, goodbye; I shall never see you any more. I am going away with someone that loves me very much. You were always too good for me. May God forgive your poor lost Nellie." Nothing more. Only an old, old story, with a vulgar clown and his wife as hero and heroine.

Joe Jeffs raised his head, Was it paint alone that gave that awful deathly look to his face and fixed glassy eyes? Was it clowning that caused the strong man's hands to shake as if he were suffering from the palsy? And, above all, was it art or nature which made that bitter cry of agony arise from the uttermost depths of a broken heart?

At that moment the call-boy's shrill voice was heard, "Mr Jeffs, the stage waits!" Mechanically the clown reeled to the door and opened it, down the narrow, dark passage, and staggered through the wing on to the brilliantly-lighted stage, and then in a voice more resembling the croak of a raven than the utterance of a human being, gave vent to the time-honoured utterance, "Here we are again!"

How the house roared at the strange voice and staggering gait! Such quiet humour! So dry, very dry! And then, after such a capital commencement, the great audience settled down with keen anticipation for the fun that was to come. And come it did. With what zest did Jolly Joe Jeffs trip up the policeman, steal the sausages, and go through the hundred and one odd tricks which go to make up the sum total of a harlequinade! The gods were in one continual roar; even the stalls and circle were mildly excited, while as for the pit, the opinion of that black, seething mass of humanity may be briefly summed up in the words of an excited old gentleman, who, carried away by his enthusiasm, flung his neighbour's hat into the air, crying, "splendid, sir, splendid! Grimaldi was a fool to Jolly Joe!" And tumbling, grimacing, tripping up, now dancing on a spade, a minute later cracking sly jokes, the clown went

A typical Victorian pantomime clown with a costume deriving from the celebrated Grimaldi

through it. Only the clown, though, for God's beautiful creation – man – was gone. When his poor, aching head swam for a moment, and he fell heavily to the ground, what a shout went up! Droll fellow, that Jeffs – very droll, and their laughter reached its culminating point when, during a hornpipe by the pretty columbine, two large tears stole down the clown's painted face, as he, in burlesque fashion, attempted to immitate it. "He's a-crying with laughter!" roared the excited gallery, and they cheered him to the echo for entering so heartily into the spirit of the thing. At last the end came. One last wild trick, clouds of smoke from the coloured fires, a last mad rally, and, amidst tremendous applause, the pantomime was over. As the band commenced to play the National Anthem, Jolly Joe Jeffs staggered off the stage, as he had staggered on. Ere he could reach his dressing-room two men stopped him. One was Mr Flies, the other Mortimer, the manager. "My boy," said the latter, taking him by both hands, and shaking them warmly, "you've surpassed yourself. If only your wife could have seen you!" That was enough. For a minute Jolly Joe stood erect, and then, with a wild, gasping cry, fell heavily to the ground. The clown was gone, but the man was there.

NIGHT THE SECOND

Ten years rolled by. Ten long, weary years they had been to Joe Jeffs, who had never given up the search for his lost darling. A few weeks after his great loss an old relative had died, leaving him a small annuity. On this he had lived, or rather existed, wandering aimlessly about the country in the hope of one day finding his wife, whom in spite of all, he loved as fondly as ever.

And this Boxing Night, he was walking down the little High Street of Milford, weary, hopeless, and sick at heart, to all appearance a bent, careworn, old man, a mere wreck of the merry fellow who ten years before had made a great theatre resound with peals of laughter at his drollery. Quickly the clown walked on, for the night was cold, and the biting east wind seemed to pierce his bones to the very marrow. When within a few yards of the little inn at which he was staying, his arm was touched.

"Buy a box of lights, sir; do buy a box, please!"

He turned. A woman, wretchedly clad, and with death stamped in every feature, stood at his elbow.

"No," answered the clown, roughly; "I don't want any," and he walked on.

But the beggar was not so easily shaken off. She detained him again, and as the wind lulled for a minute, her voice rang in his ear: "Buy a box, sir; just one box!"

At the sound Joe Jeffs turned.

"Let me see your face," he cried, hoarsely; then as the pale light of the moon fell upon it: "Nellie, dearie, don't you know me? – Joe, your husband?"

But there was no reply, for his long-lost wife lay insensible in his arms.

She was dying, the doctors said – dying of cold and want. So they told her husband, sitting by her bedside in the little inn.

"Can nothing save her?" asked the clown.

"Nothing on earth, my poor fellow – nothing on earth." And the old doctor looked out of the window and blew his nose violently, for a kind-hearted old man was the doctor, and knew something of poor Joe's story, and felt for him.

"Joe."

"Yes, darling."

"Are you sure you quite forgive me?"

A loving kiss was the only answer.

"Nellie, I won't be long," cried the clown.

"Listen!" And by a great effort the dying woman raised herself up; then suddenly: "Joe, dear, what day is it?"

"Christmas Day, Nell."

"Ah! so it is. More light, for God's sake, more light!"

The doctor made a movement of his hand, and the attendant drew back the curtains from the little window which looked upon the sea, on which lay a broad path of gold, formed of the last rays of the setting sun upon the water.

"How bright it all is, Joe,"cried the dying woman, as she sank back upon her pillow. "At last, at last! Joe, darling husband! good-bye!"

And with a sweet and happy smile on her face, Nellie went down with the sun.

Joe Jeffs still lives at Milford, but he is wonderfully changed, though. People say he is mad, and so he is, in a sad, harmless way. For as sure as Boxing Night comes round, he paints his face and dresses just like clowns do, and there in the little tap-room of the Red Lion he sings Hot Codlins in a little thin cracked voice, and tumbles in a mild and feeble way, and plays a few clownish tricks. How the villagers laugh! They know he is mad, but that doesn't take away from their enjoyment; and one of old Joe's funniest tricks is to address them all as "ladies and gentlemen", and apologise for the non-appearance of the columbine. But when all the merriment is over, old Joe, with his clown's dress still upon him, creeps down, whatever the weather may be, to the little churchyard, where, with his poor old grey head pillowed on a little marble slab inscribed 'Nellie', he pours out a bitter prayer that heaven may take him soon to her he loved so well, and ere he leaves the tomb, with great tears upon his painted face, he softly prays for Nellie too. But the end must soon come.

Each Boxing Night old Joe goes through the same performance, and the people laugh as vociferously as before. But every year he gets more feeble. He can't tumble as he used to, and his sight and memory seem failing fast, and the absent look in his face seems to denote that his thoughts are far away.

And now when people meet old Joe Jeffs, they shake their heads sadly, for they know that soon, very soon, the curtain must fall.

Murder in Rustic Surroundings
The Killing and Dismemberment of his Wife
by JOHN WILLIAM HOLLOWAY
on Thursday the 14th of July 1831
in Brighton

JOHN HOLLOWAY
Executed on 16th of December 1831
for the Murder of his Wife
whose Dismembered Body was
Discovered amid Rustic Surroundings

This horrible murder, almost unparalleled in atrocity, was discovered on Saturday, the 13th of August, 1831. On the Friday, the twelfth of the month, two men, named Maskell and Gillam, farm labourers, were passing through Rottingdean, near Preston, Brighton, when, on their arrival at a nook called the Hole-in-the-Wall, they fancied they perceived that the earth had been disturbed. They pushed away some of the mould with a stick and observed a piece of red printed cotton protruding, but at the time they took no particular notice of the occurrence. On their return home, however, to their respective families, they mentioned what they had seen, and Gillam's wife remarked that it was possible a child might be buried there. So, Elphick, the officer serving the village of Preston, was summoned to their assistance. Upon his arrival, Gillam procured a spade, for the purpose of digging round the suspected spot, and at length, at a distance of about eighteen inches only from the surface, a human thigh was found; immediately afterwards another thigh was dug up, and then a large bundle, wrapped in a dress made of the same description of cotton as that first seen, was produced. This bundle contained the trunk of a human body, but the head and arms were wanting. The body was still clothed in the stays, chemise and petticoats; and the gown, which had first attracted attention, appeared to

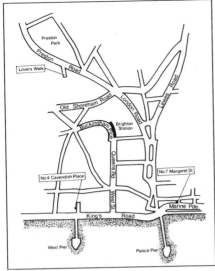

have been loosely wrapped over it, and an effort made to tie it round with a cord, which presented the appearance of a petticoat string.

Crowds of persons thronged to the spot, and amongst them was a Mrs Bishop, the wife of a labourer at Brighton, who declared that the body was that of her sister.

An investigation was now immediately set on foot, which resulted in a conviction that the husband of the deceased, John Holloway, a labourer employed at the Chain Pier at Brighton, had murdered her, and had thus disposed of her remains, in order to conceal the circumstances of her death.

During the six years which intervened between the marriage and the death of the unfortunate woman she and her husband had scarcely lived together for two consecutive months; and at length Holloway, who had quitted the Preventive Service in the year 1829 [he had been working on the Winchelsea blockade], obtained employment on the Chain Pier, which was then in the course of construction, and took a woman, named Ann Kennard [or Kennett], to live with him as his wife [their address was 7 Margaret Street, Brighton, and they lived under the aliases Mr and Mrs Goldsmith]. Mrs Holloway was then residing with her friends. Five weeks before the discovery of the murder, at which time Mrs Hollo-way was living with Mrs Symonds, at 4 Cavendish Place, North Brighton, Holloway commenced his diabolical scheme for her murder. He called upon her, and expressed a wish that their former animosities should be forgotten, and that they should again live together as they had done when they were first married. The woman, who had throughout expressed the fondest affection for him, listened to his proposals, and it was arranged that he should fetch her on a certain day, to conduct her to lodgings which he had taken for her, the locality of which, however, he did not describe. On Thursday, the 14th of July, Holloway called for his wife at Mrs Symonds's; but he first took away her boxes, in which she had previously packed her own clothes and her baby-linen. Mrs Holloway expressed some apprehension that he would not come back; but he kept his promise, and returned for her in about an hour, and took her away, attired in a gown similar in pattern to that in which her body was subsequently found wrapped. From that time she was never again seen alive. Steps were at once taken to secure her husband and his paramour. The latter was found first. She was residing at a house in Brighton, and was immediately taken into custody. On the same evening Holloway learned that inquiries had been

John William Holloway

143

No.7 Margaret Street, Brighton

No.4 Cavendish Place, Brighton

made for him, and surrendered himself into custody.

The coroner's jury returned a verdict of "wilful murder against John Holloway", and he was committed to Horsham Jail to await his trial.

A further search of the neighbourhood of Rottingdean resulted in the discovery of the missing head and legs, and on the following Saturday any doubts which might have been entertained of the guilt of Holloway were set at rest by his confession of his having committed the murder.

At his trial which took place at Lewes, on Wednesday, the 14th of December, 1831, he was remarkable for the brutality of his demeanour. When he was arraigned, his manner was such as to be fully in accordance with the atrocious nature of his crime. The court-room was excessively crowded, and when the name of the prisoner was called by the Clerk of the Arraigns a thrill of horror ran through the assembled crowd, which was audibly expressed in a murmur which gave much solemnity to the scene.

After hearing the evidence, the jury immediately returned a verdict of guilty, and the learned judge sentenced the prisoner to be executed on the following Friday, and directed his body to be given up to be anatomised. He mounted the scaffold on Friday, 16th of December, 1831, with a firm step. There was a strong expression of disgust among the spectators. He fell on his knees and prayed for a short time, after which a rope was placed round his neck and the cap drawn over his eyes. He then advanced to the front of the scaffold, and in a firm voice spoke as follows:

"Now, my dear friends. I need not tell you that sin has brought me to this untimely end. I would entreat you to be aware that there is not one among you who, if he follows a life of sin and folly, may not be brought to the same condition; for when you trifle with sin, you know not where it will end. I know I suffer justly: I have spilt innocent blood; but, however deep my guilt, I hope in the mercy of that God who has said to the penitent,'All your sins and blasphemies shall be forgiven you'. Therefore turn from your sins, and the Lord will forgive you."

After he had finished his speech he retired back on the platform, and the drop fell. The struggles of the culprit continued for some minutes.

The Brighton Trunk Murder: Number One

The Discovery of a Human Torso
on Wednesday the 6th of June 1934
in the Left-Luggage Office at Brighton Railway Station

The debate on the nature of the Perfect Murder has stimulated people's imagination for almost as long as people have tried to commit it. The fact is that fewer murders remain unsolved than might be thought, and those that do are in the main the result of brutal flights of passion that subside as quickly and inexplicably as they rise, often between people who are comparative if not total strangers. They comprise the sordid crimes rooted in greed that get hopelessly out of hand, their very pointlessness making it easy for the attacker to creep back unnoticed into the background. By any standards, the word Perfect does not come to mind in such cases. Indeed, there are those who will maintain that Murder is such a very imperfect manifestation of humankind that superlatives are *per se* inappropriate. The less pedantic might feel that a grudging acknowledgement might be extended to anybody who 'perfectly' achieves that which they set as a goal; for the murderer, perhaps, it demands more than merely 'getting away with it', and perhaps this perfection is one of those indefinable states that can only be recognized after the fact, and not compared with a blueprint. At any rate, whoever deposited the unclaimed trunk in the left-luggage office of Brighton Station on Derby Day, the 6th of June, 1934, was aiming for perfection.

Nearly a fortnight later – Sunday the 17th, to be precise – the baggage had still not been collected. Furthermore, it was beginning to give off a decidedly anti-social smell; the kind of smell that shouted out for investigation. As none of the baggage attendants had either the temerity or the stomach to approach too closely, the trunk was removed to Brighton police station; as it transpired, exactly the right place for it.

The body in the trunk was that of a woman, minus head, arms, and legs. The remainder had been wrapped round in brown paper and tied with window cord. Written on the paper in blue pencil were the letters "ford":

what had obviously been the first syllable was obliterated by blood. Not much of a clue, but since the police have been known to get a result with less, there was some degree of optimism in Brighton that night. After all, Voisin – a fellow-dismemberer – had been trapped by a faded laundry mark. The trunk itself was brand new, clearly bought for the purpose, and yielded nothing further of significance.

With their customary thoroughness, the police circulated a general request around Great Britain's railway stations, that left-luggage staff be on the look-out for other malodorous packages; they were after the rest of the Brighton body. And nor were they entirely disappointed; there was a stinking suitcase at King's Cross Station in London, and it contained four more pieces – two legs and, severed, two feet. All neatly parcelled in brown paper.

At this stage, the inspired pathologist Sir Bernard Spilsbury, the man on whose skill and experience so many murder convictions had depended, took charge of the remains. An itemized list of his findings reads:

1. Dismemberment by a person with some, though not expert, appreciation of anatomy.
2. No other injuries to the body apart from the points of dismemberment.
3. Age of victim: under 30 years.
4. Time of death: about three weeks prior to discovery.
5. Victim was in the fifth month of pregnancy.
6. From the state of care of the hands and feet, it was likely that the victim came from a middle-class background and had not engaged in any strenous or dirty occupation.

The King's Cross trunk also gave up two potentially useful clues in a face flannel and a quantity of inferior grade cotton wool packed with the lower limbs.

After extensive concentrated investigation, however, the clues had produced no leads whatever – either to the victim's identity or to that of her killer. The next step has always been a difficult decision for the police – to what extent is it productive to engage the help of the general public and the mass media? The advantages are obvious; within a space of hours descriptions, requests for assistance, even pictures, can be relayed to every home in the country via the powerful networks of newspapers, radio, and television – though police did not have this latter to consider in 1934.

The disadvantages can be imagined; with millions of amateur detectives throughout the country, the volume of input – the reported sightings, the snippets of gossip, the fears, suspicions – could be enough to grind to a standstill any investigating team that was not thoroughly prepared and organized. It happened that in this case the police were both desperate enough, and well enough organized, to realize that asking the public's help could be their only alternative to weeks of possibly fruitless searching and questioning. And so what description could be given of the girl was broadcast; details of the crime – such as they were – published. Someone surely must have missed a well-bred young woman? Someone must have heard something suspicious, seen something suspicious . . . found something suspicious? (the police were still hopeful of finding the head for identification).

The investigating officers were quite rightly refusing to admit the possibility of the perfect murder; but they were honest enough to admit that they were in need of a lot of luck.

The response was overwhelming, and hundreds of statements were made and checked in the first few days – missing women, found clothing, bought trunks . . . there were no fewer than twenty-four girls reported missing in the Brighton area alone, where police were confident that the crime originated. Investigating officers all over Britain were set to checking statements, interviewing witnesses, searching empty houses; detective agencies in Europe and the United States were checking their missing persons files. Who *was* the body in the trunk?

Two hundred police officers questioned hoteliers and guest house landladies along the length of the South Coast; Miss Gene Dennis, a professional medium, advised that the search should be narrowed to a man with dark brown hair and the initials "G.A." or "G.H.", aged about thirty-six, and a resident either of London or of Southampton. Miss Dennis was even more specific on the question of the victim . . . a manicurist with blue eyes from somewhere in Lancashire . . . "working in a white overall . . . named Dorothy Ellena Mason or something like that, and I think the crime was committed on a boat moored near Brighton. I see a toll bridge and a railway nearby. The murderer is not a murderer by type, but has been forced into this. He has worked in a wholesale seed store. . . . He is a man of an artistic type, with long slim hands and bushy hair, and I believe his name is George Henricson, or Robinson . . ."

Superintendent Frederick Wensley, formerly of Scotland Yard's Murder Squad and the man who had brought trunk murderer John Robinson to justice [see *Murder Club Guide No.1*] was enlisted as a consultant. But with the passing of a week since the body's discovery, things were looking as hopeless as ever. By the end of the month things had advanced no further; with every erroneous sighting, every half-baked theory, every new suspicion, the dossier grew fatter. And the police really were beginning to believe in the perfect murder.

To make matters worse, Fleet Street was becoming cynical; the *Daily Express* offered £500 reward for information which, it believed, was still locked in the inner recesses of someone's mind, or still being withheld out of fear or affection. Other newspapers were getting openly critical – one had discovered the whereabouts of 25 per cent of a new list of missing girls issued by Scotland Yard before the police had started. Gene Dennis stepped into the limelight again with a whole new shoal of red herrings from the world beyond. "This man was a savage, and killed for sheer revenge and the glory of hurting. She was killed because the man hated her. He was furiously jealous. He hit her and maltreated her shamefully. The fact that she was pregnant had no real bearing on his motives. He is a man of supreme vanity, and will boast of his crime. When you find him, he will confess and will glory in what he

A contemporary 'tabloid' approach to the case

has done. The murder was committed in a place that is almost public. I do not think it happened in an empty bungalow. I see a nursing home with white walls. There are two people concerned in the crime, this man and a stout woman of middle age. The head will be found in a small case wrapped in adhesive paper similar to that used on the rest of the body."

Still results were coming in negative, and with each succeeding week the trail was growing colder; the Brighton Trunk Murder had already earned itself a place in the annals of Classic Crime, it looked set to go to the top of the list of Classic Unsolved Crime.

But on Sunday, 15th July – a month after the discovery at Brighton Station – the seaside town was in a state of unconcealed excitement. Word travelled at the speed of lightning that the police had removed a black leather trunk from a house in Kemp Street, near the station. When Sir Bernard Spilsbury was seen arriving, rumours circulated that the arms and head of Brighton's celebrated corpse had been found at last. And that would have been remarkable enough; that alone would have explained the electric charge that seemed to be sparking the town. But the truth of the discovery would have defied invention by the most ghoulish imagination; police had not found the head missing from the trunk. *They had found a whole new body.* Brighton had its second Trunk Murder.

Diary of a Murderer?

The Brighton Trunk Murder Number One, as the case has been conveniently labelled, is still unsolved; and is likely, short of a miracle, to remain so. It was probably as much luck as planning and preparation that allowed its perpetrator to remain at liberty, but in an interesting postscript to his account of the case (*Trunk Crimes Past and Present*, Hutchinson, 1934), Leonard Lewis conjectured:

"Was it tantalizing our man that he could not share with another his satisfaction at the manner in which his well-laid plan to avoid detection was working out? Is there somewhere a diary, giving expression to such thoughts? Imagine how it might read:

June 18: They found the trunk at Brighton last night. It is a little earlier than I anticipated, but the hot weather has hastened discovery. Not that this matters a great deal. There is not much chance the man in the cloak-room will remember me, and surely they cannot track me through the trunk.

June 19: They have found the legs now at King's Cross. How grateful the papers should be to me for providing them with this material. What imaginative minds they have in Fleet Street! this morning there are at least a dozen suggested solutions to what they call the 'Brighton Trunk Mystery', and each suggestion bears the stamp of authenticity. Very ingenious!

The Brighton Trunk Murder: Number Two
The Killing of VIOLETTE KAYE
on or around May the 10th 1933
at 44 Park Crescent, Brighton
and the Trial and Acquittal of TONY MANCINI for her Murder

Brighton's second trunk find was, inevitably, connected in both popular and official minds with the existing enigma, and it was confidently anticipated that it would contain the hitherto missing head and arms. At the very moment that the black leather trunk was being manhandled into Brighton police sta-tion Sir Bernard Spilsbury was being driven full speed to the South-Coast resort. But speculation was wrong; the police, and Sir Bernard, had another mystery to unravel.

During the investigations into Trunk Murder

Number One the police had made extensive searches of most of the properties in Brighton – including those in Kemp Street. Number 52, however, had been split into single apartments and the several occupants were not then at home; indeed, the owner of the house had been away in London for some weeks. The police had decided to pay the house a further visit when the tenants were in residence, and in the confusion of the operation No. 52 was never searched. When the owner of the house and his wife returned they found that a number of the tenants had already left, and those that remained gradually gave up their rooms over the succeeding several weeks. This left the owners free to redecorate and take the house back into their own occupation. It was one of the house painters that first noticed the unearthly smell coming from one of the rooms.

The painter was obviously a man with a strong sense of the dramatic as well as a strong sense of smell, for he said nothing of his suspicions to the owners but went straight to the police station. After keeping watch on the house for forty-eight hours – heaven knows why – the police entered and were immediately assailed by the foul odour of decay; quite by coincidence – one of many to follow – the owners of the house had, literally, no sense of smell. When the offending corpse in its trunk had been removed, the police immediately issued a description of the man that they wished to interview – the previous tenant of the room!

Tony Mancini, a small-time crook with a string of aliases that would have filled an address book – Antoni Pirillie, Luigi Mancini, Hyman Gold, Jack Notyre (the name in which he was later charged with murder) . . . aged about twenty-six, five feet ten inches tall, sallow complexioned, and with a cast in one eye; a frequent visitor to the low dives of London's West End. Despite his Mediterranean complexion Mancini was English – in fact his real name was Cecil Lois England. It was his admiration for the Italo-American gangsters of Chicago that predisposed him to more romantic titles for himself.

Mancini had been working for some time in the Skylark cafe on Brighton's sea-front, and he had shared his modest lodgings at 44 Park Crescent with a woman he chose to refer to as his wife. She was Violette Kaye, aged

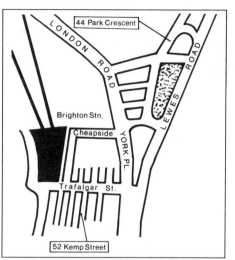

forty-two, who was quickly identified as the victim in the trunk. It was no surprise that police were anxious to contact him.

Ironically, they already had; for in yet another coincidence Tony Mancini had been interviewed in connection with the first trunk victim, for during the search for an identity for the torso police had made up lists of missing girls on one of which Violette Kaye's name had featured. Mancini had given his full co-operation including a detailed description of Violette, who he claimed had recently left him. The great difference in the two women's ages ruled Miss Kaye out as a candidate for the mystery torso and Mancini had fled back to London.

Meanwhile the background of the second victim was being carefully pieced together. Violette Kaye; also known as Mrs Violette Saunders, though she had divorced some years previously. She was one of a family of sixteen children and from her early teens had been on the stage. Dancing was what she did best, but she was also a competent singer, and had enjoyed a successful career in musical revue. Although she was forty-two, dancing had kept her trim and she was still attractive to men. At the time she met Mancini Vioette had exchanged dancing for the arguably less exacting profession of prostitution, and their relationship had depended very much on her keeping him on her 'immoral' earnings. That said, there can be no doubt that the couple shared a deep and genuine affection for each other.

In the eary morning of Wednesday July the 18th Mancini was picked up by the police while he was trudging along the London to Maidstone arterial road where it crossed Blackheath. Later in the day the prisoner was transferred to Brighton, where it seemed that the whole of the town had turned up to witness the arrival of this 'monster without parallel'. Hordes of young women in beach pyjamas and bathing costumes packed the square before the police court, hissing and booing as Mancini was hurried inside. The sight so appalled one senior police officer that he observed that it was more like the crowd at a fun-fair than a magistrates' court, and recalled the worst excesses of the old days of public executions.

Tony Mancini came up for trial at the Lewes Winter Assizes on December 10th 1934; the judge was Mr Justice Branson. Mr J. D. (later Mr Justice) Cassels KC, and Mr Quintin Hogg (later Lord Hailsham) appeared for the Crown, and Mr Norman Birkett KC led Mr John Flowers KC and Mr Eric Neve for Mancini.

Never, it must be said, was a case stronger against an accused than it was against Tony Mancini. To start with he was a known criminal – that shouldn't matter of course, not in a court of law; but it is impossible to divorce a man entirely from his past. He had admitted not only that he lived *with* Violette Kaye – a prostitute – but lived *off* her as well. Furthermore, he admitted knowing that she was dead while he had all the time pretended to the police that she had simply left him, had "gone abroad". And finally he admitted to putting Violette's body into a trunk specially bought for the purpose, and of transferring it from their lodgings at Park Crescent to Kemp Street; keeping it there at the foot of the bed and eventually fleeing to London. But at all times he was emphatic that he had not been the cause of his mistress's death; it was panic, he said, that made him hide the body after coming home and just "finding it there" in the flat; panic, and the fear that he – *a man with a police record* – would never be believed if he told the truth.

But Mancini was also luckier than he could have hoped, for in the person of his leading counsel he had perhaps the most highly regarded criminal lawyer of his time, Mr Norman Birkett. It was in great part Birkett's final address to a mesmerized jury – a speech that lasted eighty minutes, delivered entirely without notes, that turned the tables in his client's favour.

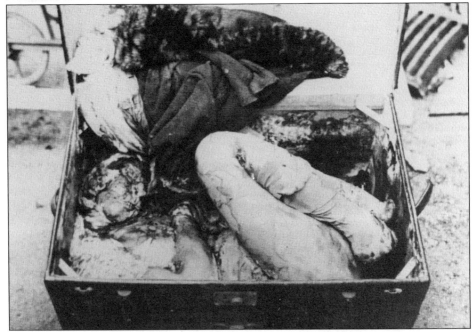

Violette Kaye, victim in the Second Brighton Trunk Murder

Having sown the seeds of doubt as to the strength of the prosecution case, Norman Birkett made deliberate capital out of Mancini's sordid background, emphasizing his client's own submission that people like him "never get a fair deal from the police". Burkett told the jury:

"This man lived upon her earnings, and I have no word whatever to say in extenuation or justification. None. You are men of the world. Consider the associates of these people. We have been dealing with a class of men who pay eightpence for a shirt and women who pay one shilling and sixpence or less for a place in which to sleep. It is an underworld that makes the mind reel. It is imperative that you should have it well in mind that this is the background out of which these events have sprung."

Birkett then summed up with an appeal direct to the hearts of the jury:

"Defending Counsel has a most solemn duty, as I and my colleagues know only too well. We have endeavoured, doubtless with many imperfections, to perform that task to the best of our ability. The ultimate responsibility – that rests upon you – and never let it be said, never let it be thought, that any word of mine should seek to deter you from doing that which you feel to be your duty. But now that the whole of the matter is before you, I think

I am entitled to claim for this man a verdict of Not Guilty. And, members of the jury, in returning that verdict you will vindicate a principle of law, that people are not tried by newspapers, not tried by rumour, but tried by juries called to justice and decide upon the evidence. I ask you for, I appeal to you for, and I claim from you, a verdict of Not Guilty."

As he paused for a brief moment, Birkett's eyes passed along the line of jurors; in the silence of the court his voice rang out: "Stand firm!"

The jury did not disappoint him; after a retirement of almost two and a half hours the foreman rose to announce the verdict that Birkett had demanded of them: "Not Guilty."

Mancini was acquitted, and Norman Birkett was hero of the hour, though of the rapturous accolades he commented cynically: "strangely enough it has given me very little pleasure . . . [Mancini] was a despicable and worthless creature. But the acquittal seems to have impressed the popular imagination."

There remains to be added a footnote: Tony Mancini avoided publicity for 40 years; but on November 28th, 1976, the *News of the World* carried a story "I've Got Away With Murder". Mancini had confessed to reporter Alan Hart. Later, Stephen Knight conducted a lengthy interview with Mancini in which he reiterated his guilt [*see Bibliography*].

The Revengeful Smugglers
The Murder of WILLIAM GALLEY and DANIEL CHATER
by BENJAMIN TAPNER, JOHN COBBY,
JOHN HAMMOND and Others
for which they were Tried at Chichester
and Executed at that place on January the 18th 1749

We do not recollect ever to have heard of a case exhibiting greater brutality on the part of the murderers towards their victims than this. The offenders were all smugglers, and the unfortunate objects of their crime were a custom-house officer and a shoe maker – named respectively William Galley and Daniel Chater. It would appear that a daring and very

extensive robbery having been committed at the custom-house at Poole, Galley and Chater were sent to Stanstead in Sussex to give some information to Major Battine, a magistrate, in reference to the circumstance. They did not, however, return to their homes, and on inquiry it turned out that they had been brutally murdered, the body of Galley being traced by means of bloodhounds, to be buried, while that of Chater was discovered at a distance of six miles, in a well in Harris's Wood, near Leigh, in Lady Holt's Park, covered up with a quantity of stones, wooden railings and earth.

At a special commission held at Chichester on the 16th of January, 1749, the prisoners Benjamin Tapner, John Cobby, John Hammond, William Carter, Richard Mills the elder and Richard Mills the younger were indicted for the murder of Daniel Chater; the first three as principals and the others as accessories before the fact; and William Jackson and William Carter were indicted for the murder of William Galley.

From the evidence adduced, the circumstances of this most horrid murder were proved, and it appeared that the two deceased persons, having passed Havant on their road to Stanstead, went to the *New Inn*, at Leigh, where they met one Austin, and his brother and brother-in-law, of whom they asked the road, and they conducted them to Rowland's Castle, where they said they might obtain better information. They went into the *White Hart*, and Mrs. Payne, the landlady, suspecting the object of their mission, sent for the prisoners Jackson and Carter, and they were soon joined by some of the others of the gang. After they had been sitting together, Carter called Chater out, and demanded to know where Diamond, one of those suspected of the robbery, was. Chater replied that he was in custody, and that he was going against his will to give evidence against him. Galley, following them into the yard, was knocked down by Carter, on his calling Chater away, and they then returned indoors. The smugglers now pretended to be sorry for what had occurred, and desired Galley to drink some rum, and they persisted in plying him and Chater with liquor until they were both intoxicated. They were then persuaded to lie down and sleep, and a letter to Major Battine, of which they were the bearers, was taken from them, read, and destroyed.

One John Royce, a smuggler, now came in, and Jackson and Carter told him of the contents of the letter, and said that they had got the old rogue, the shoe maker of

Fording Bridge, who was going to inform against John Diamond, the shepherd, then in custody at Chichester. Here William Steele proposed to take them both to a well about two hundred yards from the house, to murder and throw them in; but this was rejected, and, after several propositions had been made as to the mode in which they should be disposed of, the scene of cruelty was commenced by Jackson, who, putting on his spurs, jumped upon the bed where they lay and spurred their foreheads, and then whipped them; so they both got up bleeding. The smugglers then took them out of the house, and Mills swore he would shoot anyone who followed or said anything of what had occurred.

Meanwhile the rest put Galley and Chater on one horse, tied their legs underneath the horse's belly, and then tied the legs of both together. They now set forward with the exception of Royce, who had no horse; and they had not gone above two hundred yards before Jackson called out "Whip 'em, cut 'em, slash 'em, damn 'em!" upon which all began to whip except Steele, who led the horse, the roads being very bad. They whipped them for half-a-mile, till they came to Woodash, where they fell off, with their heads underneath the horse's belly; and their legs, which were tied, appeared over the horse's back. Their tormentors soon set them upright again, and continued whipping them over the head, face and shoulders, etc., till they came to Dean, upwards of half-a-mile farther; and here they both fell again as before, with their heads under the horse's belly, which were struck at every step by the horse's hooves.

At last the body of Galley expired, and they threw the body over the horse and carried it off with them to the house of one Scardefield, who kept the *Red Lion*, at Rake. Jackson and Carter carried Chater down to the house of the elder Mills, where they chained him up in a turf-house. Their companions in the meantime drank gin and brandy at Scardefield's, and, it being now nearly dark, they borrowed spades and a candle and a lantern and, making him assist them in digging a hole, they buried the body of the murdered officer. They then separated, but on the Thursday they met again with some more of their associates, including the prisoners Richard Mills, and his two sons Richard and John, Thomas Stringer, Cobby, Tapner and Hammond, for the purpose of deliberating what should be done with their prisoner. It was soon unanimously resolved that he must be destroyed, and it was determined that they should take him to Harris's Well and throw him in, as it was considered that that death would be most likely to cause him the greatest pain.

"The Bloody and Inhuman SMUGGLERS Throwing stones &c. on the expiring Body of DANIEL CHATER whom they had flung down Lady Holt Well"

During this time the wretched man was in a state of the utmost horror and misery, being visited occasionally by all his tormentors, who abused him and beat him violently. At last when this determination had been arrived at, they all went, and Tapner, pulling out a clasp-knife ordered him on his knees, swearing he would be his butcher; but being dissuaded from this as being opposed to their plan to prolong the miseries of their prisoner, he con-

tented himself with slashing the knife across his eyes, almost cutting them out, and completely severing the gristle of his nose. They then placed him upon a horse, and all set out together for Harris's Well, except Mills and his sons, they having no horses ready. It was in the dead of night they brought their victim to the well, which was nearly thirty feet deep, but dry, and paled close round; and Tapner having fastened the noose around his neck, they bade him get over the pales. They then tied one end of the cord to the pales and pushed him over the brink; but, the rope being short, he hung no further within than his thighs, and leaning against the edge he hung above a quarter of an hour and was not strangled. They then untied him, and threw him head foremost into the well. They tarried some time, and hearing him groan, and fearful that the sound might lead to a discovery, the place being near the road, they threw upon him some of the rails and gate-posts fixed about the well, as well as some great stones; and then, finding him silent, they left him. Their next consultation was how to dispose of their horses; and they killed Galley's which was grey, and, taking his hide off, cut it into small pieces and hid them so as to prevent any discovery; but a bay horse that Chater had ridden on got from them.

This being the evidence produced, the jury, after being out of court about a quarter of an hour, brought in a verdict of guilty against all the prisoners; whereupon the judge pronounced sentence on the convicts in a most pathetic address. The heinousness of the crime of which these men had been convicted rendering it necessary that their punishment should be exemplary, the judge ordered that they should be executed on the following day; and the sentence was accordingly carried into execution against all but Jackson who died in prison on the evening that he was condemned.

They were hanged at Chichester, on the 18th January, 1749, amidst a vast concourse of spectators.

[*From* The Malefactors Register, *London, 1776*]

Norman's Watchwords for '25

The Murder of ELSIE CAMERON
by JOHN NORMAN HOLMES THORNE
on Sunday, November the 30th, 1924
at his Wesley Poultry Farm, Crowborough

They say that it is always a mistake to trifle with the affections of women, and that many men throughout history have discovered it to their cost.

At the time he paid for his mistake, in 1924, Norman Thorne was twenty-four years of age. He left the Services, where he had enlisted as a mechanic in the Royal Naval Air Service at the end of the Great War, and took similar civilian employment with a firm of engineers. The business failed in 1922 and Norman found himself in the dole queue, with plenty of time on his hands but precious few prospects. He was living with his father at this time on the outskirts of London, and whiling away a great deal of his life in the company of Miss Elsie Cameron, a girl about his own age with whom he shared an enthusiasm for God's more eccentric manifestations in the form of Wesleyan Methodism and the Band of Hope. It was with her characteristic enthusiasm that Elsie embraced Norman's proposal of marriage.

But marriages, made in Heaven though they may be, still require at least a basic earthly funding. And it may have been with this in mind that Norman embarked upon his rather basic enterprise. Buying a small field in Crowborough with £100 of his father's money he set himself up as the Wesley Poultry Farm, eschewing the comforts of the parental home for a seven-by-twelve wooden hut in the middle of the chicken runs. With Norman, all his belongings, and probably a few chickens strayed off-course the hut was less basic than squalid, a domestic disaster that was to serve as Norman's fortress for two years. With the blindness of true love, Elsie Cameron became a regular guest at the hut; she was filled with an unreasoning optimism that found expression in one of the many letters exchanged by the couple:

> Our courtship is like a fairy-tale and will it end with 'they lived happily ever after'?

. . . Oh my treasure, how I adore you . . . if only we could get married. Oh pet, lets try to do so this year . . . We can manage in a little hut like yours; your Elsie is quite well now and there is no fear of any children for three or four years . . .

By November she was making claims of impending motherhood, and began to press Norman with greater urgency to fulfil his vows.

He resisted. She insisted.

Norman, you see, had found a new passion. It came in the person of a young dressmaker named Bessie Coldicott whom he had met at a local dance and who had occupied his heart and his bed frequently since. But if chapel had taught Norman one thing it was honesty. He might be two-timing his fiancée, but he could not conceal it from her. He wrote to Elsie on the 25th of November 1924 after she had made another attempt to browbeat Norman into wedlock:

> You seem to be taking everything for granted . . . There are one or two things I haven't told you . . . it concerns someone else . . . I am afraid I am between two fires.

Elsie replied by return admonishing her swain for his cruelty, adding that "this worry is very bad for the baby". She concluded: "I really think an explanation is due to me over all this."

Obligingly, if clumsily, Norman explained:

> What I haven't told you is that on certain occasions a girl has been here late at night . . . She thinks I am going to marry her; of course I have a strong feeling for her or I shouldn't have done what I have . . .

Elsie's response was understandable if unoriginal:

> You have absolutely broken my heart. I

Elsie Cameron, Norman Thorne, and Bessie Coldicott

never thought you were capable of such deception . . . You are engaged to me and I have first claim on you . . . Well, Norman, I expect you to marry me, and finish with the other girl as soon as possible. My baby must have a name.

On November 30th, Elsie took her complaint in person to Crowborough, where Norman, with apologies and further vague promises of wedding bells, managed to get rid of her before his appointment with Bessie.

But Elsie was a persistent girl; stubborn some might say; obstinate. Determined once and for all to get a firm date for matrimony out of her reluctant fiancé she left her home at 86 Clifford Gardens, Kensal Rise, on December 5th en route for Crowborough via Victoria station.

It gives some indication of the *laissez-faire* attitude of Elsie's parents that it was five days before they began to wonder whether she was all right. It was only on December 10th that Mr Duncan Cameron sent an almost apologetic telegram: "Elsie left Friday have heard no news has she arrived reply." Cameron pondered Norman's reply – "Not here open letters cannot understand" – for a day or so, and then informed the police of his daughter's disappearance.

Despite Norman's evident enthusiasm for showing the investigating officers around his home and estate, and posing willingly for the coterie of press photographers that had joined the bandwagon, the only clue to

emerge was the recollection of two nurserymen of seeing a young woman of Elsie's description walking towards the farm at about 5.30pm on the day of her disappearance. Confronted with this, Norman could only reiterate his willingness to help in any way he could, but regretted that the flower-growers must have been mistaken.

Meanwhile, when he was not offering useful hints to the police, it was Bessie Coldicott who was receiving the best of Norman's attentions. On New Year's Eve he wrote:

My darling Bessie . . . I have been in love twice . . . [but] Honour bright, darling, I never felt for any girl as I do for you . . . No one knows the struggle that has raged within but, dearest of pals, you have pulled me through. Love, Honour, Bessie; my watchwords for '25.

Scotland Yard were less gullible than their country counterparts when it came to Norman Thorne, and within days of Chief Inspector Gillan's arrival in Crowborough, Thorne was under arrest. While he was "helping the police with their inquiries" *they* were digging up his chicken farm. At 8.30 next morning, January 15th, Elsie's pathetic little attache case was unearthed. It was sufficient for DCI Gillan to feel confident enough to start putting the frighteners on Norman. That evening he made a statement in which he confided that he had known all along that Elsie was dead; told them where to dig her up. But he emphatically denied having been the instrument of her death. The truth according to Norman went something like this:

He was having his afternoon tea when Elsie arrived at the hut (the nurserymen, on reflection, must have been right!) Over tea and bread and butter Elsie had outlined her plans for the immediate future. She intended to stay in the hut until Norman married her! After a few hours of intermittent threats and recriminations, Norman left a very beligerent fiancée in the hut while he went out (probably in search of Love, Honour, and Bessie). When he returned at around 11.30pm he found Elsie swinging from the roof beam on the end of a washing-line.

Cutting her down with trembling hands, Norman realized that Elsie's immortal soul was now in the hands of the angels. His own fate, he came quickly to realize, was somewhat less certain; they *had* been known to quarrel – indeed, they had spent the better part of that day squabbling – what if people should think he drove poor Elsie to her final desperate act? They might even think that he . . .

Out of sight, out of mind, mused Norman; and hopefully out of trouble too. Using the hut as a makeshift operating theatre, and his

Norman's Castle, the hut at Wesley Poultry Farm

handyman's hacksaw, Norman set about rendering Miss Cameron a little less – bulky. The pieces he wrapped in newspaper and interred beneath one of the chicken runs – "the first pen inside the gate". Which is exactly where, by lamplight, the police unearthed her.

This, then, was Norman's story; the story to which he stuck throughout his trial; stuck to loyally in the face of the strongest evidence to the contrary.

The trial was held in the historic Assize Court at Lewes, and opened before Mr Justice Finlay on the 4th March. Thorne was lucky to have the services of Mr J. D. Cassels KC who, if anyone could, might have been able to help Norman out of this mess. The redoubtable Sir Henry Curtis-Bennett led for the Crown, with a formidable ally in Sir Bernard Spilsbury, the Home Office pathologist who was to present the medical evidence for the prosecution.

If the Thorne version of events were true, pondered Sir Bernard – that Elsie Cameron had been hanging for some time on a rope from a beam, then it must have been a very extraordinary rope indeed to have left no single trace on either beam or neck. There was a more plausible cause of death; Spilsbury was convinced that Elsie had died of shock following a severe beating – evidenced by the bruised state of the head and body;

compounded by a savage blow to the forehead which could conceivably have been delivered by one of the Indian clubs found in the hut. At any rate, the jury favoured this explanation and Norman Thorne, to his utter disbelief, was sentenced to hang.

And hang he did, at Wandsworth Prison on April 22nd, 1925. Ironically, it would have been Elsie's twenty-seventh birthday.

Thorne never confessed, and so for all we may ever know, Elsie Cameron could have had a hand in her own death as Norman had insisted. One thing that we can be sure about is that the dismemberment was no flash of inspiration, for found among the piles of junk in his hut was a collection of newspaper cuttings relating to the case of Patrick Mahon [see this volume]. Patrick Mahon had been tried in the Lewes court only months previously on a charge of murdering and dismembering an inconveniently pregnant girl-friend who was pressing for 'marriage'.

But there was one difference. One fact that had Norman known it might have saved both his own and Elsie Cameron's life. When Sir Bernard Spilsbury examined the remains that had been taken from the earth at the Wesley Poultry Farm, he was able to state categorically that Elsie was not, and never had been, pregnant.

Murder on The Crumbles: Death of an Innocent

The Murder of IRENE MUNRO
by JACK ALFRED FIELD and WILLIAM THOMAS GRAY
on Thursday the 19th of August 1920
on The Crumbles, at Eastbourne

It would have been unusual for a teenage girl of modest working-class parents to have undertaken a solo holiday in the 1950s, so it was all the more unusual that 17-year-old Irene Munro was planning to do just that in the summer of 1920. The situation had arisen because her mother, Mrs Munro – in service as a housekeeper to the Sinclairs of Queens Gate, South Kensington – had set her heart on a visit home to Scotland; Irene declined to accompany her, and it must have been with some misgivings that Mrs Munro bade her a fond farewell at Wapping Pier on her way to Portobello, leaving Irene to venture south.

On Monday August 16th 1920 a cheerful Irene Munro stood on the threshold of Mrs Wynniatt's boarding house at 393 Seaside, Eastbourne. After paying her £1 deposit and settling into her room, Irene took to the promenade in search of romance, adventure and postcards, in whatever order they might come. Inevitably the postcards proved the most accessible, and she bought half a dozen and dispatched them, one to her mother, the rest to friends: "Weather absolutely gorgeous . . . wish you were down here".

We know from a letter which Irene wrote in reply to one from her mother that she spent the following evening, Tuesday, on a ramble to Beachy Head where she got lost. On Wednesday she walked to Pevensey, a few miles along the coast, and back again. Still scant hint of romance and adventure.

On Thursday, after posting her letter to Scotland, Irene must have decided it was time to help adventure on its way; it can be the only explanation for her walking alone into a seaside pub and ordering a drink. The search for romance can be the only explanation for her falling willingly into the company of two men – one about her own age and the other a little older, Jack and Bill they called themselves. And when she left them to return to lunch at Mrs Wynniatt's it was with the promise to meet later on in the afternoon. Accordingly it was a light-hearted Miss Munro who left her digs at 3 o'clock, dressed to the nines in her Sunday-best green coat, and making for her rendezvous with romance outside the *Archery Tavern*.

The three companions walked eastward out of town in the direction of that wide stretch of shingle beach called The Crumbles. It happens that they were seen by William Putland and his pal Frederick Wells, who thought it a bit of a lark to follow the trio to see what they got up to. When it seemed clear that they weren't getting up to anything William and Frederick returned to the greater attractions of the town. The sighting was now taken up by a gang of workmen resting in a disused carriage from their labours on the coastal railway line; they watched Irene and her escorts until they were out of sight.

And that was the last time Irene Munro was seen alive. Except, that is, by Jack and Bill.

The next person to see poor Irene was a small boy, who on the following morning was pursuing his own adventures across the wastes of The Crumbles. Finding a corpse buried in the shingle but for a protruding foot must have put the unlucky boy off adventuring for a long time, and he screamed his way back into town to raise the alarm. When the police arrived in company with the police surgeon Dr Elworthy it needed no great feats of detection to determine that the savage battering that the girl's head had suffered was the cause of death, and that the bloody lump of stone that lay by her side was the instrument of that battering. The fact that the only thing missing was the dead girl's handbag provided at least a provisional motive for the brutal attack. By early evening Mr and Mrs Wynniatt, (who had reported the disappearance of their lodger) stood over the lifeless body in the local mortuary. Despite the difficulty of recognising her mutilated face, a tearful Mrs Wynniatt was able to identify Irene by her green coat.

It did not take Scotland Yard's Detective Chief Inspector Mercer very long to find witnesses to identify Irene's last companions, they were two local lads not noted as model citizens. Jack Alfred Field, aged nineteen, single, unemployed with a previous criminal record; and William Thomas Gray, born in South Africa, twenty-nine, married, formerly a soldier but now, like Field, living off State benefit.

By the time they stood in the dock of the Lewes Assizes on December 13th, Jack and Bill were doomed men. So tightly had the Crown built its case that the conviction of the prisoners was in no doubt. As if it were needed, Sir Bernard Spilsbury, added a further note of horror to the evidence when he expressed his opinion that Irene Munro "Probably survived a short time – possibly half an hour, but would be deeply unconscious all the time. Death might have been accelerated by the weight of shingle on the body compressing the chest. Thus death may have been due to the combined effects of shock, loss of blood and asphyxia".

The case proven, the jury returned a verdict of Guilty against both of the accused, despite a futile but spirited attempt by Jack Field at establishing an alibi as his defence; Mr Justice Avory subsequently observed: "The defence which you concocted has been demonstrated to be untrue . . . you must now prepare yourselves to undergo the penalty which the law enacts for such a crime as you have committed".

On the route to the hangman's noose, the Court of Criminal Appeal was witness to the undignified spectacle of Field and Gray turning each upon the other and passing the blame for Irene Munro's death. They were hanged at Wandsworth Prison on the morning of February 4th 1921.

Murder on The Crumbles:
The Atrocious Crime of Patrick Mahon

The Murder and Dismemberment of EMILY BEILBY KAYE
by PATRICK HERBERT MAHON
on Tuesday the 15th of April 1924
in the Officer's House on The Crumbles, Eastbourne

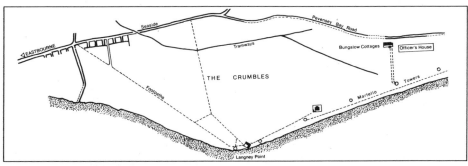

By the time Patrick Mahon had selected The Crumbles as the location for his appalling vandalism on Emily Kaye's body in April 1924 this desolate stretch of shingle beach which runs between Eastbourne and Pevensey had already acquired an unenviable reputation. On August 20th, 1920 the body of a young woman was discovered hastily buried in the shingle; her head had been murderously battered with a brick. In December of the same year Jack Field and William Gray, two unemployed ruffians, stood in the dock at the Lewes Assizes to hear sentence of death passed upon them for the crime. It is in the same historic County Hall at Lewes that Patrick Mahon stands four years later; in the same dock. His sentence

will be passed by the same judge – Mr Justice Avory; a small, thin-featured man who had amply earned his soubriquet 'The Hanging Judge' – a man responsible during his years on the bench for sending to the gallows a rogue's gallery of infamous killers.

There is coincidence too in the choice of prosecuting and defending counsels, respectively Sir Henry Curtis-Bennett KC, and Mr J. D. Cassels KC. Both had been cast in the identical role four years previously. And there is another member of the cast who is appearing four years on. He had played a minor part in the case against Field and Gray; this time it was to be a starring role. Sir Bernard Spilsbury, pathologist to the

Patrick Herbert Mahon   *Emily Beilby Kaye*

Home Office. It had been Spilsbury's task to identify the body of Emily Kaye – what was left of it – from the scraps that Mahon had left. Remains, Spilsbury confessed, which were the most gruesome he had ever seen – this from a man whose career had inured him to most horrors.

The scene has been set; the supporting cast introduced. It is time to meet the central character; time to retrace the steps that led Patrick Mahon to the dock of the Lewes Assize Court; led to his being placed at the top of the list of Britain's wickedest men.

Born into a large middle-class Liverpool-Irish family in 1890, Patrick Herbert Mahon gave little enough indication in his early years of the monster that was to develop. He proved to be a moderately good scholar, a keen and talented footballer, and a regular participant in both the sacred and the social aspects of the local Catholic church; one could also discern the blossoming good looks and easy charm that were fated to make him almost as irresistible to women as they became to him.

It was while he was at school that he met the future Mrs Mahon, and enjoyed the confidence and affection of the companion who

he was to let down so badly, and so many times, in the succeeding years. In 1910, when she was only eighteen, they married; in 1911 Mahon swindled his employers of £123 by forging cheques, and with the ill-gotten wealth began the first of a series of extra-marital affairs which were to characterize and ultimately compromise, his future. When he was eventually tracked down in the Isle of Man and returned home it was to be treated somewhat better than he deserved; the court took a lenient approach to his case and bound him over, and the ever-loving Mrs Mahon forgave him.

But for all that a pattern seems to have been set; for despite the gesture of good faith extended to him by a Wiltshire dairy company in giving him a job it was not long before Patrick Mahon had his fingers in his new master's till, to the tune of £60. This time the Assizes at Dorchester were less accommodating, and Mahon was sent down for one year.

But Mrs Mahon was characteristically understanding, and at the end of his twelve-month stretch the couple started again in the town of Calne. It may be no more than coincidence that Mahon's arrival in town was accompanied by an outbreak of un-solved burglaries – it is certain, though, that he was quickly developing a taste for horse-racing, and was frequently to be seen on the course in the capacity of bookmaker's clerk. However, such dishonesties as there were – not discounting a string of love affairs – attracted nothing by way of retribution. It was not until 1916 that Patrick Mahon step-ped back into the legal limelight.

It was in the early part of that year that the branch of the National Provident Bank situ-ated at Sunningdale was entered late at night, and for no honest purpose. Indeed, a servant girl who was disturbed by the intru-der and rose from her bed to investigate, was rewarded with a severe beating about the head with a hammer. The attacker, the in-

to the firm of Consols Automatic Aerators Ltd., at Sunbury, now a part of Greater London. In fact her integrity was held in such esteem that, when she interceded on behalf of her errant husband, Patrick was taken on as a travelling representative. It was a job at which he did surprisingly well, and perhaps it was having been provided with a legitimate reason for leaving his wife 'on business' that helped sustain his interest. Certainly he never passed up the opportu-nity to socialize with members of the oppo-site sex; sometimes, as we shall learn, in grotesque circumstances.

It was as a direct result of his job with Consols Automatic that Mahon met the un-fortunate Emily Beilby Kaye. Emily was a not unattractive woman, though at the age

The Crumbles

truder, was Patrick Mahon. Now, whatever explanation one cares to allow – stupidity, arrogance, sheer lust – Mahon's subsequent behaviour was, to say the least, extraordi-nary; for when the poor girl recovered con-sciousness she found herself embraced in Mahon's arms and being kissed by him; being asked to forgive the previous rough introduction. Not surprisingly, identification was not a problem at his subsequent trial, and Patrick Herbert Mahon was handed down a five-year sentence.

By the time he returned to the forgiving arms of his wife she had managed, by dint of hard work and resourcefulness, to rise to the responsible position of Company Secretary

of thirty-seven she remained unmarried and living at a London residential hostel for girls in Guildford Street, Bloomsbury. Perhaps she had tired of the single state; perhaps she was beginning to glimpse the spectre of a lonely old age. Whatever prompted her, she needed no great coercion to enter into an affair of the heart with Consols' new sales manager. The almost unseemly speed with which the romance developed may well have disconcerted Mahon; it is certain that the intensity with which Miss Kaye was prepared to give her passionate all was not fully reciprocated.

It was not long before Mahon was frankly worried; worried that he might be becoming a victim to a will stronger – or more desperate, or both – than his own; worried about how he could escape. Worried most of all because (though he denied it at his trial) he had made Emily Kaye pregnant, and she was now demanding that they go away together; abroad. Mahon desperate now; Emily desperate, in a different way.

It was at this stage, in the early days of April 1924, that Emily Kaye suggested – in fact, insisted on – what she called a 'love experiment'. She had long held that Patrick's resistance could be overcome if only they had an extended period alone together to allow their affections free rein, to allow their love to flower. Besides, he could hardly refuse now; not since her fortuitous discovery.

The discovery came about quite by accident when Emily was clearing out a drawer and (product of the wildest coincidence) found the drawer lined with the very newpaper that reported Mahon's trial at Guildford all those years before. It would be unlikely if this piece of knowledge – with its implicit threat of exposure – did not play a large part in Mahon's capitulation; in his agreeing to rent a bungalow on the lonely Crumbles. It may also have been the final straw that resulted in so horrible an end for Emily Kaye.

Unaware of the scheme that must by now have taken hold of Mahon's mind, Emily decided to press him further; press him to elope with her to South Africa. She had already bought herself an engagement ring and announced the forthcoming voyage to her friends and relatives; and it was probably with that wild and distant view of the future that Emily Kaye travelled on ahead of her paramour to Eastbourne; to the bungalow known as the Officer's House (it was formerly the residence of the commander of the coastguard station on that part of the beach). At any rate, she had cashed in the last of her shares before leaving – the remainder of her nest-egg had already found its way (in large part) into Mahon's pocket.

Mahon travelled down on the 12th of April from his present home at Pagoda Avenue, Richmond, where he had told his wife he was going out 'on business'. Unsurprisingly (but in the light of what was to transpire, revealing of what was hatching in his mind) he picked up a young lady named Miss Duncan on the way and arranged to meet her for supper on the following Wednesday. His only other diversion was to purchase, at a shop in Victoria Street, London, a chef's knife and a tenon saw.

The 'love experiment' appeared to begin in a friendly enough atmosphere; Emily met Mahon at the station, and they travelled thence by taxi to the Officer's House. Emily, still with high hopes of persuading Patrick out to South Africa, outlined the plan in a letter that she wrote to a friend dated Eastbourne, April 14th. On the following day, Tuesday the 15th, the couple travelled back up to London, Mahon having strict instructions to get himself a passport; this he resolutely avoided doing, and the row that his refusal instigated was to gather momentum on the return train journey to the bungalow.

Once 'home', Emily insisted that Mahon write a letter to his friends informing them of his intention to depart for Africa; Mahon equally insistent, refused.

Now, we only have Mahon's version of what happened next – poor Emily was not to survive the impassioned scene – and this is how he put that version to the court in his examination by J. D. Cassels:

Mr Cassels: You say she then got very excited, I think?
Mr Justice Avory: Very angry.
Mahon: Very angry and excited.
Mr Cassels: Tell us what was done then?
Mahon: I realized from her manner that a crisis was coming; she seemed hysterical and over-wrought.
Mr Justice Avory: This is all description; a sort of narrative. We want to know what happened, not what you thought and what you imagined, but what happened.
Mahon: I said to Miss Kaye, "Peter [a pet name], I am going to bed" . . . Miss Kaye said something, I could not catch what she did say, but as I turned by the bedroom door she flung the [coal] axe which was on the table. I barely had time to avoid it, and it struck me on the right shoulder, here; it glanced off my shoulder and hit the framework of the door . . . I was astounded by the suddenness, by the attack altogether, and in a second Miss Kaye followed up the throw. She leaped across the room, clutching at my face . . . I did my best to keep her off. We closed and struggled backwards and forwards. I

Officer's House at the time of the police investigation

realized in a minute I was dealing with a woman almost mad, mad with anger. I became absolutely uneasy with fear and fright.

Mr Justice Avory: You did?

Mahon: I did, my Lord, and with almost a last despairing throw I pushed Miss Kaye off and we both fell over the easy chair to the left of the fireplace. Miss Kaye's head hit the [coal] cauldron and I fell with her . . . I think I must have fainted with the fear and with the shock. I do not remember when I became conscious of what was happening or had happened. Miss Kaye was lying by the coal scuttle and blood had flowed from her head where she was lying on the floor . . . Miss Kaye was motionless . . . I pinched her and spoke to her and did what I could to rouse her, and she never moved or answered . . . [I remember] getting up and dashing water into Miss Kaye's face and calling her by name, and she did not answer. I think I must have gone half mad, I think I must have come out into the garden and crazy, I think, with fright and fear. I remember coming back to the bungalow later and Miss Kaye was still lying there . . . It would be hours later, I think; it would be either towards daybreak or day-break.

Mr Justice Avory: When you came back she was still lying there?

Mahon: Still lying there.

Mr Cassels: And dead?

Mahon: And dead.

Could it have been as Mahon had testified? Could it have been a horrific accident, the obvious gravity of which sent him into a delirium of panic? Or did Patrick Mahon cold-bloodedly put into execution a scheme which he had been mulling over for weeks; for which he had already purchased means of decimating the body?

It is almost certain that the jury, in opting for the latter supposition, were bearing in mind the movements of Mahon immediately after the death of Emily Kaye. Remember, he had made an appointment to meet Miss Duncan on the following day; and it is an appointment which he honoured, taking the lady for dinner in London, at the Victoria Street Restaurant. This might have been excused as a move calculated to allay suspicion. If that is true, what explanation can be given for his next move? Could there have been any justification for inviting Miss Duncan down to the bungalow to spend the Easter weekend with him; any possible justification for inviting her to share the bed in which Emily Kaye had joined him for three nights previously? Sharing a bed in the room next to which was deposited a travelling trunk containing Emily's already decapitated corpse? Because this is exactly what he did. Until Easter Monday when they caught the late train back to London.

It is not necessary to go into details of how Mahon returned the following day to Eastbourne; how he hacked his way through Emily Kaye's body in an attempt to dispose of it. Suffice to say that in his testimony Sir Bernard Spilsbury described the scene of carnage that greeted him at Eastbourne as the worst it had been his misfortune to examine.

But return now to Surrey, to Richmond, to Pagoda Avenue; and to Mrs Mahon, the wife who had proved a constant refuge. A wife who, unhappily for Mahon, was at last beginning to see through him. For some time she had been suspicious of Patrick's activities in the direction of other women; that, and a fear that he may have returned to his shady bookmaking activities on the race-course, had led her to start spying on him; had led her to retain the services of a private investigator – by name, Mr John Beard, by experience, a former detective-inspector with the railway police. It is interesting to base this next passage in Patrick Mahon's inexorable fall from grace on the recollections of Ex-Superintendent Percy Savage of the CID, the man who was to lead the Mahon investigation; the hand of retribution that was to settle on Mahon's most deserving shoulder.

Mrs Mahon had been searching in the pockets of her husband's clothes when she turned out a left-luggage ticket for a bag which had been deposited at Waterloo railway station. After consulting with Mr Beard, the two of them went together to redeem the bag which though locked revealed to Beard's exploring fingers a large knife and a quantity of blood-stained cloth. His years of detective experience served him well now. Beard handed back the bag to the attendant, and received in return the ticket, which he sent Mrs Mahon home with to return to the place whence it had been lifted. He next telephoned Scotland Yard, and spoke to Chief-Inspector Savage, voiced his suspicions, and finally accompanied the senior officer to Waterloo, where Savage managed to remove a small sample of the stained cloth from the bag for analysis – analysis which was to prove the presence of human blood. Sending detective-sergeants Frew and Thompson to wait for Mahon at Waterloo station, Percy Savage returned to Scotland Yard to wait. At 6.15 the following

Spilsbury at work in the garden of the Officer's House

morning Patrick Mahon redeemed his bag, and an instant later was flanked by two policemen:

> "We are police officers, is that your bag?"
> "I believe it is."

Told he would have to accompany his captors to the police station, Mahon replied indignantly "Rubbish!" before he was escorted there with no more ado. Savage's memory of Mahon at that first meeting was that "Mahon, who was in the waiting room, stood up and received me with a pleasant smile. he was a man above average height, and was dressed in a well-made dark brown lounge suit, a brown tie, and brown shoes. His brown soft hat, tanned gloves, and folded umbrella lay on the table. 'Chief-Inspector Savage? I've heard about you,' he said, greeting me in the most friendly manner, 'But this is the first time we have met'."

In a private room Mahon was confronted with the contents of the locked bag – a torn pair of silk bloomers, two pieces of new white silk, a blue silk scarf – all stained with blood and grease – and a large cook's knife; also a canvas racket bag with the initials "E.B.K." and some disinfectant powder. Mahon watched in silence.

"How do you account for the possession of these things?"

"I am fond of dogs, and I suppose I have carried home meat for the dogs in it."

"Dog's meat? But this is human blood."

Mahon silent.

"You don't wrap dog's meat in silk. Your explanation does not satisfy me."

"Dog's meat, dog's meat," repeated Mahon. "Dog's meat," again. Then, "You seem to know all about it."

By the early hours of the following morning Mahon had made his statement; had begun his irreversible journey to the scaffold.

All this evidence has been given to the packed Court House at Lewes. Mahon's defence – that Miss Emily Kaye had met her death by accidentally banging her head – collapsed; not least because that vital part of the anatomy' had been completely destroyed, thus rendering cause of death unascertainable. The suspicions aroused by the complete disappearance of the uterus of this obviously pregnant woman – a fact of which Mahon had denied being aware – did little to help his case. And Patrick Mahon himself, in the witness box, made a poor enough showing.

At two o'clock on that July afternoon, 1924, the foreman of the jury settled Mahon's fate; minutes later, Mr Justice Avory addressed the prisoner:

"Patrick Herbert Mahon, the jury have arrived at the only proper conclusion on the evidence which was laid before them. They have arrived at that conclusion without knowing anything of your past life, to which you yourself made reference in your statements to the police, which references have, in mercy to you, been excluded from the consideration of the jury; they did not know that you had already suffered a term of penal servitude for a crime of violence. There can be no question that you deliberately designed the death of this woman . . .

[*Mahon:* I did not.]

. . . For that crime you must suffer the penalty imposed by the law. The sentence of the Court upon you is that you be taken from this place to a lawful prison, and then to a place of execution, and that you be there hanged by the neck until you be dead, and that your body be afterwards buried within the precincts of the prison wherein you shall have been last confined before your execution. And may the Lord have mercy upon your soul."

On September 9th, Patrick Mahon faced the hangman in the execution shed at Wandsworth Prison. Which was where Jack Field and William Gray met their just end; four years previously.

Portrait of Murder
The Murder of MARGARET ROSE SPEVICK
by WILLIAM SANCHEZ DE PINA HEPPER
between Wednesday the 3rd and Sunday the 7th of February 1954
at Western Road, Hove

Margaret Rose Spevick, Pearl Hepper; two names on a school register; two normal, healthy 11-year-olds whom fate had chosen to bring together in a bond of friendship. Margaret and Pearl both attended the same school in Victoria, in south-west London; they lived in the same area, not far from the school – the Spevicks at Embankment Gardens, Chelsea, the Heppers at Ormonde Gate in the same Royal borough; the Hepper family also had a seaside flatlet at Hove.

What more natural, then, than that Mrs Spevick should receive a letter on January 17th, 1954, from Pearl's father, inviting Margaret down to the coast to convalesce after an unfortunate fall had resulted in a simple fracture of her arm?

William Hepper was sixty-two, and had a modest local reputation as an artist. One of his reasons for inviting young Margot (as she was affectionately known) to stay in Hove was to paint her portrait. He had assured her mother that all Margaret's medical requirements would be attended to, and there were fond farewells when Hepper collected her on February 3rd, and returned with her to the South Coast.

On the following day Mrs Spevick received a postcard: "Enjoying myself. Having a splendid time . . ." On Sunday of the same week, Mrs Spevick arrived, as arranged, to visit her daughter in Brighton; she had expected to be met at the station, not least because she did not know the Heppers' address, but after two hours' wait she was obliged to return on the London train, where she promptly visited the Ormonde Gate house. Finding no-one at home, Mrs Spevick began to feel twinges of anxiety, and with commendable sleuthing discovered the Hove address and sped back to the coast. There she waited outside the one-room flatlet as she had previously waited at the station – in vain, and with mounting misgivings. So long did she wait that a neighbour, the tenant of another of the flats, a Mrs Holly, took pity on her evident distress and together they enlisted the help of the caretaker to get into Hepper's flat.

It was Mrs Holly's misfortune to find Margaret. She had been first into the room, first to see a child's foot sticking out from the edge of the bed: "I pulled back the blankets," she wept, "and saw the little girl lying naked. She was dead." The pitiful sight was made the more macabre by the presence, next to the bed, of an artist's easel. Propped on it was the unfinished portrait of Margaret Spevick.

The police lost little time in putting together evidence of this unhappy child's last days. Margaret had been seen with Hepper two days previously by the same Mrs Holly who had found her corpse. On that same Friday, in the evening, a Major Davey had visited Hepper and talked to the girl. Hepper had spoken of going to Gibraltar. The local police checked town and port transport along the south coast, while their counterparts in London sought Hepper in his known haunts in the capital. The newspapers carried Hepper's portrait, as did the cinemas; and for only the second time in that medium's existence, police collaborated with BBC television in broadcasting the wanted man's description, the announcement being made by popular broadcaster Donald Gray.*

But it was from abroad that the clue came to William Hepper's hiding-place. Friends in Gibraltar had received a card for him postmarked 'Irun', the little Spanish border town where Hepper had spent the past three days sight-seeing. It was Detective Inspector Reginald Bidgood of the Hove CID who negotiated Hepper's extradition, and escorted him back from the gaol at San Sebastian where he had been detained.

On July 19th 1954 William Sanchez de Pina Hepper appeared on his trial before Mr Justice Jones. The brutal rape and murder of a child will always, and rightly, arouse public anger; add a touch of xenophobia – Hepper was half-Spanish – and a reputation as an artist (always synonymous with 'weirdos') and William Hepper must have felt a very lonely man standing there in the dock of historic Lewes Assizes. But he had one champion: his defence was in the more than capable hands of Mr Derek Curtis-Bennett, the great Sir Henry's son.

Hepper's defence had originated as far back as the time of his extradition (if not before), when he told DI Bidgood in San Sebastian on February 20th, in reply to a request to explain Margaret's death: "That is impossible. I cannot remember since I lost my money in Brighton until I come round a few days ago." On his behalf, Curtis-Bennett submitted to the court that Hepper was a victim of a mental disorder known as paranoia. Indeed, Hepper's father had died in confinement in a Madrid asylum.

Hepper's story was that, on arriving in Hove with Margaret on the evening of February 3rd, he found a letter bearing the news that his brother was dangerously ill in Spain and he would have to rush to his sick bed. Both he and Margaret were terribly unhappy that their holiday should be so truncated. He gave her a spare key, and a ten-shilling note for her fare home if she left while he was abroad. On the following evening Hepper suffered a severe attack of asthma, and went walking on the beach to take in the sea air; when he returned he took some tablets with a glass of brandy and fell into a deep sleep.

The first time was in the search for William Pettit who killed Mrs Rene Brown at Chislehurst, Greater London, in October 1953.

What follows is Hepper's recollection of that night as he told it in the witness box:

Hepper: I had a terrible dream; I saw my wife coming into the room with a man I know very well and I got up from the chair and followed almost in the dark to the corridor outside my room.

Mr Justice Jones: Whom did you follow?

Hepper: The man. My wife stayed in the room. The man disappeared in the dark. I went back into the room and had a discussion with my wife and accused her of infidelity.

Mr Justice Jones: This is still a dream, isn't it?

Hepper: Yes, my Lord . . . Then we had like a fighting, and she fell on the floor, suffering from pain because we had a fight. Later, I woke up and found nobody in the room. It was about six o'clock in the morning. I took the first train to Victoria, where I buy a ticket as far as Paris. I don't remember reaching Spain.

Hepper's quite irrational accusations of his wife's infidelity were not entirely new to his paranoia. While he was incarcerated in San Sebastian two months previously he had written a very eccentric letter to the Spanish Ambassador in London, which contained the passage: "On the night of my wedding I bore an enormous disillusion. She [Mrs Hepper] was not what I believed before. I continued to love my wife madly as on the first day, but she treated me coldly . . ." He claimed she later told him, "My heart always belonged to another man whom I loved with passion. I always hated you." Hepper had also sent a similar letter to Dr Hugh Gainsborough, his physician at St George's Hospital in London, which the doctor testified he thought an untrue and scurrilous slight on a devoted and long-suffering wife.

There was a minor drama in court the next day when the prisoner collapsed on the ground when his name was called. A doctor summoned to attend him told Mr Justice Jones: "I cannot find any physical cause for his collapse. His pulse is normal. He is just lying down and will not speak to me, and will not even co-operate to the extent of taking smelling salts." A genuine psychotic attack, or a cynical attempt to give credence to his defence?

There next followed a succession of physicians and psychiatrists arguing for and against William Hepper's legal culpability. Dr Alexander Willson Watt, a specialist at the Royal County Hospital, testified that he thought Hepper was a paranoiac: "It is my belief", he said in evidence, "that on the night of February 4th, and the morning of February 5th, Hepper was the prey of his delusions."

This medical opinion was rebutted by prosecution witness Dr John Matheson, principal medical officer at Brixton Prison, where he had had ample opportunity to examine the accused and members of his family during Hepper's remand awaiting trial. He had concluded that the prisoner was not, at the time of the crime or since, legally insane.

The jury took just under an hour and a half to find Hepper guilty of Margaret Spevick's murder. Asked if he had anything to say before sentence was passed, the prisoner replied: "I think it is quite unfaithful – I mean, incorrect. I did not do it."

On the 11th of August William Hepper, the man who, according to his own account, had been a successful wool merchant, a translator for the BBC, a spy for the United States Intelligence Service, a key figure in the International Brigades during the Spanish Civil War, and an exhibiting artist of at least passable talent, was hanged at Wandsworth Prison. There is no doubt that he was the killer of little Margaret Spevick. What is in doubt, perhaps, is his mental accountability for the crime; for if he was not insane, then he could have convincingly added acting to his list of creative achievements.

The Coward's Weapon: 2

Strychnine shares with aconitine the quality of being a particularly brutal poison, causing the sufferer agonies before depriving him of his reason and his life. For this reason little mercy has been shown towards the users of this terrible drug.

Nux vomica, or poison berry, is said to have been known to the Arabians as far back as the fifth century. The first reliable record of the existence of the berries *Strychnos nux vomica* in the pharmacy is met with in the text-books of medicine in the seventeenth century, where the powdered berries are recommended for poisoning vermin and birds.

The *Strychnos nux vomica* shrub from which the valuable seeds are obtained, is a member of the botanical family Loganiaceae, and has the dark shiny leaves typical of that family. When in seed, it produces long, cylindrical beans, or pods, from which a number of disc-shaped seeds about the size of a 5p piece are extracted. The seeds are slightly hollow on one side, and the centre of the opposite side is raised correspondingly. They are covered with fine silky hairs, which radiate from the centre to the edge, and give the seed a very striking appearance owing to the reflection of the light falling on it. In colour *nux vomica* seeds are light brown, greenish-grey, or silver grey, according to the state of maturity at which they were gathered. They are very tough, and difficult to powder in a mortar.

The active principle of *nux vomica* is, as mentioned above, strychnine, but the seeds also contain another alkaloid called brucine, which resembles strychnine in all its characteristics, but is only one-sixth of its strength. It was with this drug, Dumas tells us (in his novel *The Count of Monte Cristo*), Madame de Villefort attempted to poison half a household. With brucine there is no need to do more than mention that every description applied to strychnine applies equally to the related brucine, and recording the fact that in the last century a number of brewers were heavily fined for putting brucine into their beer to enhance its bitterness.

Strychnine gives a colourless solution of an intensely bitter taste, which can be distinctly detected in even the weakest dilutions. It is a very powerful poison, and it must be considered that a dose of one-third of a grain administered by mouth, or one twentieth of a grain injected, constitutes a dangerous dose. One and a half grains (100 milligrams) is generally set as the fatal dose, though one-third of a grain is known to have been fatal within twenty minutes.

The symptoms of strychnine poisoning are very marked. Some time after the administration of the drug, the victim experiences a sense of restlessness, accompanied by a feeling of impending suffocation. Then the face is drawn into a characteristic grin, due to the contraction of the facial muscles. This grin is known as the *risus sardonicus*. Following this the muscles are violently and spasmodically contracted, the patient being bent and doubled up into all sorts of shapes. At one moment he may be bent double like a bow, resting on his heels and head; at the next he may be jerked off the bed through violent contractions of his other muscles. These paroxysms last for several minutes, and are succeeded by a period of rest, during which the sufferer complains of great exhaustion, and of intense thirst. Then another attack comes on, and the patient suffers further agony. The muscles of the stomach become hard and tense, the face livid, the eyeballs staring and prominent. Still the patient is fully conscious, though often unable to speak owing to the fixture of the jaw by a variety of lockjaw. The slightest touch will often throw the sufferer into violent convulsions. The pulse becomes so rapid during the spasmodic attacks as to be uncountable. As the effect progresses the attacks follow one another with increasing rapidity, and in one of them the victim dies from suffocation, due to the paralysing of the respiratory muscles. There may be an interval between the administration of the drug and the onset of the symptoms of two or even three hours, but once the symptoms are developed it is a question of speedy death or speedy recovery.

Hanging in Chains

". . . but they kill'd him, they kill'd him for robbing the mail. They hanged him in chains for a show."[1]

(Alfred, Lord Tennyson, *Rizpah*)

There gradually arose, side by side with the capital punishment of hanging on the gallows the custom of publicly exposing human bodies upon gibbets as warnings to others.

In England, we gather from the *Vocabulary of Archbishop Alfric* of the tenth century, and from early illuminated manuscripts that the gallows ('galga') was the usual mode of capital punishment with the Anglo-Saxons. It can scarcely be doubted that in certain cases, as with the Romans, the body of the fordemned remained *in terrorem* upon the gibbet. As Robert of Gloucester states in 1280: "In gibet hil were an honge."

In the numerous enactments concerning the administration of the criminal law, from the 'Statute of Westminster the First' in 1277, to the Act of George II in 1752, no recognition is given to the hanging of bodies of criminals in chains. Such treatment was rather devised by the State than by the law. However, in Chauncy's *History of Hertfordshire,* it is stated:

> Soon after the King came to Easthampstead to recreate himself with hunting, where he heard that the bodies which were hanged here were taken down from the gallowes, and removed a very great way from the same; this so incensed the King [Richard II] that he sent a writ, tested the 3rd of August, Anno 1381, to the bailiffs of this borough, commanding them on sight thereof, to cause chains to be made, and to hang the bodies in them upon the same gallowes, there to remain as long as one piece might stick to another, according to the judgement; but the townsmen, not daring to disobey the King's command, hanged the dead bodies of their neighbours again, to their great shame and reproach, when they could not get any other for any wages to come near the stinking carcasses, but they themselves were compelled to do so vile an office.

Again, during the Second Northern Rising in 1536, the Duke of Norfolk hanged and quartered (as the usual punishment for high treason) 74 men at Carlisle, but the bodies of Sir Robert Constable and Ashe were hung in chains at Hull and York respectively, as special cases.

The numerous references to the gibbet by Shakespeare show how common they were in his day.

In Scotland, Lord Dreghorn, writing in 1774, says, "The first instance of hanging in chains is in March 1637, in the case of one Macgregor, for theft, robbery, and slaughter; he was sentenced to be hanged in chenzie on the gallowlea till his corpse rot." Thus hanging in chains formed part of the sentence in Scotland which it never did in

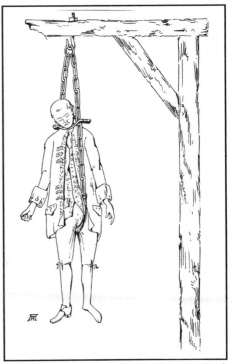

In 1752 Captain Lowry suffered at Execution Dock for piracy, and was hung in chains by the side of the Thames

England for any crime, if we except the solitary instance at Easthampstead in 1381.

It will be convenient to give a variety of examples further illustrating the subject:

We can learn from the parish registers of Bourne, in Cambridgeshire, that Richard Foster, his wife, and his child, were buried on Shrove Wednesday 1671. All three were murdered the preceding Sunday by a miscreant named George Atkins. He evaded the law for seven years, but was finally captured, hanged, and gibbeted on Caxton Common, adjoining Bourne.

In 1674 Thomas Jackson, a notorious highwayman; was executed for the murder of Henry Miller. He was hung in chains on a gibbet set up between two elm trees on Hampstead Heath, one of which retained the name "Gallows Tree".

In 1690 one William Barwick, while out walking with his wife at Cawood, a few miles south of York, threw her into a pond, drowned her, drew her out, and buried her there and then, in her clothes. Barwick's brother-in-law's suspicions arose, and enquiries were set about; the man confessed, and was duly tried, condemned and executed at York, and hung in chains by the side of the fatal pond. A curious part of this case was that Barwick's brother-in-law was urged to action in consequence of his having seen, or fancied he saw, a few days after the murder, the ghost of his sister by the side of the water, at midday.

For other examples in the early years of the eighteenth century the following will suffice to show how thick the gibbets were near London:

Edward Tooll: executed on Finchley Common, February 1700, and afterwards hung in chains.

Michael Von Burghem: executed at the Hartshorne Brewery, June 1700, and hung in chains between Mile End and Bow.

William Felby: executed at Fulham in August 1707, and hung in chains there.

Herman Brian: executed in St James's Street, near St James's House in October 1707, hung in chains at Acton Gravel Pits.

Richard Keele and *William Lowther:* executed on Clerkenwell Green, 1713, conveyed to Holloway, and hung in chains.

John Tomkins: executed at Tyburn in February 1717, with 14 other malefactors; hung in chains.

Joseph Still: executed on Stamford Hill, and hung in chains in the Kingsland Road.

John Price: executed on Bunhill Fields, and hung in chains near Holloway, 1717 [see *Murder Club Guide No.1*].

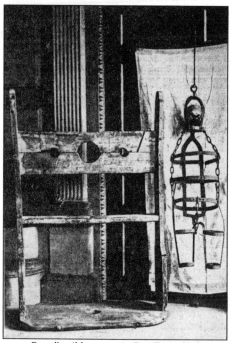

Breed's gibbet, now in Rye Town Hall

In 1742 John Breeds, a butcher of Rye, conceived a violent animosity against Mr Thomas Lamb of the same place, and as the old Statute of High Treason would put it, "Compassed and imagined" his death. He was tried and found guilty, and condemned to death and to be hung in chains. For this purpose a gibbet was set up in a marsh at the west end of town, later called Gibbet Marsh. The carcass of Breeds swung for many years on the morass, and when all but the upper part of the skull had dropped away the chains and frame were rescued by the Corporation of Rye.

In 1747 Christopher Holliday was beaten to death with his own staff by one Adam Graham, on Beck Moor, near Balenbush, on the English side of the Border. Graham was executed at Carlisle, and his body hung in chains upon a gibbet twelve yards high on Kingsmoor, with twelve thousand nails driven into it to prevent it being swarmed, or cut down and the body carried off.

By this time it became usual for the court, in atrocious cases to direct that the murderer's body should be hung upon a gibbet in chains, near the place where the fatal act was committed; but this was no part of the legal judgment. By an Act of 25 George II (1752), gibbeting in chains was first legally recognized. By this statute it was enacted that the body should, after sentence delivered and execution done, be given to the surgeons to be dissected and anatomized, and that the judge might direct the body afterwards to be hung in chains, but in no wise to be buried without dissection. This Act seems to have cleared the way considerably, and from this date gibbeting rapidly increased. It may here be recalled that the idea of being gibbeted was ever a very terrifying one to the sufferer, and many a strong man who had stood fearless under the dread sentence broke down when he was measured for his irons.

At Newgate, as at other gaols, it was the custom after execution to convey the body into a place grimly called 'The Kitchen'. Here stood a cauldron of boiling pitch, and into this the carcass was thrown. It was shortly after withdrawn, packed in chains, and these cold-riveted – truly "fast bound in misery and iron". We can picture the brutal work, with, no doubt, the coarse jesting when the malefactor was finally riveted up in what was called "his last suit".

A notorious highwayman, John Whitfield, was executed and gibbeted on Barrock, near Wetheral, Cumberland, about the year 1777. It is said he was gibbeted alive, and that the guard of a passing mail-coach put him out of his misery by shooting him. Later a sergeant was reduced to the ranks for shooting at the dead body in chains of Jerry Abershaw, a notorious brigand, on Wimbledon Common.

Towards the year 1808, a man named Thomas Otter, alias Tom Temporal, was hanged at Lincoln for the murder of a woman with whom he cohabited. It appears that she had followed him when he returned to Nottinghamshire where his wife lived. At the junction of the two counties he turned on her like a wild beast, and slew her, and flung her body into a drain dividing the two counties. He was executed and hung in chains on the

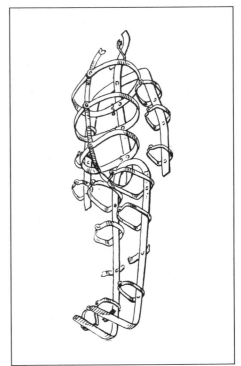

Miles's Irons, 1791

fatal spot. Subsequently, some inquiring tomtits made their nest and hatched seven young ones in the upper part of the iron frame where the head was fixed, and a local poet produced the following riddle:

10 tongues in one head
9 living and one dead
1 flew forth to fetch some bread,
To feed the living in the dead.

(*Answer:* The tomtit that built a nest in Tommy Otter's head)

The last example of hanging in chains is that of a man named Cook, a bookbinder, who murdered Mr Paas with the iron handle of his press at Leicester [see *Murder Club Guide No. 4*], in 1834. He was sentenced to death and the body ordered to be gibbeted. This was done in Saffron Lane, outside the town, and the disgraceful scene around the gibbet, as described by an eye-witness, was like a fair. A Dissenter mounted upon a barrel and preached to the people, who only ridiculed him, and the general rioting soon led to an order for the removal of the body. In the same year (4 William IV) Hanging in Chains was abolished by Statute.

APPENDIX THREE
The Early Abolitionists and the Capital Punishment Within Prisons Bill

And naked to the hangman's noose
The morning clocks will ring
A neck God made for other use
Than strangling in a string.
            (Housman, *Shropshire Lad. IX*)

For all practical purposes, the early modern period of reform towards abolition had its beginning in Italy in 1764 with the publication of Cesare Beccaria's *Essay on Crimes and Punishments.* Here Beccaria expounded his belief that, since man was not his own creator, he did not have the right to destroy human life, either collectively or individually. He did, however, capitulate on two significant points: the first, to allow an execution if it would prevent a popularly elected government being toppled by revolution; the second, to accept execution if it was the only way to deter others from committing a crime – which latter was effectively the claim of retentionists both before and after Beccaria.

These radical ideas found their way into English debate through Jeremy Bentham and Sir Samuel Romilly. Bentham (1748-1832) embraced abolition on purely political reasoning as part of his precocious theories of 'free-thinking'; however, he was constrained to admit that the death penalty produced a far stronger impression on the public mind than any other form of punishment, and maintained that it could be justified for the crime of murder. Bentham is quick, though, to add this warning: judges and witnesses are fallible, yet once executed there is no remedy for the punishmnt of death. All chance of reform or of gain from productive labour by the convicted person ends on the scaffold.

The movement for the widespread elimination of capital punishment – or at least its wholesale application – can properly be said to have begun in 1808, when Sir Samuel Romilly petitioned Parliament to remove some of the more than 200 capital offences on the statute. The retention of most of these petty crimes as capital charges was,

even ignoring the humanitarian argument, a great disadvantage to the proper and effective conduct of law-enforcement. It was not unnoticed that people from whom, say, a sheep had been stolen would prefer not to bring charges if it meant that the miscreant's death on the scaffold would be on their conscience. Juries too were refusing to bring in positive verdicts for the same reason, and magistrates and judges were increasingly liberal with their reprieves. It was even suggested by some cynical old lags that they would *rather* be indicted on a capital charge because the chances of getting off scot-free were greater.

This reduction in the draconian list of capital crimes became a particularly popular preliminary target for the repealers; while there were enlightened men and societies prepared to go as far as to bring into question the use of capital punishment in any form, for any crime.

Prominent among these was William Allen, a chemist, Member of the Royal Society and Fellow of the Linnean Society. Any instinctive feelings of justice would have been greatly reinforced by his adherence to the Quaker faith, and as early as 1809 he founded the first society with a specific mandate to campaign against capital punishment – the Society for the Diffusion of Knowledge Respecting the Punishment of Death and the Improvement of Prison Discipline. In this work he was helped by fellow-Quaker Peter Bedford and by Basil Montagu, a friend of Bentham and Romilly. An interesting byproduct of Montagu's commitment was his publication, in 1809, of *Opinions of Different Authors Upon the Punishment of Death,* an anthology of historic and contemporary thought on the subject.

A new, more ambitious society was founded in 1828 – the Society for the Diffusion of Information on the Subject of Capital Punishment. William Allen was its London chairman, and its members included the prison reformer Sir Thomas Fowell Buxton, who was also instrumental in the ending of slavery in the British colonies, the Reverend Daniel Wilson (later Bishop of Calcutta) and Lord Suffield. The Society promoted its cause in part by the publication of five pamphlets under the title *The Punishment of Death,* and achieved some modest success as a pressure group on Parliament.

The Society for Promoting the Abolition of Capital Punishment succeeded this latter group in 1846, and benefited from the infusion of new radical blood in the persons of Thomas Beggs and Alfred Dymond, Secretary of the Society and another Quaker. The lobbying of Parliament, and in particular of the Home Secretary, on matters relating to abolitionist policy was relentless.

Dymond himself in 1865 published an important and influential book of anecdotes under the title *The Law on its Trial: or, Personal Recollections of the Death Penalty and its Opponents.* On the approaches to the Home Secretary, Dymond recalled, "The London deputations hunt him down like a deer; they watch the private entrance to the Home Office like revenue officers snaring a false coiner. They sight his exit as he escapes by the front staircase; raise the hue and cry down Parliament Street; circumvent him as he darts through the Members' entrance and buttonhole him in the lobby."

But the anti-hanging crusade was beginning to touch the hearts of the people as well, and public sympathy was being gradually mobilized "to agitate Parliamentary inquiry for the abolition of capital punishment" (*The Times,* November 22nd, 1856).

The movement was no longer a London-based intellectual talking shop, it had become an evangelical machine of the reformists: "Educate, proselytize, and agitate" became the key to the campaign strategy.

Among these new evangelists were Alfred Dymond (Secretary of the Society for the Abolition of Capital Punishment from 1854 to 1857). The great orator and statesman John Bright spoke for the Society, as did Charles Gilpin, who in 1849 persuaded Charles Dickens to speak out against public executions. (Dickens did not think that it was realistic to expect total abolition.)

In 1866 a group of London Quakers set up

JACK KETCH'S LEVEE
OR, THE
GREAT SENSATION SCENE AT NEWGATE.
BY AN EX OFFICIAL.

CONTAINING AN ACCOUNT OF

THE BARBAROUS CUSTOMS OF THE OLDEN TIMES:

TRIALS BY BATTLE; DEATH PUNISHMENT OF THE INNOCENT;

200 Crimes Punishable by Death reduced to 1

Showing also that the Gallows is no Corrective but a fearful Promoter of Crime.

PRICE 1d.]   PUBLISHED BY C. ELLIOT, SHOE LANE.   [PRICE 1d.

the Howard Association – its name and aims rooted in the work of the highly respected eighteenth-century philanthropist and prison reformer John Howard. This Association assumed the responsibilities of the Society for the Abolition of Capital Punishment under that Society's former leader, William Tallack. The Howard Association also extended its brief to embrace the wider problems of the rehabilitation of prisoners and reform of the penal system. The SACP struggled on but a short time under the leadership of Thomas Beggs. But even in modified form, the strict abolitionists had already lost, if not the war, then at least the present battle. In 1866 a Royal Commission on Capital Punishment went only as far as the abolition of *public* executions. With this blow the Society finally disbanded, leaving the Howard Association to incorporate the abolitionist views in its broader mandate.

During the nineteenth century there was an abundance of printed propaganda – particularly of broadsheets and pamphlets, many of which dealt with such moral issues as the abolition of the death penalty. The styles varied in direction, many following the tradition of satire characteristic of the previous two centuries – Charles Gilpin's *Grand Moral Spectacle* of 1847, for example.

Edward Gibbon Wakefield, a colonial statesman, was imprisoned himself for three years in 1826 for abducting and marrying an heiress. This gave him valuable first-hand knowledge of criminals and the state of prison life that was to prove so valuable a background to his subsequent reformist campaigning. Wakefield was a vociferous critic of the penal code, and through a series of savage satirical pamphlets was a great influence on later reformers. Before his vitriolic pen few were safe, he treated with equal contempt the lawyers and the judges, the clergymen and executioners; he included the comfortable classes who bought special seats at public executions, and digested the Gallows Reports the next morning along with their breakfast.

Public Lessons

or

THE HANGMAN

By G. J. Holyoake.

[Two days after this Letter appeared the TIMES had a leader which might be taken as a summary of its statements (so closely was it analogous to them), and admitting that public executions were disastrous in London; but arguing that the Hangman's Lessons told on those who were absent, treating the Gallows as a school where only those pupils profit who do not attend! The STANDARD afterwards published a poem strenuously deploring the effect upon the public of the appearance at the gallows of two Teachers together—the Clergyman and the Strangler, the one preaching Mercy and the other Murder. And lastly, the Grand Jury at Manchester have since protested against executions, public or private, in that city, and advised that executions shall take place WITHIN THE PRECINCTS OF THE GAOL for the hundred of Salford.]

[FROM THE "MORNING STAR," NOVEMBER 16, 1864.]

FIFTH THOUSAND.

LONDON:

F. FARRAH, 282, STRAND, W.C.

[One Penny Each. Four Shillings per Hundred for Distribution.]

A contemporary of Wakefield was George Jacob Holyoake, whose *Public Lessons of the Hangman* (1864) was directly prompted by his witnessing the execution of Franz Müller [see *Murder Club Guide No. 1*]. Although it was an exaggeration (on the title page of the pamphlet) to suggest that *The Times* newspaper was directly influenced by his words, or even the Grand Jury at Manchester, it is certain that Holyoake was a very popular pamphleteer and polemicist, and one who was at his most sensational when dealing with the iniquity of public executions.

Of the very few middle-class publications that espoused the cause of abolition, *Punch* was perhaps the most consistent. Indeed, its first issue made clear its opposition to "that accursed tree which has its roots in injuries". Douglas Jerrold, the author and actor, contributed many fine reformist pieces to *Punch,* as predictably did one of the paper's founders, Henry Mayhew, who was already celebrated for his mammoth study *London Labour and the London Poor,* and was an active member of the Committee for the Abolition of Capital Punishment. On November the 13th, 1849 *Punch* published John Leach's cartoon on the public execution of the Mannings [see *Murder Club Guide No. 1*] The Great Moral Lesson at Horsemonger Lane Gaol, beneath which appeared a poem – *The Lesson of the Scaffold; or, the Ruffian's Holiday:*

> *Each pubic-house was all alight, the place just like a fair;*
> *Ranting, roaring, rollicking, larking everywhere,*
> *Boozing and carousing we passed the night away,*
> *And ho! to hear us curse and swear, waiting for the day.*

But by 1850 even *Punch's* crusading spirit flagged with the decline in editorial influence of men like Jerrold and Mayhew.

The *Eclectic Review* was another respectable journal which often published the written views of members of the Society for the Abolition of Capital Punishment. It was this magazine that had strong words to say over the defection of Charles Dickens from the abolitionist camp; strong words that resulted in an acrimonious exchange between the novelist and the magazine over the benefits to be derived from private executions. The *Eclectic Review* believed that behind the closed doors of prisons, all manner of abuses of power might take place in the name of justice.

It was often the very fact of public executions that excited demands for their abolition; vociferous demands from such eloquent sources as the essayist and novelist William Makepeace Thackeray who in

August 1840 was so appalled by seeing the execution of François Benjamin Courvoisier that he wrote the lengthy essay 'Going to see a man hanged' for *Frazer's Magazine* – at that time a platform for the abolitionists [see *Murder Club Guide No. 1*]. But *Frazer's* too succumbed to the growing tide of conservatism, and in 1864 it was printing hardline retentionist articles by the noted jurist James Fitzjames Stephens.

Of the others, the *Spectator* maintained a consistent, though cautious, policy of attacking the barbarity of public executions, but remained uncommitted to the total abolitionist cause. Until 1864 – just two years before private hangings were recommended by the Royal Commission – the *Spectator* was still hesitant, opting in the end for a kind of semi-private ceremony carried out in a specially built hall at Newgate and attended not only by the usual gamut of clergy and physicians, etc. but also by a "body of witnesses specially admitted to testify to the identity and to the fact of death, and the absence of all cruelty" (*Spectator,* February 27th, 1864).

In *Good Words* (April 1865), Henry Rogers in an article headed 'On Public Executions' made it clear that his reasons for supporting private executions were that their effect would be beneficial to potential criminals – the principle being that a man killed in secret could not be turned into a martyred hero on the public platform. The air of mystery about a secret hanging would, Rogers reasoned, still ensure that the concept of retribution would deter the ambitions of potential malefactors, without the unseemly spectacle of the public excecution. In short, Rogers felt happy enough with capital punishment as a penalty, at least for murder, that he was unprepared to have its retention jeopardized by the outcry at public executions. "The hour is surely at hand", he argued, "when England must abolish either public executions or capital punishment."

We have seen how attendance at the public hanging of Courvoisier prompted Thackeray to speak out against such spectacles. In the same crowd on that July day in 1840 was another of the country's great writers. The scene that he witnessed caused Charles Dickens to pen several lengthy 'letters' to his own newspaper, the *Daily News:*

I was present myself at the execution of Courvoisier. I was purposely on the spot from midnight of the night before, and was near witness to the whole process of the building of the scaffold, the gathering of the cowd, the gradual swelling of the concourse with the coming of day, the hanging of the man, the cutting of the body down, and the removal of it into Prison. From the moment of my arrival when there were but a few score boys in the street, and all those young thieves, and all clustered together behind the barrier nearest the drop – down to the time when I saw the body with its dangling head being carried on a wooden bier into the gaol – I did not see one token in all the immense crowd of any emotion suitable to the occasion. No sorrow, no salutary terror, no abhorrence, no seriousness, nothing but ribaldry, debauchery, levity, drunkenness and flaunting of vice in fifty other shapes. I should have deemed it impossible that I could ever have felt any large assemblage of my fellow-creatures to be so odious.

(February 28th 1846)

Thus did that great social commentator apply himself to one of the great debates of his day. But it was not to be a comfortable dialogue. Dickens made it quite plain that, though he abhorred the practice of capital punishment, he equally abhorred the crime of murder and those who perpetrate it. By the time of the trial of the Mannings in 1849, three years after Courvoisier, Dickens had made an uneasy peace with his conscience and concentrated his efforts on the reform of capital punishment – which in effect meant simply the abolition of *public* executions. On November 15th, he expressed to Charles Gilpin the opinion that abolition would never be accepted in England, and that its supporters would be well advised to concentrate on the immediate evil of public hangings. A letter to *The Times* of November 19th 1849 puts Dickens' own model for the procedure into the public arena:

From the moment of a murderer being sentenced to death, I would dismiss him to the dread obscurity . . . I would allow no curious visitors to hold any communication with him; I would place every obstacle in the way of his sayings and doings being served up in print on a

Sunday for the perusal of families. His execution within the walls of the prison should be conducted with every terrible solemnity that careful consideration could devise. Mr Calcraft the hangman [see Appendix to *Murder Club Guide No. 3*] – of whom I have some information in reference to this last occasion – should be restrained in his unseemly briskness, in his jokes, oaths, and his brandy. To attend the execution I would summon a jury of 24, to be called the Witness Jury, eight to be summoned on a low qualification, eight on a higher; and eight on a higher still; so that it might fairly represent all classes of society. There should be present likewise, the governor of the gaol, the chaplain, the surgeon and other officers. All these should sign a grave and solemn form of certificate (the same in every case) on such a day, on such an hour, in such a gaol, for such a crime, such a murderer was hanged in their sight. There should be another certificate from the officers of the prison that the person hanged was that person and no other; a third that the person was buried.

Such open apostasy earned Dickens the public vilification of the hard-line abolitionists, and at a meeting he was accused of "possessing a homicidal disposition". True or not, it was only another ten years before Dickens went full circle and allied himself to the retentionist lobby.

In 1854 the French writer and revolutionary, Victor Hugo, motivated by the execution of the murderer Tapner on the island of Guernsey, added his criticism of barbaric English justice; the climate of feeling against the French being what it was, he was ignored.

Two years later arch-abolitionist William Ewart failed to get the House of Commons to inquire into the question of capital punishment. The Lords, however, had already appointed a Select Committee on Capital Punishment, the report of which strongly recommended that executions should take place "within the precincts of a prison, or in some place securing similar comparative privacy". The fact that almost everybody else disagreed mitigated against any such recommendation being implemented.

On May the 3rd 1864 Ewart again pressed the government to inquire into capital punishment; surprisingly, they responded by setting up a Royal Commission, whose brief was to examine the whole question, and in particular public executions. It became clear that a new feeling of moderation was pervading informed opinion.

In the following year John Hibbert's 'Capital Punishment Within Gaols Bill' received its first reading; it turned out to have been a premature action, as it was necessary to withdraw the draft Bill until the House had received the report of the Royal Commission. This eagerly awaited Report was finally released in January 1866, and eight weeks later Hibbert reintroduced his Bill. Ironically, it was from the staunch abolitionists that much of the opposition to private executions came. They reasoned – perhaps with justification – that the hiding away of the execution would have the effect of obscuring the main issue of total abolition; that it was the gross nature of the public spectacle that would eventually turn public opinion against it. Once again John Hibbert was obliged to withdraw his Bill.

A new Bill embodying the main recommendations of the Royal Commission on Capital Punishment surfaced in March 1866, and wound its weary course through both Houses until after its third reading, the 'Law of Capital Punishment Amendment Bill', as it was named, was scrapped by the Home Secretary, Spencer Walpole, in late July.

The following year saw another attempt made with the Capital Punishment Within Prisons Bill and predictably the diehard abolitionists proved its worst enemy. In what was becoming a tiresome regularity, the Bill was withdrawn.

When Gathorne Hardy, a dedicated privatizer and active member of the former Royal Commission, assumed the post of Home Secretary on Walpole's resignation in May 1867 it was a clear signal for the reintroduction of the ill-fated 'Within Prisons' Bill. While Hardy was most enthusiastic in his support of the Bill, he made it quite clear that for the foreseeable future there was no possibility of abolition – particularly in the contentious debate on murder, and the recently abandoned 'Murder Law Amendment Bill'. Again it was the abolitionists who presented the most consolidated opposition. Stephen Gaselee. Serjeant-at-

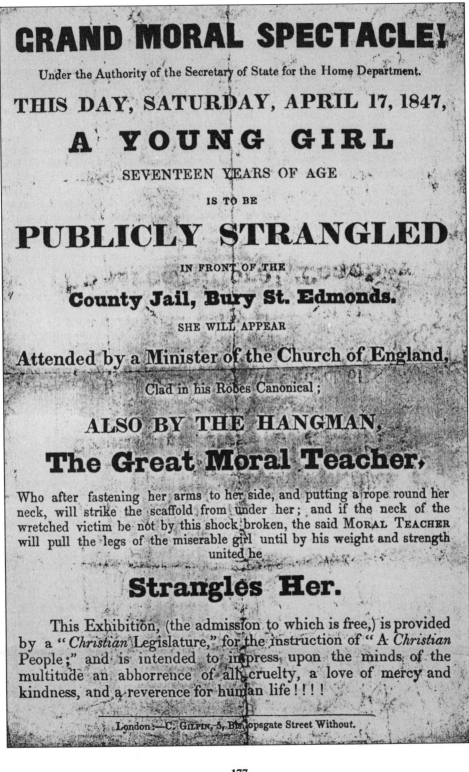

GRAND MORAL SPECTACLE!

Under the Authority of the Secretary of State for the Home Department.

THIS DAY, SATURDAY, APRIL 17, 1847,

A YOUNG GIRL

SEVENTEEN YEARS OF AGE

IS TO BE

PUBLICLY STRANGLED

IN FRONT OF THE

County Jail, Bury St. Edmonds.

SHE WILL APPEAR

Attended by a Minister of the Church of England,

Clad in his Robes Canonical;

ALSO BY THE HANGMAN,

The Great Moral Teacher,

Who after fastening her arms to her side, and putting a rope round her neck, will strike the scaffold from under her; and if the neck of the wretched victim be not by this shock broken, the said MORAL TEACHER will pull the legs of the miserable girl until by his weight and strength united he

Strangles Her.

This Exhibition, (the admission to which is free,) is provided by a " *Christian* Legislature," for the instruction of " A *Christian* People;" and is intended to impress upon the minds of the multitude an abhorrence of all cruelty, a love of mercy and kindness, and a reverence for human life ! ! ! !

London:—C. GILPIN, 5, Bishopsgate Street Without.

law and a radical, observed that executioner Calcraft was bungler enough with his public duties; what carelessness might he not be capable of secure behind walls! Another suggestion (not perhaps as fatuous as it might sound) was that if there were no public scrutiny of the dispatch it would be possible for a wealthy felon to procure a substitute. This was countered by Sir George Bowyer, the Bill's seconder, who claimed that for £1,000 one could already escape hanging – public or not.

Much discussion centred around Charles Gilpin's claim in opposition that, "if hanging be acknowledged to be so unclean a thing that it is no longer to be tolerated in the broad sunlight, the English people will have none of it". Charles Newdigate, in his attack both on abolitionists and on private executions, presented a 3,000-signature petition from residents of Birmingham, who thought the Home Secretary far too generous with his remissions already!

Gilpin proposed an amendment to the Bill "that in the opinion of this House it is expedient, instead of carrying out the punishment of death within prisons, that Capital Punishment be abolished".

The philosopher and founder of the Utilitarian Society John Stuart Mill (in the 1840s an outspoken abolitionist) then rose to voice his dissent from the amendment, and with that ungentlemanly babble and turmoil which is still characteristic of Parliamentary divisions, Gilpin's clause was voted. Thus was total abolition once again defeated – by 127 votes to twenty-three. It was significant, however, that the main argument of the Bill – the abolition of public executions – met with success.

Three days before the 'Capital Punishment Within Prisons Bill' received Royal Assent (on May 29th, 1868), Michael Barrett, the Fenian who had conspired to cause the Clerkenwell explosion, was hanged [see *Murder Club Guide No. 1*]. As it turned out, it was to be the last execution in public to take place in England, and Calcraft's usual clumsiness earned him the customary spite of the mob, and he was jeered with cries of "Come on,

body-snatcher! Take away the man you killed!"

The provisions of the new Act dictated that future executions would be carried out inside the prison in which the condemned was held at the time of sentencing. The responsibility for the practical aspects of the hanging lay in the hands of the Sheriff, and the statutory presence was required of the Gaoler, the prison surgeon, and the chaplain. The right to attend executions was extended to local and visiting justices and, at the discretion of the sheriff, to relatives of the prisoner and "other persons". That these other persons included newspaper reporters was a source of intense irritation to the still vociferous abolitionists. One reformer, Frederick Hill, spoke for them all when he said, ". . . but the brutalizing effect of an execution is but diminished not banished. The cheap newspapers carry the account of the final scene of disgrace and pain far and wide, and it is eagerly read by all who are eagerly attracted by baneful excitement", (*An Autobiography of Fifty Years: Times of Reform*, 1894).

Further safeguards to the proper conduct of an execution were made in the requirement for a surgeon's examination following death, and a coroner's inquiry carried out within twenty-four hours.

On the morning of the 13th of August 1868 Thomas Wells stepped on to the scaffold [see this volume]. The spectacle of young Wells's last convulsions was spared the roar of the spectators. This was a small victory in what was to be another 100 years struggle against capital punishment. Writing of the Wells execution, the *Morning Advertiser* warned:

When we turn . . . to the account of the calm and apparently satisfactory manner in which the culprit met his doom, we cannot think . . . the system yesterday is an act of mercy to the man who is the wretched hero of the day. . . . We are not reconciled to capital punishment by the fact that it was yesterday carried out in the least offensive manner of which it is capable.

Ye Hangmen of Old England

Ye hangmen of Old England
How sturdily you stood,
A-smoking pipes by Tyburn Tree,
A-swigging pots in the Old Bailee,
And strung up all you could.
(from an old ballad)

Hanging, as an instrument of judicial execution, entered England by way of the Anglo-Saxons, who had inherited the method from their German ancestors. It became the established punishment for a great many crimes when Henry II organized trial-by-jury and the assize courts in the twelfth century. By the Middle Ages, the power to try, sentence and hang felons was vested in every town, abbey, and manorial lord.

Executions until the present century were extremely crude affairs – carried out publicly and often preceded and succeeded by additional barbaric torture. Elaborations like hanging, drawing and quartering became popular spectator events; the prisoner was cut from the gallows while still alive, and his entrails torn out before his eyes, he was then beheaded and quartered – the head, being exposed on a pole as a grim public warning. The first such punishment was meted out to one Maurice, a nobleman's son convicted of piracy in 1241.

But even at best, a simple hanging was little better than slow strangulation – sometimes lingering on for hours; indeed, it was considered a great act of kindness on the part of the executioner to allow some relative or well-wisher to pull on the victim's legs, and so hasten death.

With the last public hanging in 1868,* and the confinement of such practices to the execution shed of prisons, a more enlightened and humane procedure was developed to dispatch the prisoner with the greatest speed and least pain. The act of hanging became a science based on the accurate relationship of weight to distance, and the hangman became its craftsman.

---

* The execution of the Fenian Michael Barrett.

This is a description of the 'enlightened' method, still in use when the last person was hanged in England:

The executioner with his assistant arrives at the prison of execution on the day before the event. He is given details such as the weight and height of the condemned man, and is allowed to note his build and manner by peeping through the death cell's judas-hole.

Using a sack filled to the weight of the man to be hanged, the executioner adjusts the 'drop' of the rope – too short a drop, slow

William Marwood, who served as public hangman 1874-1883

strangulation – sometimes lingering on for hours; indeed, it was considered a great act of kindness on the part of the executioner to allow some relative or well-wisher to pull on the victim's legs, and so hasten death.

With the last public hanging in 1868,* and the confinement of such practices to the execution shed of prisons, a more enlightened and humane procedure was developed to dispatch the prisoner with the greatest speed and least pain. The act of hanging became a science based on the accurate relationship of weight to distance, and the hangman became its craftsman.

This is a description of the 'enlightened' method, still in use when the last person was hanged in England:

The executioner with his assistant arrives at the prison of execution on the day before the event. He is given details such as the weight and height of the condemned man, and is allowed to note his build and manner by peeping through the death cell's judas-hole.

Using a sack filled to the weight of the man to be hanged, the executioner adjusts the 'drop' of the rope – too short a drop, slow strangulation; too long a drop, decapitation. The trap on which the condemned stands consists of two hinged sections connected by long bolts. The executioner checks the smooth withdrawal of the bolts and the opening of the trap when the lever is pulled.

On the following morning, the executioner enters the condemned cell, straps the prisoner's arms behind his back and leads him to the gallows trap, where the assistant to the hangman straps the prisoner's legs together. The white hood over the head is followed by the noose, the knot of which is drawn tight to the left of the jaw and held in position by a sliding metal washer.

The executioner pulls the well-greased lever...

Many discrepancies are encountered in attempting the task of listing The Hangmen of Old England, but the following represents an attempt to make sense out of the available records. Some exist merely as disembodied names – like Bull, known to be active in 1593 (in the reign of Elizabeth I), though nothing more is recorded of him. Some became household names – like Jack Ketch, himself no better than the villains who

swung from his rope; a man despised even beyond the despised rank of hangman. Some like William Calcraft attracted legends so extravagant that even this extravagant character could not live up to them, a character it is said who, in his professional capacity favoured the short drop, so that he could leap on to the back of the still-conscious victim and thus strangle him. Some, like James Berry and Albert Pierrepoint, changed their views so sharply that conscience hastened their retirement – Berry in 1892 and Pierrepoint in 1964. Both subsequently spoke strongly in favour of abolition; Berry claiming "My experiences have convinced me we shall never be a civilized nation while executions are carried out in prison."

Bull	1583
Derrick	1601
(Assistant: G. Brandon)	
Gregory Brandon	1616 (active)-ca. 1640
Richard Brandon	ca. 1640-1649
Lowen	1649
Edward Dun	164(9)-1663
Jack Ketch	1663-1686
(In 1686 Ketch was replaced for a short period by Pasha Rose)	
John Price	1714-1715
William Marvell	1715-1717
Banks	1717-1728
Richard Arnet	
John Hooper	1728-1735
John Thrift	1735-1752
Thomas Turlis	1752-1771
Edward Dennis	1771-1786
William Brunskill	1786-1814
John Langley	1814-1817
James Botting	1817-1820
James Foxen	1820-1829
William Calcraft	1829-1874
William Marwood	1874-1883
Bartholomew Binns	1883-1884
James Berry	1884-1892
James Billington	1894-1902
William and John Billington	1902-1905
Henry Pierrepoint	1905-1911
Thomas Pierrepoint	1903-1948
James Ellis	
Albert Pierrepoint	1940-1964

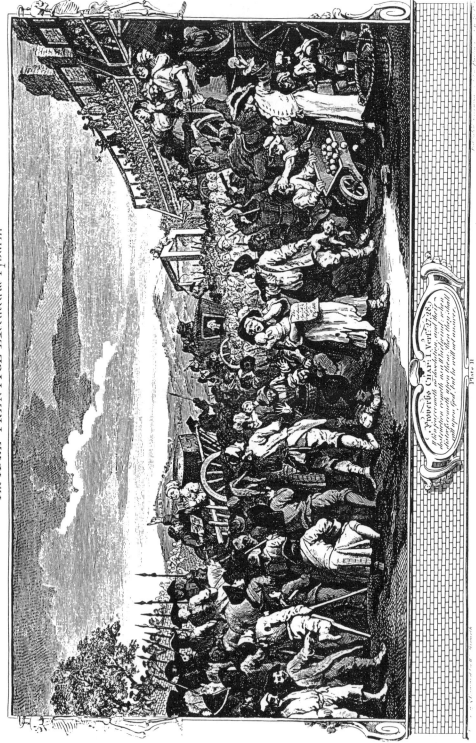

Select Bibliography

The following Bibliography makes no claim to completeness, and when one single volume is considered to provide a balanced, reliable account of a crime, this title alone is listed; for example, one in the remarkable Notable British Trials series. Published by William Hodge, the 83 volumes provide an unparalleled panorama of British crime, notably the crime of Murder. It is a matter of regret that the series is now long out of print and only occasional single volumes appear on the second-hand book shelves.

Tribute must also be paid to the publishers of this present series of *Guides* for their consistent, imaginative programme of publishing of true-crime books; the Harrap list is particularly strong in the field of the forensic sciences. Happily, many of these are either in print or periodically reprinted.

For many of the historical cases (for example, that of The Waltham Blacks) there are few reliable modern sources. In this event contemporary references (most of them used by the authors in compiling this *Guide*) have been cited, though they are not freely available outside the national archives and book depositories.

As a postscript, this may be an appropriate occasion on which once again to thank the staff of the British Library Reading Room for their unfailing courtesy and expertise. Much of this Series was compiled at desk T9, and it is no exaggeration to say that it would have been far poorer in content were it not for the BL resources.

ARDEN, Alice *et al*
Arden of Faversham, Edward White. First edition entered at Stationers Hall, 1592.
Arden of Faversham, Anita Holt. (*About Faversham*, No.7), Faversham Society, Faversham, 1970.

BAKER, Frederick
The Alton Murder. Illustrated Police News Edition, London, 1867.

BRIGHTON TRUNK MURDER No. 1
Trunk Crimes Past and Present, Leonard Lewis. Hutchinson, London, 1934.

BRIGHTON TRUNK MURDER No. 2: TONY MANCINI
Perfect Murder, Bernard Taylor and Stephen Knight. Grafton, London, 1987.
Crime Cases of 1934, Roland Wild. Rich and Cowan, London, 1935.

BUCKFIELD, Reginald Sidney
The Trial of Reginald Sidney Buckfield, ed. C. E. Bechhofer Roberts. (Old Bailey Trials series), Jarrolds, London, 1944.

CHEVIS CASE
The Power of Poison, John Glaister. Christopher Johnson, London, 1954.
Poison Mysteries Unsolved, C. J. S. Thompson. Hutchinson, London, 1937.

DADD, Richard
The Late Richard Dadd, Patricia Allderidge. Tate Gallery, London, 1974.
The Rock and Castle of Seclusion, David Greysmith. 1973.

DYER, Ernest
Murders Most Strange, Leonard Gribble. John Long, London, 1959.

They Couldn't Lose the Body, Bruce Sanders. Herbert Jenkins, London, 1966.

FIELD, Jack Alfred, and GREY, William Thomas
Notable British Trials, ed. Winifred Duke, 1939.

FOX, Sidney Harry
Notable British Trials, ed. F. Tennyson Jesse, 1934.
The Sound of Murder, Percy Hoskins. John Long, London, 1973.
Mostly Murder, Sir Sydney Smith. Harrap, London, 1959.

GWINETT, Ambrose
The Life and Unparalleled Adventures of Ambrose Gwinett, Isaac Bickerstaffe. 1825.

HEPPER, William Sanchez de Pina
The Child Killers, Norman Lucas. Barker, London, 1970.

HOLLOWAY, John
The Seaside Murders, ed. Jonathan Goodman. Allison and Busby, London, 1985.

LUARD CASE
Savage of Scotland Yard, Percy Savage. Hutchinson, London, 1934.
Perfect Murder, Bernard Taylor and Stephen Knight. Grafton, London, 1987.
Consider Your Verdict, Horace Wyndham. W. H. Allen, London, 1946.

MAHON, Patrick
Famous Trials: Patrick Mahon, ed. George Dilnot. Geoffrey Bles, London.
Mr Justice Avory, Gordon Lang. Herbert Jenkins, London, 1935.
Trunk Crimes Past and Present, Leonard Lewis. Hutchinson, London, 1934.

MANCINI, Tony (see BRIGHTON TRUNK MURDER No. 2)

MAPLETON (alias LEFROY), Percy
The Railway Policeman, J. R. Whitbread. Harrap, London, 1961.

MONEY CASE
Murder by Persons Unknown, Hargrave Lee Adam. Collins, London, 1931.

NIEMASZ, Hendryk
Francis Camps: Famous Case Histories, Robert Jackson. Granada, London, 1983.

SANGRET, August
War on the Underworld, Edward Greeno. John Long, London, 1960.
Evidence for the Crown, Molly Lefebure. Heinemann, London, 1955.

SMITH, George Joseph
Notable British Trials, ed. Eric R. Watson, 1922.
Life and Death of a Ladykiller, Arthur La Bern. Leslie Frewin, London, 1967.
George Joseph Smith, Frederick J. Lyons. Duckworth, London, 1935.

THORNE, Norman
Notable British Trials, ed. Helena Normanton, 1929.

VAQUIER, Jean-Perre
Notable British Trials, ed. R. H. Blundell and R. E. Seaton, 1929.

WALTHAM BLACKS
A History of the Blacks of Waltham. London, 1723.

WELLS, Thomas
Dover Chronicle and Kent and Sussex Advertiser, Dover, July-August 1868.

WILLAMS, John
The Winchester Tragedy, M. Thomas. 1815.

WREN CASE
Murder Most Mysterious, Hargrave Lee Adam. Sampson, Low, Marston, London, 1932.
Hambrook of the Yard, Walter Hambrook. Robert Hale, London, 1937.

APPENDICES

THE COWARD'S WEAPON
The Coward's Weapon, Terence McLaughlin. Robert Hale, London, 1980.

Reports of Trials for Murder by Poisoning, George Lathom Browne. Stevens and Sons, London, 1883.
Poison Mysteries Unsolved, C. J. S. Thompson. Hutchinson, London, 1937

HANGING IN CHAINS
Punishments of Former Days, Ernest W. Pettifer. EP Publishing, Wakefield, 1974 (reprint).

THE EARLY ABOLITIONISTS
The Lesson of the Scaffold, David D. Cooper. Allen Lane, London, 1974.

GENERAL REFERENCE BOOKS

The Guilty and the Innocent, William Bixley. Souvenir Press, London, 1957.
Sir Bernard Spilsbury: His Life and Cases, Douglas G. Browne and Tom Tullett. Harrap, London, 1980.
The Murderers' Who's Who, J. H. H. Gaute and Robin Odell. Harrap, London, 1979.
Murder Whatdunit, J. H. H. Gaute and Robin Odell. Harrap, London, 1982.
Murder Whereabouts, J. H. H. Gaute and Robin Odell. Harrap, London, 1986.
The Railway Murders, Jonathan Goodman. Allison and Busby, [London], 1985.
The Seaside Murders, Jonathan Goodman. Allison and Busby, [London], 1984.
Murders of the Black Museum, Gordon Honeycombe. Hutchinson, London, 1982.
Francis Camps, Robert Jackson. Hart-Davis MacGibbon, London, 1975.
Poisoner in the Dock, John Rowland. Arco, London, 1960.
Forty Years of Murder, Professor Keith Simpson. Harrap, London, 1978.
Cause of Death, Frank Smyth. Orbis, London, 1980.
Companion to Murder, E. Spencer Shew. Cassell, London, 1960.
Clues to Murder, Tom Tullett. Grafton Books, London, 1986.
Strictly Murder, Tom Tullett. Bodley Head, London, 1975.
A Casebook of Murder, Colin Wilson. Leslie Frewin, London, 1969.
Encyclopaedia of Murder, Colin Wilson and Patricia Pitman. Arthur Barker, London, 1961.

Index

Index

Index

An Invitation To Join

THE MURDER CLUB

The publication of this series of *Guides* has been timed to coincide with the Club's Public Membership launch.

Criminology will no longer be the exclusive domain of scientists, lawyers and writers, The Murder Club enables every one of its Members to become an arm-chair detective.

You, the readers, are invited to join in the Club's fascinating research programmes, to contribute your ideas to its publications and entertainments, its 'Notorious Locations' tours and presentations.

Or simply sit back and enjoy the regular packages of intriguing true-life crime material prepared by The Murder Club *exclusively* for its Members, stimulating the imagination with a little fireside detective work.

Membership benefits for 1988–1989 include, among other features:

★ The Murder Club's own unique badge, membership card, and personal Certificate of Membership. (Dispatched with Introductory Membership Pack.)

★ *The Murder Club Bulletin,* a two-monthly magazine devoted to all aspects of real-life crime – new cases, old cases, cases to marvel at, cases to solve. A fully illustrated miscellany of information and entertainment; plus full news of Murder Club activities in Great Britain and abroad. (Dispatched to Members bi-monthly.)

continued overleaf

- -

THE MURDER CLUB

APPLICATION FOR MEMBERSHIP

I enclose the sum of £25*, being the annual Membership Fee of The Murder Club. I understand that this entitles me to all the benefits listed above and outlined in the introductory Membership Pack.

Name _____

Address _____

_____

_____

Signature _____

Please send completed form and remittance to:
The Murder Club
35 North Audley Street, London W1Y 1WG

*Due to high overseas postal rates, a small supplement of £5 will be charged to Members outside the British Isles.

★ *Murder World Wide,* a series of illustrated booklets covering Classics of Murder from around the world. Each issue is complete in itself and a printed slip-case will be presented to contain each series as an annual 'volume'. (Dispatched to Members monthly.)

★ *Cabinet of Crime,* a companion series of monthly publications dealing with immortal cases from the annals of British murder. Specifications as *Murder World Wide.*

★ *The Black Museum,* title of The Murder Club's own mail-order catalogue with a difference. A unique illustrated document covering a wide range of publications, facsimiles, posters, prints, photographs and objects, exclusively produced by the Club to enable its Members to build up their own 'home Black Museum' of thought-provoking conversation pieces. (Published annually with bi-monthly supplements.)

★ The Murder-Book Club. A service offered to Members through our contact with the specialist publishers of popular true-crime books. A two-monthly list of available titles will be issued – many of which are available through the Club at lower than publishers' catalogue prices. (Updated bi-monthly.)

★ Concessionary prices and privileges on a wide range of Murder Club and related products, entertainments, and activities.

For Annual Membership including Introductory Membership Pack and monthly supplements, please complete the form overleaf enclosing the sum of £25.

Or send £2.50 (deductible from Membership) for further information.